EARLY

Technology, Function, Style, and Interaction in the Lower Southeast

Edited by
Rebecca Saunders and Christopher T. Hays

THE UNIVERSITY OF ALABAMA PRESS
Tuscaloosa

Typeface: Bembo

∞

The paper on which this book is printed meets the minimum requirements of American
National Standard for Information Science–Permanence of Paper for Printed Library
Materials, ANSI Z39.48–1984.

Library of Congress Cataloging-in-Publication Data

Early pottery : technology, function, style, and interaction in the lower Southeast /
edited by Rebecca Saunders and Christopher T. Hays.
    p. cm.
  Papers originally presented at the Society for American Archaeology meetings in
2000.
  Includes bibliographical references and index.
  ISBN 0-8173-1420-2 (cloth : alk. paper) — ISBN 0-8173-5127-2 (pbk. : alk. paper)
  1. Indian pottery—Southern States—Themes, motives. 2. Indian pottery—Southern
States—Classification. 3. Mississippian pottery—Southern States—Themes, motives.
4. Excavations (Archaeology)—Southern States. 5. Indians of North America—Southern
States—Antiquities. 6. Poverty Point culture. 7. Southern States—Antiquities. I. Saunders, Rebecca, 1955– II. Hays, Christopher T. (Christopher Tinsley), 1957– III. Society
for American Archaeology.
  E78.S65E16 2004
  738.3′089′97075—dc22

                                                                    2004010598

Early Pottery

Contents

List of Figures

Figures / ix

List of Tables

Acknowledgments

This volume was generated from a series of papers given at the Society for American Archaeology meetings in 2000. The editors would like to thank all the participants of that symposium. To the authors included here, thanks for putting up with our questions and comments as we stumbled our way through our first edited volume. Thanks especially to Judith Knight of The University of Alabama Press, who kept us informed and (mostly) on time. Thanks also to the stalwart copy editor, Kathy Cummins, for controlling hyphenations and all the other wayward minutiae that would have distracted from the fine efforts of the authors included here had we been left to figure this out for ourselves.

Early Pottery

I

Introduction

Themes in Early Pottery Research

Rebecca Saunders and Christopher T. Hays

When pottery appeared at the close of the Middle Archaic period (8000–5000 B.P.), the lower Southeast (Figure 1.1) contained a complex social landscape that included small, mobile, hunting and gathering groups as well as semisedentary and possibly transegalitarian groups. These peoples constructed large earthen mound complexes in Louisiana and shell mound complexes in Florida (Russo 1996a; Saunders 1994; Saunders et al. 1994). Despite the apparent limitation of having little but lithics from which to derive models, social information on these groups has expanded in recent years, and it is clear that there were complex interregional ties that affected even those groups with little extraregional trade (e.g., Sassaman 1994, 1995a, this volume). Nevertheless, the introduction of pottery, with its oft-cited plasticity and durability, greatly expands our information on social groups and boundaries and on the interaction between groups in the lower Southeast in the Late Archaic period (5000–3000 B.P.). Indeed, technological and stylistic studies of early pottery in the lower Southeast have uncovered evidence for a great deal of interaction at a variety of scales. The chapters in this volume provide a broad, comparative sample of early pottery and the attendant issues of its appearance and distribution, vis-à-vis interaction, in many Late Archaic cultures in the lower Southeast. Taken together, the chapters provide information on the function, both technological and social, of early pottery, as well as on the temporal and areal extent of Late Archaic interactions.

SPACE AND TIME

The areal and temporal focus of this volume is on pottery traditions that developed in the Atlantic and Gulf coastal plains between about 4500 and 2500 radiocarbon years before present (rcybp)[1] (Figure 1.2). The authors discuss pottery assemblages from sites in an area that extends from the south

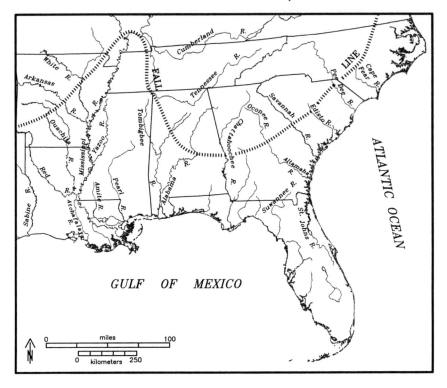

Figure 1.1. The lower Southeast.

Atlantic coast to the Lower Mississippi River Valley (LMRV) (Figure 1.3).
It is the similarity in surface decoration and vessel forms in the pottery
throughout this region—and the interaction that this implies—that makes
the areal coverage a cohesive unit. These similarities were noted even as
basic cultural chronologies were still being formulated (e.g., Ford 1952), and
they were central to Walthall and Jenkins's (1976) formulation of the Gulf
Formational stage and the recognition of the Gulf tradition (Jenkins et al.
1986) in early coastal pottery.

While elsewhere in the East pottery ushers in the Woodland period (by
ca. 3000 rcybp), it appears much earlier in the lower Southeast. The earliest
dates are from Rabbit Mount, an inland site on the Savannah River (two
dates of ca. 4500 B.P. were obtained, which calibrate to over 5000 B.P.; see
below), but pottery may actually have developed first along the coast (Sassaman 2002, this volume). After its debut, interaction among groups pro-
pelled the spread of pottery relatively quickly throughout the Savannah and
St. Johns River valleys.

Curiously, pottery does not move out of the south Atlantic coastal plain

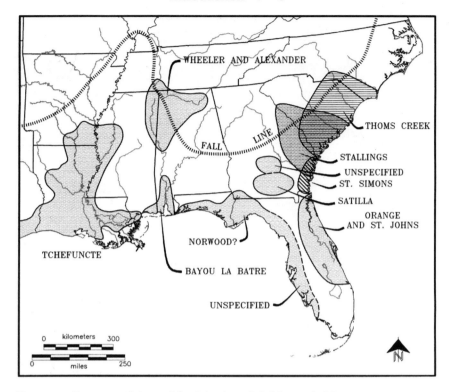

WHEELER AND ALEXANDER

THOMS CREEK

FALL LINE

STALLINGS

UNSPECIFIED
ST. SIMONS

SATILLA

ORANGE
AND ST. JOHNS

NORWOOD?

TCHEFUNCTE

BAYOU LA BATRE

UNSPECIFIED

kilometers
0   300

miles
0   250

N

Figure 1.2. Pottery traditions of the Atlantic and Gulf coastal plains.

for almost a thousand years. When pottery does begin to move westward, it may have arrived as a long-distance trade item. Evidence presented in this volume by Hays and Weinstein suggests that the earliest pottery in the LMRV is the Florida pottery type St. Johns, which appears at Poverty Point (16WC5) between 3420 and 3285 B.P. Gibson and Melancon (this volume), on the other hand, argue for the precedence of a locally made ware. Whether pottery arrived as an idea, and was first locally produced, or as an item, through long-distance trade, the westward movement of early pottery is clearly linked with long-distance exchange.

Though there are discrete stylistic traditions within the area considered in this volume, the overarching Gulf tradition contains a suite of surface decorations and vessel forms that distinguish it from its counterparts north of the Fall Line. Early potters on the lower Atlantic coastal plain and in the LMRV used a wide variety of decorative treatments, including punctation in random and linear patterns, drag and jab punctation, incising, simple stamping, and occasionally rim bosses (Jenkins et al. 1986; Walthall and Jenkins 1976). Vessel forms of the Gulf tradition evolved from the large,

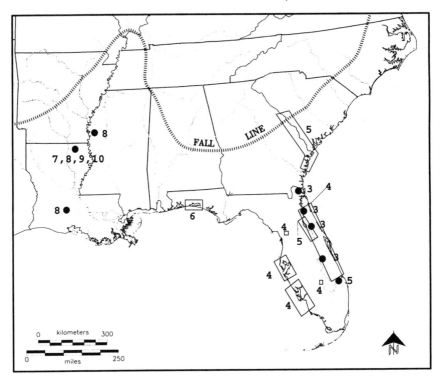

Figure 1.3. Locations of assemblages discussed in this volume. Numbers are chapter numbers.

open basins of the early Stallings and Orange traditions to more typically Woodland small beakers and bowls, and some of the later pottery of this tradition (e.g., St. Johns, Tchefuncte, and Alexander) has distinctive podal supports. By contrast, the decorative treatments on the earliest pottery north of the Fall Line primarily consist of fabric or net impressions and cord marking, and many of the earliest vessels north of the Fall Line are relatively large with barrel shapes and sometimes pointed bases (e.g., Fayette Thick and Swannanoa).

OVERVIEW OF GULF TRADITION POTTERY TYPES AND CONTRIBUTIONS OF THIS VOLUME

To give the reader a sense of the development of the type names and the current problems in the discrete traditions, we provide an overview of the types and culture history of pottery in the Gulf coastal plain. Following Walthall and Jenkins (1976), we have divided the region into two sections, eastern and western. The eastern section includes the Stallings (Claflin

1931), Thoms Creek (Griffin 1945a), St. Simons (Holder 1938), Orange (Griffin 1945b), and St. Johns (Griffin 1945b) pottery series, while the western section incorporates the Norwood, Bayou La Batre (Wimberly 1950, 1960), Wheeler (Haag 1939; Sears and Griffin 1950), Alexander (Griffin 1939; Haag 1939), and Tchefuncte (Ford and Quimby 1945) series. Thoms Creek, Wheeler, and Alexander wares do not play a large part in the chapters in this volume, but they are included in this discussion for the sake of completeness.

Early Pottery in the Lower Atlantic Coastal Plain

In the eastern portion of the study area, a plethora of early pottery types have been described (see Cable 1993; Sassaman 1993a; Shannon 1986, 1987; Stoltman 1972a; Trinkley 1976, 1980 for more exhaustive accounts of the development of these types). Over the years, type names have been winnowed and, while there remains debate over some nomenclature, it is generally agreed that three distinct pottery wares (*sensu* Rice 1987:484; as a group of types, Shepard 1980:319) emerged between 4500 and 4000 rcybp: Stallings, Orange, and Thoms Creek. Coastal variants of Stallings and Thoms Creek have been proposed; these are discussed further below. In addition, a separate Norwood ware (Phelps 1965), theoretically distinguished from Orange by a sandy paste and simple stamping (Bullen 1972), has been defined for the Florida panhandle area (see discussion in White 2003). Some consider Norwood a regional variant of Orange and thus not a discrete type (e.g., Milanich 1994). Others (e.g., White 2003) find the Norwood concept so poorly defined as to be useless as a taxonomic entity. However, simple stamping and stick impressing do distinguish a panhandle fiber-tempered assemblage from a typical Orange collection (sandy pastes do not: see Cordell, this volume; Saunders, this volume) and evoke connections to Wheeler fiber-tempered pottery. In addition, until recently, the earliest dates for fiber-tempered pottery in the panhandle did not predate ca. 3400 B.P. (Campbell et al., this volume; Kimbrough 1999).[2] These dates, along with the simple stamping, generally have relegated fiber-tempered pottery in west Florida to the western series of fiber-tempered types, and we discuss it in the western section. As fiber-tempered wares moved westward, a fourth ware, St. Johns, appeared in eastern Florida; a sandy ware appeared shortly thereafter (Russo and Heide, this volume).

Orange and Stallings Wares

Stallings (Claflin 1931) is a fiber-tempered ware found in the Savannah River valley and portions of the adjacent coast stretching from the Savannah to the Edisto River drainage (Figures 1.1 and 1.2). To the south, in southern Georgia and eastern Florida, another fiber-tempered ware with a distinct suite of surface treatments, called Orange (Griffin 1945b), is found. Orange wares occur along the Florida Atlantic coast and into peninsular Florida. Orange has also been recovered from sites on the west coast of Florida, in the Glades area, and in the panhandle (Shannon 1987), though it is unclear whether these were trade wares or were locally produced. Cordell addresses this issue in Chapter 4 of this volume.

The earliest dates for Stallings are 4450 ± 135 and 4475 ± 95 rcybp (GXO-343, GXO-345) (Stoltman 1966); these dates, on wood charcoal, render Stallings the earliest pottery in the United States. The dates are from the same stratigraphic level in two different units separated by some 27 m at the Rabbit Mount site. They date the basal level of a Stallings shell midden in the Savannah River swamp in southeastern South Carolina. Corrected and calibrated, these dates extend back to between 5569 and 4654 B.P.[3] The extreme young end of this range is some two hundred years older than the oldest Orange pottery. At present, the earliest secure date for Orange is from the Cock Fight site (8DU7460) at 4447 (4301) 4127 2cal B.P. (Beta-50154) (Russo et al. 1993). Nevertheless, Sassaman (2002, this volume) suggests that Orange and Stallings were derived from a single plain, fiber-tempering tradition, with stylistic divergence occurring around 3800 B.P. as pottery surface decoration developed.

Both Orange and Stallings fiber-tempered wares display the "vesicles," small holes or linear tracks, characteristic of pastes with burned-out organics. Vesicles are generally common to abundant in Orange wares, at least in northeast Florida, while inclusion abundance appears to be more variable in Stallings (Sassaman, this volume). In some cases carbonized fibers are present (these could be AMS dated). Spanish moss is the most commonly cited temper (e.g., Simpkins and Allard 1986), although Wyman (1875) and Brain and Peterson (1971) suggested palmetto fibers as the tempering agent. Both wares were apparently hand modeled initially and then later coil built.

Orange vessels, as the name implies, commonly have an exterior and interior fired color in the orange range, though sherds have a thick, almost black core. This suggests rather high firing temperatures of short durations. Stallings sherds are also characterized by dark cores. Exterior and interior surfaces are darker than those of Orange wares, with oxidized ranges in the yellows and browns (Griffin 1943:160). These are generalities, however, and individual plain sherds are not sortable to type on the basis of fired color.

Decorated Orange and Stallings pottery sherds are relatively easy to differentiate on the basis of surface treatment. Orange has a distinctive suite of narrow-lined, rectilinear incised motifs. Curvilinear elements do occur, though these designs, called Tick Island Incised, are rare and restricted in time and space. Small (1–2 mm), tear-shaped or circular punctations are sometimes added as minor elements alongside incised lines, but they are never used as the sole or even the principal element in a motif. In contrast, Stallings wares display relatively bold punctation with a variety of implements; punctations may be arranged in a random, linear, or curvilinear fashion. Drag and jab is also common. Incising, simple stamping, and designs that combine different techniques, such as punctation and incising, are present but less common and may be temporally sensitive, as is the relative frequency of punctation in general (though see Sassaman 2002:401–402). Orange and Stallings Plain wares may also be differentiated on the basis of lip thickness, lip form, paste texture, paste inclusions, interior and exterior surface treatment, and vessel form (Shannon 1987). Shannon's research also suggested that sandy pastes occurred significantly more often in Stallings and Norwood than in Orange and Wheeler wares. However, as Cordell's and Saunders's research results indicate (this volume), there are areal differences in paste inclusions for Orange wares, as well as differences within assemblages. As a group, northeast Florida Orange wares, for instance, can be quite sandy, but, individually, sherds in a component may have pastes that range from no sand inclusions to abundant sand inclusions.

Finally, Stallings vessel forms can be divided into three types: a shallow, wide-mouthed basin with a flat to semiflat base; a small, slightly restricted-mouth basin; and an unrestricted bowl form with a rounded base (Sassaman 1993a:144). The basins represent earlier, indirect-heat cooking methods, while bowls are associated with direct heating. Rare carinated and recurved bowl forms are also found. Sassaman (this volume) uses the prevalence of bowls at the Stallings Island (9CB1) site to suggest feasting activities at that site, as well as an overall emphasis on serving during the Late Archaic that resulted in intensification of pottery production at that time. Orange vessels also began as shallow basins, which became deeper through time (Bullen 1972; Milanich 1994). Bowl forms do not appear in traditional Orange culture chronologies until quite late in the sequence (late Orange 4–5), but Saunders (this volume) has identified bowls at the Rollins Shell Ring site (8DU7510) in the Orange 3 period.

Thoms Creek

Thoms Creek (Griffin 1945b), another early ware, differs from Orange and Stallings in that it contains little or no fiber but a range of sand sizes and abundances. Some have argued that quartz inclusion size and frequency are temporally diagnostic (e.g., Cable 1993) and have used these characteristics to establish types. Others, however, insist that these paste attributes reflect only clay source variability. In one of the most exhaustive studies of Thoms

Creek wares, Trinkley (1980) concluded the latter and argued against using the size of sand inclusions as the basis for establishing different types.

Thoms Creek wares overlap in distribution with Stallings along the Savannah River and in southern South Carolina, but they become the dominant ware north of the Santee River. Thoms Creek and Stallings types approach identity in terms of surface decoration, with the exception of a finger-pinching treatment (called Awendaw by some) that is restricted to the Thoms Creek series and occurs only along the coast. Indeed, sorting of Stallings and Thoms Creek pottery is not as simple as it might appear. Sassaman (1993a:80), Saunders (2002a), and Trinkley (1980:18), among others, note the difficulty of segregating Stallings pottery with little fiber and Thoms Creek pottery with incidental vegetal inclusions. In this volume, Sassaman notes that in the Cosgroves' collection of Stallings vessels from Stallings Island (the type site!), 70 percent of the pastes have only rare fibers and 80 percent have sand inclusions.

Stallings is considered by some to be incontestably ancestral to Thoms Creek (Cable and Williams 1993; Sassaman, this volume; Stoltman 1972a), and it is true that no Thoms Creek site has yet produced a date as old as the oldest dates on fiber-tempered wares from South Carolina and Florida.[4] Others (e.g., Trinkley 1980), however, stress the contemporaneity of the two types for most of their time ranges and conclude that the exact temporal relationship between the wares is unresolved at present. The stratigraphic evidence is unclear. In a number of sites, "pure" Thoms Creek components underlie those with both types. In others, assemblages with only Stallings sherds appear below mixed Thoms Creek/Stallings components. There has not been enough study of the dates, intersite and intrasite distributions, vessel forms, and site functions of these contradictory examples to indicate whether there are temporal, cultural, or functional reasons for the conflicting data or whether they arise from site formation processes.[5] It would not be surprising, however, if Stoltman's (1972a) early conjecture were true. Noting the probable coexistence of Stallings and Thoms Creek in coastal South Carolina, he noted that Thoms Creek might indeed be descended from Stallings but that we should "allow for the possibility that such a descent was a localized rather than a pan-regional development" (Stoltman 1972a:56).

Like Stallings and Orange wares, Thoms Creek vessels could be hand modeled or coil built; Trinkley (1980:9) does not indicate that there is a temporal factor to this difference in construction method. Fired color is variable, running the gamut from reds to blacks. The vast majority (78 percent) are incompletely oxidized with dark gray or black cores. Vessel forms include two bowl forms, one with an open and one with a slightly constricted mouth, and a deep, unrestricted jar.

Coastal vs. Interior Variants

A number of researchers have postulated coastal variants for both Stallings and Thoms Creek wares, although attempts to incorporate this variation into types have tended to confuse rather than clarify the literature. Stallings was proposed as a type by Claflin in 1931. However, Holder (1938) called the fiber-tempered ware recovered during his 1936–1937 excavations on St. Simons Island, Georgia, "St. Simons." This typology was taken up by Waring (1968b) at the Bilbo site (9CH4) near Savannah, Georgia; by Caldwell and Waring (1939) for excavations in Chatham County, Georgia; and by Kelly (1938) for his excavations in Macon, Georgia. Waring (1968b:160) believed that fiber-tempered wares from inland sites were thinner than coastal wares; that they were more uniform than coastal wares; that punctations were smaller, neater, and more varied; and that interior assemblages contained simple stamping on bases and carinated vessel forms, both of which were absent from coastal assemblages. Griffin was a strong opponent of the concept of a coastal variant. He (Griffin 1943) concluded that there were no significant differences between coastal and interior assemblages, a position reiterated in a larger study by Sears and Griffin (1950).

This disagreement has not been resolved. Given the poor taxonomic control over coastal Georgia fiber-tempered pottery that persists today, it is not surprising that Marrinan (1975) chose not to type the fiber-tempered wares recovered from her excavations at the shell rings on Cannon's Point, St. Simons Island, though drawings of sherds show both Orange- and Stallings-like motifs.[6] DePratter (1979, 1991), Elliott and Sassaman (1995), and Cable (1993), to name a few, continued to use the St. Simons terminology for coastal Georgia fiber-tempered assemblages, while Stoltman (1972a) and Trinkley (1986:159) maintained that coastal and interior assemblages are not divergent enough to warrant a distinct nomenclature. Indeed, Stoltman (1972a:42) argued that the first two of Waring's differences were not sortable and that incidences of the latter two attributes were so rare in Stallings assemblages that their lack in coastal assemblages was simply not significant (Sassaman discusses the low frequency of carination in the middle Savannah River valley in this volume). Elliott and Sassaman (1995) relied on a different set of attributes to distinguish St. Simons from Stallings. They noted that "assemblages from the Georgia coast are dominated by plain pottery and sherds have a consistently fine paste" (Elliott and Sassaman 1995:50). They also pointed to differences in design element frequency. However, element frequency and the dominance of plain pottery are assemblage-level observations and cannot produce a sortable pottery type.[7] Paste attributes for St. Simons have yet to be systematically quantified and compared, though Sassaman's (1993a) comparison of fiber and grit abundance in interior and coastal sherds indicates similar fiber abundances but sandier pastes in the interior. Most recently, Sassaman (2002:402) has written that early, plain ware coastal and interior assemblages cannot be distinguished. Data on stylistic aspects of later, decorated assemblages are still unavailable, but Sassaman did note that spatial distributions of this later ware indicate regionalization. He appears to accept the St. Simons nomenclature on geographic grounds alone (Sassaman 2002:404).

A similar controversy over Thoms Creek ware typology dogs work in the northern portion of the study area. The ware was first defined by Griffin (1945a) from a site near Columbia, South Carolina. Early coastal sandy-paste wares have been variously called Awendaw, Horse Island, or Thoms Creek (see Cable and Williams 1993; DePratter et al. 1973; Elliott and Sassaman 1995; Trinkley 1980 for more in-depth discussion). At present, Cable (1993:178) seems in favor of retaining a Horse Island type for fine-sand pastes and restricting the designation Thoms Creek to sherds with coarse-sand pastes. As noted above, this runs counter to Trinkley's conclusion that paste inclusions should not be used as an attribute of a type. Trinkley (1983) has subsumed both Horse Island and Awendaw under Thoms Creek. Trinkley's typology, then, would suggest a homogeneous style area extending from the coast throughout the coastal plain to Columbia, South Carolina.

Finally, Snow (1977) has defined a Satilla and an Ocmulgee series for fiber-tempered pottery in the Ocmulgee Big Bend area of the southern Georgia coastal plain. Both have sandy pastes. Satilla decoration includes simple stamping and check stamping; the former suggests ties to Norwood while the latter may indicate a progression into early Woodland Deptford wares. Ocmulgee wares are predominantly plain. The few designs present could be Orange, St. Simons, or Stallings (Elliott and Sassaman 1995:61). Other pockets of diversity exist as well. Some sherds depicted by Elliott and Sassaman (1995:figs. 16, 17) from Jenkins County, Georgia (on the Ogeechee floodplain near Midville), are more elaborately and closely punctated than typical Thoms Creek. Some linear elements look like Lake Borgne Incised (a Tchefuncte/LMRV type), which, like the Jenkins County sherds, often has multiple surface treatment techniques on a single vessel. Elliott and Sassaman (1995:61; Sassaman 2002) suggest that all of these assemblages are late, though none have been radiocarbon dated.

St. Johns

St. Johns pottery is found in greatest abundance in the St. Johns River basin and along the adjacent coastline of northeast Florida. Like its predecessor, Orange, it has been recovered throughout most of Florida.

Goggin (1952:99) described St. Johns pottery as including "a variety of differently decorated pottery types, all on a distinct chalky paste." Until relatively recently the cause for the distinctively chalky feel of this pottery was uncertain. Microscopic analysis of St. Johns pottery has revealed that the chalky feel is attributable to the presence of freshwater sponge spicules in the paste, which slough off the sherds when handled (Borremans and Shaak 1986:127–128). Recently, Rolland and Bond (2003) suggested that the sponge spicules in St. Johns pottery are most likely an intentional temper added during the manufacturing process.

Early St. Johns pottery is always coiled. Podal supports are sometimes found on unrestricted jars; the presence of podal supports on Tchefuncte pottery in the LMRV is often cited as influenced by St. Johns, though the direction of influence has not been rigorously established. Small side lugs, perhaps copied from steatite vessels, also occur, though rarely.

Surface decoration of early St. Johns wares is said to be derived from Orange 4 designs, and Orange 4 designs are considered a devolution from the "apogee" (Bullen 1972) of Orange surface decoration in the Orange 3 period. Simple incised designs predominate, but some finger pinching (not an Orange technique) and punctating also occur. Incising is common on early sites, but surfaces become overwhelmingly plain by A.D. 100. Red filming on an otherwise plain surface (Dunns Creek Red), however, is common (Milanich 1994:247).

The Transitional Period

The appearance of St. Johns pottery marks the beginning of the "Transitional" period in Orange assemblages. The dates for this transition are usually cited as between about 3000 and 2500 rcybp, but there have been for some time outlier dates suggesting an earlier introduction. Indeed, at the J-5 site (8JA8) on the Florida panhandle, Bullen (1958a, 1958b, 1972) found St. Johns pottery associated with Orange wares in a context dated to 3150 ± 250 rcybp (2cal 3979 [3375, 3369, 3363] 2754). At the Palmer/Hill Cottage (8SO2) shell midden site on Tampa Bay, Bullen and Bullen (1976) recovered Orange, "semi-fiber-tempered," St. Johns, and sand-tempered wares from a level dated to 3350 ± 120 rcybp (2cal 3985 [3677] 3380). Heide (2000) gives a review of more of these "transitional" dates. In this volume, Russo and Heide contribute six additional calibrated intercept dates of between 2951 and 3340 B.P. from contexts containing sand-tempered and spiculate pottery from the Joseph Reed Shell Ring site (8MT13; see below).

More generally, the transition from the Archaic to the Woodland period in the Southeast is described as *including* a gradual change in pottery paste inclusions from fiber to sand or grit for Stallings and from fiber to a semifiber-tempered pottery, sometimes with sponge spicules as the major paste inclusion, in the Orange area. Though Bullen's (1959) criteria were more rigorous, a transitional component is routinely invoked whenever any combination of the aforementioned tempers/inclusions are found in sherds, or sherds with the different paste inclusions are found in the same provenience. This current usage takes a beating in this volume. Cordell, Sassaman, and Saunders all demonstrate that sand is a major inclusion in some fiber-tempered pastes long before the so-called Transitional period (as did Shannon [1987] some time ago).

Current thinking on Transitional period pottery assemblages is also confounded by data presented by Russo and Heide on a pottery assemblage from the Joseph Reed Shell Ring in Martin County, Florida. At Joseph Reed, which is at about the same latitude as the northern shore of Lake Okeechobee, Russo and Heide found sherds with abundant sponge spicules—indistinguishable from St. Johns—in proveniences dated to 3425 B.P. (corrected; 2cal 3575 [3318] 3275). Uncorrected (3060 ± 80 rcybp), the date is consistent with the beginning of Bullen's Transitional period, so the date would not have surprised Bullen. However, the location of the find certainly would have. Russo and Heide's excavations were in an area thought marginal to all but the latest (Glades) pottery developments in southeast Florida, and this early instance of spiculate pottery is well south of the St. Johns heartland. Sandy wares do appear later in the Joseph Reed stratigraphic sequence in the same proveniences as the spiculate ware. Dates on these sandy sherds are less secure but still appear quite early for the region (ca. 3280 B.P., corrected). One other curious aspect of this assemblage is that no fiber-tempered pottery was found at the site, even in proveniences below the spiculate wares (which may be preceramic), though fiber-tempered wares are found in the area in sites dated to ca. 4000 B.P. Russo and Heide offer some very interesting ideas about site function and the interaction patterns that may have produced this anomalous assemblage.

Western Subregion

Our knowledge of early ceramics from the western portion of the study area is based primarily on data from archaeological surveys and excavations in the Tombigbee River watershed and the LMRV (e.g., Jenkins and Krause 1986; Phillips 1970). As a result of this work, the archaeological sequences in these areas are relatively well known and they have well-developed ceramic typologies based on the type-variety system. But, as might be expected, we know less about the earliest pottery in the region than we do about the later sequences.

Jenkins et al. (1986) have developed the most comprehensive model for the introduction of pottery to this region. They noted that early Wheeler shows close similarities to the Stallings series, while the typical shape of Wheeler pottery (the flat-based beaker) is probably from St. Johns and hence a product of St. Johns–Wheeler interaction on the 3150 rcybp time level (Jenkins et al. 1986:548). This interaction is most clearly evidenced at the Poverty Point–era Claiborne site (22HA501, née 22HC35), since it contains Wheeler and St. Johns pottery and soapstone vessels. They proposed that fiber-tempered pottery and soapstone were initially traded into the Tombigbee River watershed, LMRV, and Gulf Coast through the vast Poverty Point trading network (as did Ford and Webb 1956:106). They consequently considered the earliest pottery type in the western section to be fiber-tempered pottery. The authors also noted that early St. Johns pottery is present in association with Wheeler pottery at the Claiborne site at the mouth of the Pearl River in Mississippi, but they did not speculate on how it was traded into the area from its heartland in eastern Florida.

Most fiber-tempered pottery along the northern Gulf coast is classified under the type name of Wheeler, but some fiber-tempered pottery in panhandle Florida is assigned the type name Norwood. The other well-known early pottery types in the western portion of the study area include Alexander, Bayou La Batre, Tchefuncte, and St. Johns.

Wheeler

The fiber-tempered Wheeler series is centered in the western Tennessee River valley of northern Alabama and west Tennessee, but it is also found in eastern Mississippi, western Alabama, and, in small numbers, eastern Louisiana (Jenkins and Krause 1986:33; Weinstein 1995). Wheeler vessel forms include flat-bottomed, wide-mouthed beakers and simple bowls that are typically plain; surface decorations include punctations, dentate stamping, and simple stamping. In general, punctations and simple stamping are the preferred decoration on early Wheeler pottery, while dentate stamping is most common in later assemblages (Jenkins et al. 1986:45). Hays and Weinstein (this volume) report finding a fiber-tempered podal support in an assemblage from Poverty Point; to date, this is the only one known for a Wheeler vessel or, indeed, for any fiber-tempered vessel. Jenkins and Krause (1986) suggested a general range of 3000–2500 B.P. for early Wheeler pottery (e.g., Broken Pumpkin phase) in the Tombigbee watershed.

Norwood

Phelps (1965) defined the Norwood series to categorize the fiber-tempered pottery found on the Florida Gulf coast. He included two types, Norwood Simple Stamped and Norwood Plain, but he acknowledged that the plain pottery "includes some sherds which would readily be identified as Orange, Stallings, or Wheeler Plain if viewed out of regional context, but [these] are generally rougher in appearance, less well-made, than the 'type' sherds in other series" (Phelps 1965:65). According to Phelps, the decorative patterns on Norwood Simple Stamped sherds are distinct from Wheeler Simple Stamped motifs. Specifically, Norwood surfaces have parallel dowel impressions along with some crossed simple stamping that lead directly to motifs associated with its descendant series, Deptford Simple Stamped. Tempering material in the series gradually shifts over time from fiber to sand, with the presence of at least a little fiber in the paste ("semi-fiber-tempered") being used as the criterion for distinguishing between the Norwood and Deptford series (Phelps 1965:66). Some archaeologists differentiate Norwood from Orange wares by the presence of sand in the paste of Norwood, but, as is demonstrated in this volume, Orange wares may contain abundant sand, and sherds typed as Norwood do not always contain sand (Milanich 1994:97). Milanich (1994:95) noted that Orange and Norwood surface treatments are commonly found in the same assemblages in northwest Florida. The distribution of Norwood is concentrated between the Apalachicola and Suwannee Rivers along the Gulf coast in Florida but extends into the southwest corner of Georgia (Phelps 1965:66). West of the Apalachicola River, however, the fiber-tempered pottery is all plain (Phelps 1969:3). Milanich and Fairbanks (1980) dated Norwood to about 4000–3000 B.P.

Some archaeologists working in Gulf coastal Florida have opted to disregard the type name Norwood because they feel it cannot be consistently distinguished from other fiber-tempered series, particularly when the sherds are plain, which is the case for the vast majority of fiber-tempered pottery in the region (e.g., Campbell et al., this volume; White 1999). Other archaeologists, however, continue to use the Norwood type in their identifications of Gulf coastal Florida fiber-tempered sherds at sites such as 8WA420 (Kimbrough 1999) and 8JE875 (Davis et al. 1994), particularly when the sherds have the characteristic simple stamping. Hays and Weinstein (this volume) have identified what appears to be a Norwood Simple Stamped sherd at Poverty Point. It has wide interior stamping, which is typical of the Norwood series and unknown in any other fiber-tempered pottery.

Alexander

Alexander pottery is a coarse sand-tempered pottery that is concentrated in the Tombigbee drainage and the western middle Tennessee River valley, but it has been found as far north as Kentucky, as far west and south as Louisiana, and as far east as central Kentucky (Dye and Galm 1986:28). The major decorative treatments are rectilinear/geometric incising, fingernail punctating, and zoned dentate stamping (Jenkins et al. 1986; O'Hear 2001). The incising is arranged in either parallel or crossed lines, resulting in diamond, rectangular, circular, and triangular patterns. Rim treatments vary considerably and may include fabric impressing, notching, ticking, and nodes. Podal supports are common and vessel shapes include globular jars and bowls and, less frequently, boat-shaped vessels. Jenkins and Krause (1986) assigned the Alexander series to the Henson Springs phase with the earliest dates beginning about 2500 B.P. and extending to 2100 B.P. O'Hear (2001) bracketed the Alexander series as beginning about 2800 B.P. and extending to about 2400 B.P. Alexander pottery is often found in conjunction with Wheeler pottery, which suggests that they were being used contemporaneously. While this complementarity in paste types recalls the situation with Stallings and Thoms Creek, Alexander and Wheeler do not share the close correlation in surface decoration that occurred with the former two types.

Bayou La Batre

Bayou La Batre is a coarse-textured, sand-grit-tempered pottery that commonly has dentate stamping and impressing with a scallop shell; plain rocker stamping is a minority treatment. Vessel forms include beaker-like pots and simple bowls. Bayou La Batre has a more limited distribution than most of the other early ceramic types, with the largest samples being found in the Mobile Bay area at the famous Bryant's Landing site (1BA176; Trickey and Holmes 1971). Small samples of it have also been found in the lower and middle Tombigbee River area, the Pascagoula Basin, and the Mississippi Sound area (Blitz and Mann 2000:22; Chase 1972). It has not been identified in Louisiana, but Phillips (1970) noted that it is very difficult to distinguish Bayou La Batre from the sandy Mandeville series of Tchefuncte that is found in the Pontchartrain phase of the Lake Pontchartrain area (Weinstein 1986). Bayou La Batre pottery is poorly dated, with the earliest date coming from the Bryant's Landing site (3140 B.P.), but there are also radiocarbon assays postdating 2500 B.P. (Brose 1985).

Tchefuncte

Tchefuncte is a distinctive pottery series that has a poorly wedged, temperless paste that appears contorted and/or laminated in cross section (Gertjejansen et al. 1983; Phillips 1970; Weinstein and Rivet 1978). Tchefuncte has an unusually wide variety of decorative styles (i.e., drag and jab, punctations, incising, stamping); archaeologists have identified at least six distinct types of decorative motifs, and each of these contains anywhere from two to six varieties (Hays and Weinstein 2000; Weinstein and Rivet 1978). Podal supports of various styles (e.g., teat and wedge shaped) are also characteristic of Tchefuncte pottery. Vessel forms are limited primarily to small bowls and beakers. Tchefuncte pottery is found primarily in the LMRV, with a distribution that ranges from southern Arkansas to southern Louisiana and from western Texas to western Alabama (Weinstein 1995).

Tchefuncte is widely acknowledged as the earliest indigenous pottery series in the LMRV (e.g., Jeter et al. 1989; Phillips 1970). The beginning date for this ware has traditionally been cited as around 2500 B.P. (e.g., Shenkel 1980), although Jenkins et al. (1986:551) suggested that it may be as early as 2800 B.P. at the Jaketown site (22HU505). Recent radiocarbon assays from strata containing early Tchefuncte pottery support an even earlier starting point of around 3400 to 2800 B.P. These early dates were obtained from materials at several sites, including Bayou Jasmine (16SJB2; Hays and Weinstein 2000), Cross Bayou (16CT354; Gibson 1991), and Poverty Point (Hays and Weinstein, this volume).

Gibson (1995) has argued that the Tchefuncte decoration complex was developed independently in the LMRV, possibly at or around the Poverty Point site, and several chapters in this volume evaluate this hypothesis directly or indirectly. Gibson and Melancon discuss this possibility with reference to early pottery from several sites (Jaketown, Meche-Wilkes [16SL18], Ruth Canal [16SM20], and Poverty Point). Ortmann and Kidder's computer-aided petrographic analysis of Poverty Point pottery provides some support for Gibson's hypothesis. They conclude that the Tchefuncte sherds they examined were manufactured on site. By contrast, Stoltman's petrographic analysis of three Tchefuncte sherds from Poverty Point suggests that they were not manufactured on site. Hays and Weinstein use several lines of argument to suggest that it is highly unlikely the Tchefuncte complex developed at Poverty Point itself.

St. Johns

The final early pottery type in the LMRV discussed here is the early St. Johns series. Previous discussions of Poverty Point–era sites in the western part of the study area have made little or no mention of this pottery type (e.g., Jeter et al. 1989), perhaps because it had only been found in small amounts at two sites: Claiborne (Gagliano and Webb 1970) and Poverty Point (Haag 1990). Hays and Weinstein's analysis of Poverty Point pottery (this volume), however, makes the case that St. Johns pottery was probably the earliest type at Poverty Point and that it definitely was the most numerous type in the early stages of the site's construction and use. Moreover, they discuss two radiocarbon dates (averaging 3352 B.P.) that bracket a St. Johns Incised sherd at Poverty Point, which makes it the earliest dated pottery in the LMRV. Note that this is coeval with the St. Johns pottery recovered at the Joseph Reed Shell Ring site (Russo and Heide, this volume).

To date, St. Johns has not been identified at any other sites in the LMRV and it has not been found at all in the Tombigbee watershed. It seems reasonable to suggest, however, that its extreme scarcity may be, in part, because it is not identified as such when it is recovered outside of Florida. For example, St. Johns pottery may be mistyped as Tchefuncte pottery because it appears to the naked eye to have no temper. However, St. Johns paste is not laminated, and sherds generally have a distinctive fired color and core in addition to the microscopic sponge spicules noted above. Alternatively, when Blitz and Mann (2000:23) refer to early pottery sherds in the Mississippi Sound area that are temperless but are not Tchefuncte, it seems probable that at least some of these are St. Johns sherds that have not been microscopically inspected.

POTTERY AND PEOPLE

We have spent some time discussing Late Archaic pottery types and radiocarbon dating for the earliest pottery in the United States. Such culture-historical discussion has been criticized, and rightly so, when it is an end in itself. However, culture history is an absolute necessity to frame and address research designed to take us further. In other words, answers to almost all of our processual and postprocessual questions are available only after our data are firmly grounded in time and space. This is very clear in the body of papers presented here. Almost all authors lament the lack of adequate radiocarbon data for comparing assemblages. And we are not so far along that we cannot be surprised by radiocarbon dates anymore—for example, Russo and Heide's dates on spiculate pottery from the Joseph Reed site—or by information developed using simple stratigraphic principles, such as Hays and Weinstein's evidence that the bulk of early pottery at Poverty Point is St. Johns (cf. Gibson and Melancon, this volume).

But the taxonomic, typological, and stratigraphic arguments presented in this volume reverberate beyond simple culture history. Implicitly or explicitly, the pottery wares or assemblages discussed in this volume are equated with Late Archaic ethnic groups. While ideally cultures should be defined from a number of different data sets, including other categories of material culture, the truth is that many Late Archaic coastal cultural inventories are remarkably sparse (Marrinan 1975:108; Saunders 1999), and pottery assemblages are the most accessible and informative data available for defining ethnic groups (though see Sassaman, this volume, who uses distinctive bannerstones). Once such ethnic groups are established (whether these have an etic reality or are just heuristic devices), examination of stability and change in production techniques and attributes of pottery form and style, through either space or time, can imply far-reaching changes in cooking technology, directions of cultural influence, and, less directly, social processes.

Issues in the Origin and Use of Early Pottery

As befits a volume on early pottery, many of the chapters included here consider the factors involved in the invention, spread, and use of early pottery. These are essentially questions about how early pottery functioned in Late Archaic societies—on utilitarian as well as social and ideological levels (to borrow the ideas, if not the specific terminology, from Binford [1962]). This discussion is as old as culture history. While this is not the place for an exhaustive review, it is interesting to note that, through time, researchers have felt quite differently about the significance of the invention and adoption of pottery. In some of the earliest culture histories (Morgan 1878; Tylor 1871), the presence of pottery distinguished "lower barbarism" from "upper savagery"; the latter represented "a new epoch in human progress in the direction of an improved living and increased domestic conveniences" (Morgan 1878:12–14, quoted in Rice 1999:3). And pottery continues to be seen as an important innovation in most parts of the world (see reviews in Barnett and Hoopes 1995; Brown 1989; Rice 1987, 1999; Smith 1986).

Southeastern archaeologists, however, have been less than impressed with the "container revolution" (Smith 1986:30). Caldwell (1958:15) noted clear continuity between preceramic and ceramic levels at both interior and coastal shell middens and concluded that "earthenware was just another innovation in a continuing way of life." Stoltman (1972a:54) considered Stallings pottery "a late and non-disruptive additive trait (origin unknown) in an on-going shellfish-based economy" and noted that its introduction was not accompanied by "any significant changes in the archaeological record." Milanich (1994:86) stated that "the available evidence suggests few if any differences in Late Archaic lifeways before and after the appearance of fiber-tempered pottery" in Florida (see also White 2003:78). Indeed, by the beginning of the Late Archaic period, "several regional cultural adaptations were established that changed little over the next several thousand years" (Milanich 1994:86). As can be seen, these indications of cultural continuity were based primarily on settlement and subsistence patterns and artifact assemblages. With more emphasis on social action, however, and more subtle analyses, some southeastern archaeologists portray pottery as playing a major role in culture change. Smith (1986:30), for instance, presaged some more-recent arguments by noting that pottery had "an inconsequential initial impact on cultural systems [but] . . . significant long-term consequences."

With these contradictory opinions in mind, it is useful at this point to examine briefly the various theories for the origins and initial use of pottery. In a comprehensive review of the origins of pottery worldwide, Rice (1999; see also Brown 1989; Hoopes and Barnett 1995) could place most origin hypotheses into four main categories: the architecture hypothesis, the culinary hypothesis, the resource-intensification hypothesis, and the social/symbolic-elaboration theory (although many researchers combine elements of some or all of these in their explanations for the origin and use of pottery). In the architecture hypothesis, the origin of pottery is found in the technological isomorphism of wattle and daub and other architectural traditions that use clay and pottery production. This hypothesis is used primarily in Old World reconstructions and addresses only origins and not subsequent use. The other hypotheses place more emphasis on use. In the culinary hypothesis, pottery is an adaptation that enables greater productivity by increasing efficiency in food preparation, by detoxifying some previously inedible resources, by improving nutrition to the young and infirm by producing softer foods, and by increasing storability of foods. This hypothesis is closely tied to the Neolithic revolution model that associates (but no longer specifically equates; Rice 1987:9) sedentism, agriculture, and pottery production and is an essentially functional/adaptational rationale. At face value, the resource-intensification models that tie pottery origins to climatic changes at the end of the Pleistocene seem similar to the culinary hypothesis, but while culinary models tend to generalize, there is more emphasis on resource abundance in specific environments and seasons in the resource-intensification model. Within this category, however, there is still no agreement on whether resource abundance or scarcity is the prime mover; either might trigger changes depending on historical circumstances. Finally, the social/symbolic-elaboration theory emphasizes the fact that much early pottery is quite elaborate and is found in contexts that cannot be described as strictly utilitarian. In this scenario, pottery emerges first not as a utilitarian item, as depicted in the other models, but as a prestige technology, the knowledge of which may have been controlled by shamans or other ritual specialists.

The theory most cited in this volume is one forwarded in a series of papers by Hayden (1990, 1995a, 1995b, 1996a, 1996b); Hayden's theory ultimately seeks to explain the emergence of complexity throughout the world (Hayden 1998). In terms of the origins and uses of early pottery, Hayden combines elements of the latter three of the hypotheses described by Rice.

According to Hayden (1995a, 1998), pottery, like other new material technologies, emerged initially as a prestige technology. He notes that this was true even for what today are considered mundane materials like iron, aluminum, and even plastic, which was initially used primarily for elite jewelry (Hayden 1995a:259). These elite items—portable manifestations of surplus labor—are manipulated by aggrandizers, who appear worldwide, along with prestige technologies, first among complex hunter-gatherers (Hayden 1998:11, 17). Both the complex hunter-gatherers and their prestige items appear first in areas of abundant resources, especially those rich in r-selected species like estuarine fish and shellfish, which are difficult to overexploit. These abundant resources allow for a reduction in mobility and an increase in territoriality, both important contributors to increased complexity because intergroup relations become more complex. Aggrandizers emerge to control these intergroup relations. The hosting of feasts is one of the primary means by which aggrandizers in these societies control those relations and gain prestige. In the context of these feasts, pottery might first be expected to occur as food-serving vessels, and "specialized production of highly decorated forms should occur" (Hayden 1995a:261). At sites where groups converge, such as feasting sites, decoration of pottery might be used to assert social identities and boundaries (Kelly 1991). If early pottery is relatively crude, it might have been used to process prestige foods rather than for display (Hayden 1998:29). Russo and Heide adhere to this model in their chapter, as do Hays and Weinstein; Gibson and Melancon use Hayden's model as one explanation for pottery at Poverty Point but note that pottery may also have been used to prepare "fast foods" or to deliver drinking water to work gangs busy building mounds. Although by the time the Rollins Shell Ring was constructed fiber-tempered pottery had become a widely available "practical technology" (Hayden 1998), Saunders's research into design frequency at shell ring vs. amorphous midden sites also speaks to the presence of "highly decorated forms" as special-purpose wares found predominantly at ring sites.

Another issue addressed by several authors is the puzzling barrier to the spread of pottery, as a prestige or a practical technology, to the west. As noted above, after its inception around 4500 rcybp, fiber-tempered pottery does not move west out of the lower Atlantic coastal plain and peninsular Florida for over 1,000 years. A widely accepted model for the eventual movement of fiber-tempered pottery was forwarded by Jenkins (1982; Jenkins et al. 1986), who characterized the individuals participating in soapstone exchange west from sources in the Alabama-Georgia piedmont as the agents of change. According to this model, the "individuals participating in soapstone exchange were the primary sources of the diffusion of innovation and . . . the development and maintenance of such relationships were pre-conditions for the westward spread of pottery" (Sassaman 1993a:223). The relatively late date of the arrival of pottery into western areas was simply a factor of the absence of appropriate avenues for transport. In contrast to the model of Jenkins and colleagues, in which steatite exchange was a positive factor in the spread of pottery, Sassaman (1993a) proposed that steatite exchange was, in fact, the barrier. He envisioned active resistance to the spread of pottery by those who controlled the exchange of steatite in the Late Archaic period. These individuals would have viewed pottery as a direct threat to their prestige and power and consequently would have worked to halt or at least impede its adoption. (There is precedent for this hypothesis in Old World archaeology, where some data indicate that stone bowls impeded the adoption of pottery at Ali Kosh, Halln Cemi, Cyprus, Jericho, and Jarmo [Hayden 1998:29].) In this volume, the chapters by Campbell, Thomas, and Mathews and Hays and Weinstein employ Sassaman's hypothesis to explain the slow adoption of pottery in their respective regions. Gibson and Melancon, however, argue against the model by pointing out that steatite appears at Poverty Point after pottery and that trade relations at Poverty Point were far too complex to have been controlled in any sense by a single special interest (Sassaman [2002:419] has responded to this).

This volume comes at an exciting time in which new theories are coalescing to provide a glimpse of a much more interesting Late Archaic cultural landscape than has existed heretofore. The players are active, the situations dynamic, and the results are indirectly documented in the archaeological record, which we are continuously relearning to interpret.

ORGANIZATION OF THE VOLUME

We have arranged the chapters in this volume to go from east to west, following the chronological sweep of pottery across the Gulf coastal plain. In Chapter 2, Sassaman discusses the divergent pathways by which pottery technology spread along the south Atlantic coast. He uses new chronometric and technofunctional data on Orange and Stallings pottery to illustrate the effects of ecology and intergroup politics on technological exchange. Saunders follows with an analysis that attempts to determine whether a "prestige" Orange culture pottery existed. She examines technological and stylistic attributes of Orange pottery from the Rollins Shell Ring in Florida and compares the Rollins assemblage with pottery assemblages from other contemporaneous Orange sites. She also notes the homogeneity of designs between distant Orange assemblages and considers long-range interaction a likely source of this homogeneity. Cordell's chapter examines paste variability in Orange pottery from Florida to define regional production characteristics. The data are then used to explore interregional trade between Late Archaic populations in Florida. In their chapter, Russo and Heide discuss the Joseph Reed Shell Ring site in southeast Florida, where two types of pottery were recovered, one with a paste with sponge spicule inclusions and the other with a paste with sand inclusions. Both of these are found at the Joseph Reed site in contexts dated earlier than are generally recovered in their respective heartlands. The chapter by Campbell, Thomas, and Mathews examines the incidence and distribution of fiber-tempered pottery in the Elliotts Point complex of northwest Florida. They argue that the paucity of fiber-tempered pottery in those sites is directly related to the control of trade routes by local entrepreneurs engaged in the Poverty Point exchange networks.

The next four chapters are based on research carried out on pottery on or near the Poverty Point site. As noted above, many archaeologists have highlighted the important role this site played in the movement of pottery across the Gulf coastal plain. In the first chapter in this series, Hays and Weinstein discuss the stratigraphic and horizontal context of a large sample of sherds that they analyzed from the site. They use these data to evaluate broad research questions on the origin and function of pottery at Poverty Point. Principal among their conclusions is that St. Johns was the earliest pottery at Poverty Point. Gibson and Melancon examine the evidence for early pottery in the LMRV at several sites including Poverty Point, Jaketown, Meche-Wilkes, and Ruth Canal. They conclude that pottery with clay and other inclusions and bearing Tchefuncte designs appears in contexts preceding or coeval with fiber-tempered materials. The next two chapters use petrographic thin-section analysis to evaluate whether different pottery types from the Poverty Point site were manufactured locally. Ortmann and Kidder use a computer-aided petrographic analytical technique and conclude that local manufacturing was an important part of the ceramic industry. Stoltman uses a more traditional petrographic analysis and concludes that most of the sherds examined were probably imports.

These disagreements over similar data should not distress us. Instead, they should be taken to indicate a vigorous field of research, and one that is likely to produce new data, and new disagreements, for some time to come.

2

Common Origins and Divergent Histories in the Early Pottery Traditions of the American Southeast

Kenneth E. Sassaman

The oldest pottery traditions in the American Southeast consist of fiber-tempered wares whose origins arguably can be traced to a single source. The probable locus of origin for all lineages of fiber-tempered pottery in the south Atlantic, peninsular Florida, and the eastern Gulf Coast is most likely the south-central coast of present-day Georgia and northeast Florida. Although radiometric assays for the earliest pottery in this coastal area are scarce, this pottery dates to at least 4500 radiocarbon years B.P., or roughly 5200–5000 calendar years B.P. (all dates hereafter are reported as uncalibrated radiocarbon years B.P.; assays without correction for fractionation but made on samples of wood charcoal are treated *as if* they were corrected because the standard for correction is wood). Shortly thereafter the innovation spread north and south along the Atlantic coast and into the Savannah and St. Johns River valleys. Subregional traditions began to appear after 4200 B.P., with northeast Florida and the Savannah River region diverging into the distinctive Orange and Stallings series by 4000 B.P. While these emergent traditions are best known from the elaborate decorations applied to vessel surfaces, new data on the chronology, technology, and function of early pottery provide a more nuanced perspective on the causes of subregional variations. In this chapter I take an expressly technofunctional perspective on Orange and Stallings to explore causes for variation in these early traditions, paying particular attention to patterns of interactions among regional groups that both enabled and thwarted technological change.

The data I draw upon here consist of technofunctional and stylistic attributes of sherds from dozens of sites in the Savannah, Ogeechee, and St. Johns Basins, as well as on the coasts of South Carolina and Georgia. Currently the database includes values for 2,014 Stallings and related vessel lots from 34 sites in the greater Savannah River region and 599 Orange vessels from seven sites in the middle St. Johns. I should note that the Florida research is in its nascent stages; data from coastal Florida assemblages are particularly wanting, although ongoing research is beginning to fill this void.

COMMON ORIGINS

Both the Stallings and Orange fiber-tempered pottery series began with plain, flat-bottomed basins that functioned as containers for indirect-heat cooking (i.e., "stone boiling"). The shallow profile and wide orifice of these vessel forms provided easy access for transferring thermal media, and the flat bottoms effectively radiated heat upward from an internal source. The vesicles left from carbonized fibers in the paste curtailed conductive heat loss, although the generally thin walls and wide orifices of these vessels clearly were not conducive to effective insulation of internal heat. The limited incidence of sooted exterior surfaces on rim portions is consistent with an indirect-heat method of cooking. Of the 332 plain Stallings basins with noneroded exterior surfaces, only 22 (6.6 percent) have definite or probable traces of soot; of the 256 plain Orange basins examined to date, only 7 (2.7 percent) bear soot. As we will shortly see, these figures stand in stark contrast to the high proportions of sooted surfaces in certain assemblages of decorated vessels, showing not only that cooking methods varied over time and across forms but also that the lack of sooted surfaces among plain basins cannot be blamed on taphonomic factors. It is important to note that the absence of soot alone is not terribly diagnostic of vessel function, as Saunders (this volume) points out. However, to paraphrase Ralph Linton (1944), it may not always be possible to tell whether a particular vessel was used for prolonged cooking over an open fire, but it is easy to determine, on the basis of morphological and technological attributes of vessels, whether they were suited to this task. Early fiber-tempered basins clearly were not conducive to prolonged, direct-heat cooking.

At 4465 ± 95 B.P., the oldest radiocarbon assay for fiber-tempered pottery in the region continues to be one from Rabbit Mount (38AL15) on the Savannah River (Stoltman 1966). This date on charcoal is corroborated by a second sample spatially independent of the first. Two other Savannah River sites have provided assays in excess of 4200 B.P., and several more sites have assays in excess of 4000 B.P. (Sassaman 2002). With minor exception these associations involve plain fiber-tempered pottery with thickened or flanged lips.

Given the distinct possibility of inundated coastal sites older than 4200 B.P., coupled with problems dating marine shell, there is good reason to believe that early pottery sites on the coast will prove to be the oldest in the region and hence the ultimate source of the innovation. If the 4190 ± 90

B.P. date on oyster shell reported by Marrinan (1975:48) from the base of the Cannon's Point Marsh Ring (9GN57) was not corrected for isotopic fractionation, then we are justified in adding 400 years to the estimate. Other coastal Georgia sites with early dates for pottery include the anomalous 5000 ± 180 B.P. from a hearth at 9Cam167 (Kings Bay) coupled with a second assay of 4260 ± 100 B.P. (Calvert et al. 1979:109). Both age estimates were made on carbonized wood. Other charcoal samples associated with plain fiber-tempered pottery at Sapelo Shell Ring 1 (9MI1-1; Simpkins 1975) and Bilbo (9CH4; Williams 1968:330) are dated ca. 4120 B.P. The Cock Fight site (8DU7460) in the Timucuan Preserve of northeast Florida has recently produced a corrected date of 4330 ± 80 B.P. on shell immediately below a level with plain fiber-tempered pottery (Vicki Rolland, personal communication, 2001).

A tentative model for the origin and regional spread of fiber-tempered pottery during the period 4600–3800 B.P. is presented in Figure 2.1. Based primarily on chronometric data, the model posits a common origin for plain, flat-bottomed vessel technology on the south coast of Georgia, ca. 4600–4500 B.P., followed by rapid spread into the lower Savannah region and to the mouth of the St. Johns from 4500 to 4200 B.P. A final expansion into the middle Savannah and middle to upper St. Johns occurred from 4200 to 3800 B.P. With the possible exception of the central Florida Gulf Coast (Bullen 1972), all other occurrences of fiber-tempered pottery in the greater Southeast, including those of the Ocmulgee Big Bend, the Oconee, the Chattahoochee, and the Florida panhandle, postdate 3800 B.P. and consist of assemblages that pale in comparison to heartland Orange and Stallings assemblages in terms of density and frequency.

In the geographical expanse of early fiber-tempered pottery shown in Figure 2.1, at least two and possibly four distinct cultural formations are recognized in the centuries prior to the emergence of pottery. Centered in the upper and middle Savannah River valley were members of the Late Archaic Paris Island phase (Elliott et al. 1994). Radiocarbon dates for this phase fall between 4500 and 4200 B.P., although it most likely arose from local Middle Archaic traditions dating to at least 5800 B.P. As I have shown elsewhere (Sassaman 1998), members of the local successor to Paris Island— the Mill Branch phase of 4200–3800 B.P.—never adopted pottery despite prolonged interaction with pottery-using groups. These decidedly nonpottery traditions mark the northernmost and farthest interior extent of *early* fiber-tempered pottery in the Southeast.

The southern end of the geographic extent of early fiber-tempered pottery was home to cultures of the Mount Taylor tradition. Although poorly known, Mount Taylor has origins extending to at least 5500 B.P., when shell

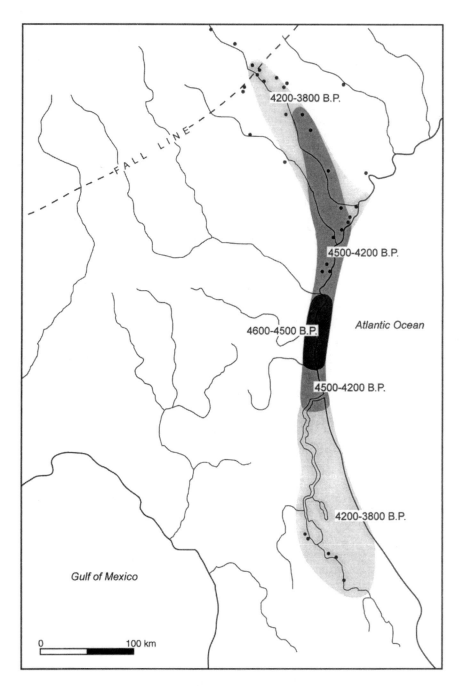

Figure 2.1. Hypothetical model of the origins and spread of fiber-tempered pottery (dots indicate Stallings and Orange sites from which technofunctional data on pottery have been derived).

middens began to accumulate at sites on the middle St. Johns. At least one such midden, Harris Creek on Tick Island (8VO24), was initiated as a mortuary mound (Aten 1999). Later mounds of Mount Taylor or descendant cultures include the earthen Tomoka Mounds of coastal Volusia County (8VO81; Piatek 1994). A coquina shell midden at the base of a 3-m-high conical mound (Mound 6) at Tomoka yielded a corrected date of 4460 ± 70 B.P. Other contexts and dates for prepottery components in the St. Johns region show continuity from Mount Taylor times to the Orange period (Milanich 1994:86–88; Russo et al. 1992).

Interactions between middle Savannah and northeast Florida prepottery groups are apparent in the regional distribution of bannerstones (Figure 2.2). Although generally rare in Florida, bannerstones are not all that uncommon in the St. Johns region, considering especially that lithic materials for manufacturing these items are over 350 km distant. Northeast Florida sites such as Tomoka Mound 6 (8VO81), the Thornhill Mounds (8VO58), and several shell middens have produced several examples of a variety of bannerstone Knoblock (1939) referred to as the Southern Ovate (Douglass 1882; Goggin 1952:126–127; Moore 1894). This form is highly diagnostic of the Paris Island phase of the Savannah River valley. In fact, two locales of manufacture have been documented in the piedmont of the Savannah (Sassaman 1998). During the subsequent Mill Branch phase a more elaborate variety of bannerstone known as the Notched Southern Ovate was made and distributed throughout the Savannah Basin but rarely exported outside this region. One example from Hardee County, Florida (Purdy 1996:71), is almost certainly from the middle Savannah.

Inasmuch as the regional distribution of bannerstones made in the middle Savannah mimics the regional distribution of early fiber-tempered pottery, the mechanisms that account for bannerstone distributions apparently enabled the spread of vessel technology. I hasten to add, however, that groups with individuals making bannerstones in the middle Savannah never adopted pottery, although they clearly interacted with pottery-using people through soapstone and perhaps shell bead exchange, as well as bannerstone exchange.

Unfortunately, little is known about prepottery groups in the area between the middle Savannah and middle St. Johns. One poorly defined complex tentatively called the Allendale phase (Sassaman et al. 2002; Whatley 2002) consists of diagnostic stemmed and notched hafted bifaces with possible affinities to the Benton tradition of the Midsouth (note that one Southern Ovate bannerstone was found in a burial at the Perry site [1LU25] in the Tennessee River valley [Webb and DeJarnette 1942]). Allendale phase lithics have been found at the base of two shell middens in the coastal plain

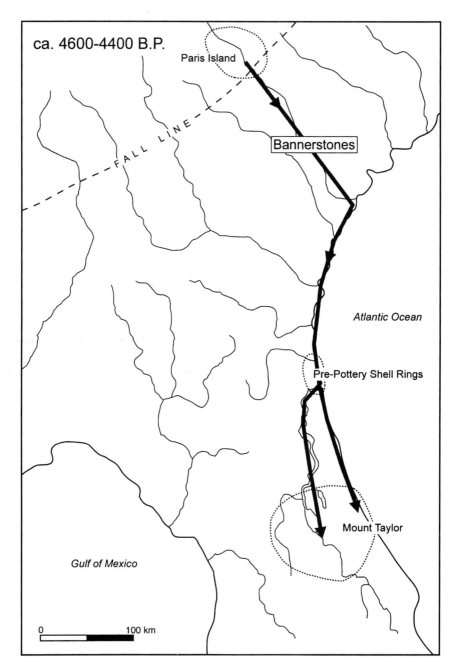

Figure 2.2. Hypothetical model of bannerstone exchange from the middle Savannah to the St. Johns region among preceramic populations.

along the Savannah River valley and these components appear to be the immediate predecessors of early Stallings culture, presumably dating to ca. 4800–4400 B.P.

The other significant prepottery population consists of the elusive coastal dwellers. Until recently archaeologists were divided between two opposing views on coastal settlement: (1) that the coast was incapable of sustaining a human presence until after 4200 B.P. (that is, until after sea level rise had slowed sufficiently to permit the development of productive estuaries) and (2) that any evidence for coastal occupations prior to this time was destroyed by transgressions of the shoreline (see Russo 1996b). New evidence for prepottery shell deposits dating to as early as 5600 B.P. has been found by Mike Russo and colleagues working at the Timucuan Preserve north of Jacksonville. Clearly the coast sustained relatively permanent populations long before pottery appeared, although too little is known about them to speculate on possible roles in bannerstone exchange and other regional interactions.

In sum, fiber-tempered pottery predating 4000 B.P. appears to have a common origin on or near the south coast of Georgia and was geographically circumscribed at this time to the Savannah and St. Johns Basins and the intervening coasts of Georgia and northeast Florida. An existing conduit of interaction between prepottery groups at distal ends of this expanse undoubtedly facilitated the spread of early pottery, although not in the direct sense that they themselves carried this knowledge or actual craft from place to place. Indeed, the distal components of this line of interaction were either late to adopt pottery or, in the case of the Paris Island and Mill Branch phases, resistant to its adoption altogether. Parenthetically, both the Paris Island/Mill Branch and Mount Taylor traditions involved the local extraction of freshwater shellfish (unionids in the middle Savannah, *Viviparus* in the middle St. Johns, and coquina on the coast). Whereas shellfishing among Mount Taylor groups has long been recognized, only in the past few years has an equivalent subsistence pursuit been recognized for the middle Savannah prior to the Stallings period, owing largely to a new suite of radiocarbon dates from a thick stratum of mussels at Stallings Island (9CB1) (Sassaman 1999b).

DIVERGENT HISTORIES

Despite overall similarity in the form and technology of the Southeast's earliest fiber-tempered wares, subtle differences between early Stallings and Orange pottery reflect differences in the ecology and lithology of the respective locales. The plain, flat-bottomed basins that dominate Stallings assemblages prior to 3800 B.P. have an average orifice diameter of 36.3 ± 6.1 cm and walls that are on average about 9.0 ± 1.8 mm thick (measured 3 cm below lip). Orange basins are smaller and thin walled, with an average orifice of 21.6 ± 6.7 cm and average wall thickness of 8.0 ± 1.8 mm. Both appear to be hand modeled and generally oval or round in plan, although some Orange Plain vessels have rectangular shapes with one or more "spouted" corners and lug handles, features completely absent on Stallings basins.

As noted earlier, soot is rarely observed on Stallings and Orange basins. In the Savannah region vessels were clearly used as containers for indirect-heat cooking. The region was home to a soapstone cooking-stone technology whose roots can be traced to the late Middle Archaic (ca. 5800 B.P.). Where soapstone outcrops in the lower piedmont of the Savannah River, cooking stones are found by the hundreds in Paris Island and Mill Branch phase assemblages (Ledbetter 1995; Wood et al. 1986). They were also exported downriver to early Stallings communities of the lower Savannah (Sassaman 1993a; Stoltman 1974) and continued to be used through classic Stallings times after lower Savannah groups relocated to the middle Savannah after 4000 B.P. Despite changes in technology that rendered vessels better suited for direct-heat cooking, the traditional method of stone boiling was never relinquished through the entire Stallings sequence in the middle Savannah (Sassaman 1993a, 2000).

Stone suitable for indirect-heat cooking is rare in the St. Johns, and soapstone, or any other rock, for that matter, was not routinely imported for this purpose. As on the Georgia coast, baked-clay objects may have been a substitute for rock, although the frequency of these items is generally low. The Bluffton collection at the Florida Museum of Natural History includes only nine specimens, averaging about 200 g each. Early pottery assemblages from the north coast of Florida appear to be void of these items (Saunders, this volume; Michael Russo, personal communication, 2001). As Saunders (this volume) suggests, flat-bottomed Orange basins may have been used over embers, a technique that would not routinely produce soot on upper walls of vessels. In this regard, it is noteworthy that the thin walls of Orange Plain vessels are matched by equally thin bases (8.2 ± 2.7 mm at Bluffton [8VO22]). While such thin bases would afford good thermal conductivity to these vessels, the ultimate evidence for direct-heat cooking will come from use-alteration data (i.e., thermal attrition of basal sherds), which, unfortunately, are too few at this point to judge.

The actual foods processed in early vessels and the means by which this was accomplished may account for much of the interregional variation in form and technology. St. Johns shell middens with early Orange pottery consist largely of freshwater snails (*Viviparus*), and early coastal counterparts are often dominated by coquina (*Donax variabilis*). Both types of shellfish are minute compared to oysters and clams and thus likely required some sort of container for cooking. The small, flat-bottomed Orange basins would have been ideal for quick snail and coquina processing. We can imagine that the lugs and spouts of such vessels enabled the entire vessel to be lifted and its liquid contents poured into serving containers.

The larger and thicker Stallings basins, on the other hand, appear to have been used for rendering oil from hickory nuts, perhaps among other tasks (Sassaman 1995b). Although hickory does not constitute a major arboreal component of the coastal plain locales in which early Stallings pottery first appears, the spread of pottery technology into the Fall Zone of the middle Savannah, where hickory was prevalent, is seemingly tied to the mass processing of mast resources. The Victor Mills site (9CB138) in Columbia County, Georgia, exemplifies such intensive use of mast (Sassaman, unpublished data). This small, single-component site overlooking the middle Savannah floodplain contains scores of large storage pits, enough to hold an estimated 1,800-plus bushels of nuts. Dating to ca. 4000 B.P., the pits at Victor Mills contain plain fiber-tempered pottery, soapstone slabs, and large nutting stones.

Technologies within and between the various centers of fiber-tempered traditions diverged markedly after about 4000 B.P. Stylistically, the Stallings and Orange series bear little similarity, with the former dominated by linear punctations and the latter by incising. Intuitively, the divergence between the ware groups would appear to be explicable in geographic terms alone; that is, Stallings and Orange communities were seemingly circumscribed in noncontiguous subregions. Although the intervening area of coastal Georgia contains assemblages with elements of both traditions, unique stylistic treatments, such as grooving and separate punctates over incisions, may warrant a separate taxonomic class, heretofore known as St. Simons (De-Pratter 1979; Sassaman 1993a:195–198).

Even within subregions of stylistic similarity, such as the riverine Stallings sites of the greater middle Savannah, local variations in the technology of contemporaneous pottery are apparent. For instance, 97 percent of 166 punctated Stallings vessels from sites in the middle Savannah proper were tempered with fiber, and only about one-fifth of these have visible aplastics (generally fine sand) in the paste. In contrast, only 24 percent of 183 punctated vessels from sites along nearby Brier Creek contain fiber, and almost two-thirds of these include visible aplastics. Over two-thirds of the 139 vessels lacking fiber were tempered with sand; the remaining vessels lack any sort of visible aplastics. Finally, 550 vessels from sites of the adjacent Ogeechee River are split evenly between fiber and sand tempered, with only one of the fiber-tempered specimens lacking visible aplastics. Chi-square tests of association indicate that none are these interareal differences in paste are likely due to chance alone (Sassaman and Rudolphi 2001).

Similarly divergent patterns are evident in mean vessel wall thickness. Middle Savannah vessels are the thinnest on average, with a mean of 8.5 ± 1.9 mm. Brier Creek vessels are a bit thicker at 9.9 ± 1.9 mm on average, while Ogeechee River vessels are especially thick at 11.8 ± 1.9 mm on average. Difference of means tests using Student's t distribution reveal strong nonrandom tendencies in all pairwise comparisons (Sassaman and Rudolphi 2001).

Increasing the scale of comparison to encompass the entire region of Stallings pottery, coastal as well as riverine, we find further divergences in terms of vessel function. Despite overall morphological similarity and clear stylistic similarity with riverine assemblages, coastal Stallings vessels post-dating 3800 B.P. are often sooted (42 percent, or 82 of 194 vessels examined; Sassaman 1993a:159), a pattern clearly indicative of routine direct-heat cooking. From this point forward coastal wares were modified to improve thermal efficiency: vessel walls became thinner, the ratio of orifice diameter to volume decreased, and fiber temper gave way to sand. This is hardly a surprising trend given the lack of suitable raw materials for indirect-heat cooking on the coast. What is remarkable is that similar technological changes took place at interior riverine sites, but throughout the Stallings period in this subregion, pots were not routinely used over fire (less than 5 percent of over 300 vessels show traces of soot). Recent excavations at Mims Point (38ED9), Ed Marshall (38ED5), and Stallings Island (9CB1) have produced abundant, well-preserved, and well-dated assemblages of sherds to show that this variation in use alteration cannot be attributed to taphonomic factors (Sassaman, unpublished data).

Technofunctional variation among Orange pottery might be best explained in temporal terms if the culture-historical sequence constructed by Bullen (1954, 1955, see also 1972) over 50 years ago were to hold up to modern data, but apparently it does not. In brief, Bullen proposed a sequence of four or five subperiods spanning the fourth millennium before present. Essentially, the sequence entails a roughly 350-year period of exclusively plain fiber-tempered pottery, followed by the introduction and apogee of incised fiber-tempered wares, followed by a transitional period in which sponge spicules and sand became prevalent in pastes, leading eventually to the St. Johns tradition of (nonfiber-tempered) chalky, spiculate wares after 3000 B.P. Analyses of Orange pottery have traditionally divided assemblages into plain, decorated, and chalky wares as if these reflected sequential temporal phases. This was certainly the approach I took in a recent paper

(Sassaman 2002) in which I concluded that variations in form and function of Orange pottery parallel the trend toward direct-heat cooking evident on the coast of South Carolina.

New AMS dates for incised sherds from the middle St. Johns valley refute my inferences about technofunctional change in Orange pottery. Seven assays on soot from samples from three sites show that incised Orange pottery in the middle St. Johns dates from ca. 4100 to 3600 B.P. and is thus coeval with assemblages dominated by plain basins (Sassaman 2003a). Moreover, recent petrographic analysis by Ann Cordell (this volume) reveals that incised Orange sherds from the middle St. Johns often contain sponge spicules. In short, plain basins and incised fiber-tempered vessels are coeval over the period 4000–3600 B.P., and spiculate pastes date as early as 4000 B.P. in Orange incised vessels from the middle St. Johns. It follows that technofunctional variation in Orange pottery needs to be explained as a consequence of function or culture, not time.

Variation in the technology and function of Orange vessels from the middle St. Johns is rather marked indeed. Whereas only 7 of 256 (2.7 percent) plain basins bear traces of soot, 180 of 266 (67.7 percent) incised vessels are sooted. A similar proportion (64.4 percent) of 73 fiber-tempered vessels with spiculate pastes are sooted. In terms of vessel size, orifices average 21.6 ± 6.7 cm for plain basins and 29.6 ± 8.8 cm for incised vessels. Presumably vessel height parallels these differences, although metric data are insufficient to substantiate this. We now have good evidence that coiling was common to Orange Incised vessels (Endonino 2000), an innovation that would have enabled taller vessel profiles.

Vessel wall thickness generally covaries with vessel size. Orange Incised pottery from the middle St. Johns is especially thick, 11.3 ± 2.8 mm, compared with Orange Plain at only 8.0 ± 1.8 mm. Coupled with the porous paste, thick-walled Orange pottery was not especially efficient in transferring heat. However, the addition of sponge spicules to the clay may have improved thermal conductivity over that of fiber-tempered vessels. By the time fiber stopped being added to clay, perhaps as early as 3500 B.P., wall thickness had decreased markedly. Among the techniques used to achieve thinner walls was rigorous scraping of interior vessel walls prior to firing.

Technofunctional data on coastal Orange pottery are yet too few to make definitive comparisons with middle St. Johns River assemblages. However, Saunders's (this volume) vessel data on the 3700–3600 B.P. Rollins Shell Ring site (8DU7510), coupled with some preliminary observations from a few other northeast Florida coastal sites (Jim Mallard, personal communication, 2001), reflect an extremely low incidence of sooted sherds. This stands in sharp contrast to not only the middle St. Johns assemblages of equal age but also those of coastal Georgia and South Carolina. Because all of these sites are in areas with little to no local stone, the availability of rock suitable for stone boiling is alone insufficient to explain the development of direct-heat cooking technology.

Saunders (this volume) also emphasizes that the Rollins assemblage, along with that of the coastal Summer Haven (8SJ46) site to the south (State of Florida 1995), boasts an unusually high percentage of decorated pottery. Her observation that many contemporaneous sites in the region contain few decorated pots is bolstered by recent dates from Blue Spring Midden B (8VO143) on the middle St. Johns, where a virtually pure plain Orange assemblage dates to 3800–3500 B.P. (Sassaman 2003b). In contrast, assemblages from the contemporaneous Tick Island (8VO24) and Mouth of Silver Glen Run (8LA1) sites, some 22 km downriver from Blue Spring, are dominated by incised Orange pottery (Sassaman 2003a). Thus, both riverine and coastal settings for Orange pottery involved occupations where highly decorated vessels were used and discarded, as well as coeval settlements involving primarily, if not exclusively, plain wares. It remains to be determined whether technofunctional differences parallel these intersite patterns in surface treatment.

If interassemblage differences in the incidence of decorated pottery cannot be explained in temporal terms alone, we should consider further the possibility of functional specialization among sites. Saunders (1999) has suggested that shell "ring" sites such as Rollins were nodes of regional interaction, where groups congregated to feast on the bounty of estuarine resources (see also Michie 1979). Implicit to this line of reasoning is some degree of settlement hierarchy, whereby particular locations on the landscape were not only locations of aggregation but also nexuses of symbolic power. In the past few years archaeologists have increasingly regarded shell rings and shell mounds as monumental constructions of ranked societies (Claassen 1996; Russo 2004), not simply the accumulated refuse of egalitarian foragers (e.g., Milner and Jefferies 1998).

None of the shell accumulations in the middle Savannah evoke images of monumentality, as all investigated to date are either downslope dumps or amalgams of shell-filled pits. Nonetheless, there is sufficient patterning in the interassemblage variation of pottery and other data to suggest that Stallings Island was the "center" of a regional population. The classic Stallings period of ca. 3800–3500 B.P. involved intensive settlement at Stallings Island, Mims Point, Ed Marshall, and several other locations on the middle Savannah, as well as nearby enclaves on Brier Creek and the Ogeechee River. As mentioned before, these clusters of contemporaneous settlement

yield pottery assemblages that are stylistically indistinguishable, but technologically distinct. With independent data on the handedness of potters, I
have suggested (Sassaman and Rudolphi 2001) that consistency in pottery
technology within each of its three riverine locales of occurrence was a
result of postmarital residence patterns that ensured generational continuity
among related potters. Patterns of decorative expression and pottery function, however, crosscut residential clusters to unite riverine Stallings communities in a regional culture apart from its coastal counterparts. These differences of material expression reflect the multiple communities of practice
potters participated in, communities that were constituted not simply
through residential proximity and inheritance but also through affiliations
that evolved with changes in social identity (e.g., from daughter to daugh-
ter-in-law) over the course of potters' lives.

Feasts at Stallings Island were among the likely opportunities for groups
allied through marriage to renew and negotiate social obligations amongst
themselves. Like Rollins Shell Ring, Stallings Island boasts an unusually
large percentage of decorated wares. More important, Stallings Island is one
of the few sites in the middle Savannah to yield vessels with carinated rims,
some as much as 50 cm in diameter. We have known about these forms since
the publication of the Cosgroves' 1929 expedition to Stallings Island (Claflin 1931:plate 11), but only recently has the entire collection been available
for study. William Claflin's portion of the 1929 assemblage was delivered to
Harvard's Peabody Museum a few years ago and integrated with the remaining collection. I recently spent a week sorting through all the pottery,
isolating and collecting data on carinated rim sherds. Below I summarize in
brief some of the salient findings of this analysis as they pertain to inferences about social integration and feasting.

One hundred thirty of 913 vessel lots identified in the Stallings Island
collection include carinated rim profiles. This amounts to over 14 percent
of the vessel assemblage. Only two other sites in the middle Savannah have
produced carinated rim sherds, one with two examples (Tinker Creek
[38AK224]) and the other with a single occurrence (38MC494). Similar
forms are entirely absent in the lower coastal plain and coastal assemblages
of Stallings affiliation, as well as in those from sites along Brier Creek and
the Ogeechee River. In some cases the absence of this minority form may
be simply a matter of sample bias, but in most cases sample sizes are sufficiently large (100 or more vessel lots) to preclude this possibility. Thus,
Stallings Island stands alone as the only site with more than a trace of carinated vessels.

Surface treatments on vessels with carinated rims are diverse. Although the majority involve some form of decoration, nearly one-quarter are plain and another third are merely simple stamped. The balance consist of 20 percent drag and jab punctate, 4 percent separate linear punctate, 8 percent incised, and 10 percent with multiple treatments, usually a combination of simple stamping and punctation or incising. The prevalence of simple-stamped surface treatments runs counter to assemblages of classic Stallings times (ca. 3800–3500 B.P.) and would seem to suggest that the typology established for relative dating of Stallings pottery (Sassaman 1993a:106) does not apply to carinated forms. That the carinated vessel assemblage at Stallings Island either predates or postdates classic Stallings times finds little support in recent radiocarbon dating (Sassaman 1999b). Nevertheless, there is much to recommend that carinated forms were made, used, and discarded toward the end of classic Stallings times, just prior to abandonment of the middle Savannah at ca. 3500 B.P. Especially noteworthy in this respect is the prevalence of sandy pastes. Although all but 2 percent of the assemblage contains the diagnostic fiber tempering of Stallings wares, 70 percent contain only minor traces of fiber, and 80 percent include visible aplastic inclusions, generally fine to medium sand. This trend toward increasingly sandier pastes and reduction in fiber continues into the Thoms Creek and Refuge phases of the Early Woodland period, as does the prevalence of simple-stamped surfaces and, in the case of the Thoms Creek tradition, recurvate rim profiles reminiscent of carinated bowls (Sassaman 1993b:131–132). Moreover, roughly 10 percent of the carinated vessel lots from Stallings Island include simple-stamped or incised lip treatments, attributes that are common in the Thoms Creek phase of the middle Savannah (Phelps 1968). In short, the carinated assemblage from Stallings Island appears to have accumulated during the waning years of classic Stallings times and hence may have been part of a cultural response to conditions (social, political, ecological, or otherwise) that ultimately led to regional abandonment.

The formal and technological properties of carinated bowls from Stallings Island provide some basis for inferring function. In overall design the Stallings Island vessels are highly reminiscent of Mississippian carinated bowls. In his study of Barnett phase (northwest Georgia) Mississippian vessel function, Hally (1986) makes a strong case that this form was used primarily to prepare and serve large quantities of liquid-based foods in highly social contexts. The low, flat profile of the form and its wide orifice provide good access to contents while remaining stable and spill resistant. These same properties render carinated forms inefficient for prolonged cooking, suggesting to Hally (1986:288–289) that those with soot (43 percent of his sample) were used to reheat foods prepared in vessels better suited to cooking. Carinated bowls in Hally's Barnett phase sample fall into two size

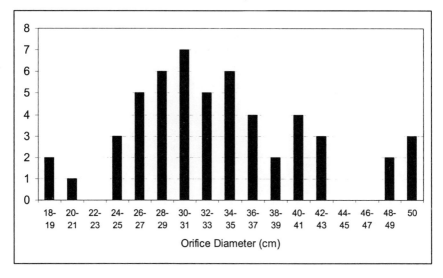

Figure 2.3. Absolute frequency distribution of carinated vessels (n = 53) from Stallings Island (9CB1) by orifice diameter.

classes: small bowls with orifice diameters in the range of 15–25 cm and large bowls ranging from 28 to 42 cm in orifice diameter.

Carinated bowls from Stallings Island do not cluster neatly into distinct size classes, although the entire range conforms moderately well to that of the Barnett phase. With a few exceptional outliers at either end, the frequency distribution of orifice diameters for Stallings Island specimens (n = 53) is unimodal (Figure 2.3), with a mean of 33.3 cm and standard deviation of 7.8 cm. There are no strong tendencies for orifice diameter to covary with surface treatment, paste attributes, or wall thickness, although those vessels with either incising or multiple surface treatments are, on average, the widest (incised = 40.3 ± 8.4 cm; multiple = 38.6 ± 7.6 cm). Clearer distinction among vessels is found in the frequency distribution of rim height, which is more suggestive of bimodality (Figure 2.4). Only 2 (5.7 percent) of the 35 vessels with rim heights in the upper mode (i.e., >37 mm) are plain; 20 of 78 (28.2 percent) in the lower mode are plain. If, as Hally (1986:283) suggests, the upper rims of carinated bowls were decorated to communicate information about social identity or status, Stallings potters may have manipulated rim height to fulfill social as well as technological needs. Overall vessel size may also be expected to covary with degree or scale of social interaction (e.g., Blitz 1993), so the taller rims might be expected to occur on the largest vessels. Whereas those with tall rims (>37 mm) have orifice diameters averaging larger (34.6 ± 9.2 cm) than

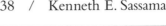

Figure 2.4. Absolute frequency distribution of carinated vessels (n = 106) from Stallings Island (9CB1) by rim height.

those with short rims (32.7 ± 7.0 cm), the difference is not statistically significant. Data on total vessel height or volume are too few to test this hypothesis.

These new data on the carinated vessel form at Stallings Island foreground the possibility that a significant "push" for intensified production and use of pottery was increased demand for serving vessels, not cooking vessels (see Rice 1999). The extent to which such incentives were driven by the aggrandizing behaviors of would-be "big men" (Hayden 1995a) would have depended on local historical circumstances. Irrespective of social intensification, the regular use of pottery vessels for serving purposes is expected to have led to higher rates of pottery production and consumption by virtue of short use-life. Ethnoarchaeological studies worldwide provide data to show that serving vessels last an average of only 1.5 years, compared to 2.2 years for cooking vessels and 5.2 years for storage vessels (Mills 1989; Rice 1987:table 9.4). Thus, increased demand for serving vessels in particular had the greatest potential for production intensification of vessels in general (cf. Brown 1989). The appearance of carinated forms at Stallings Island at ca. 3500 B.P. coincides not only with the waning years of occupation in the middle Savannah but also with the widespread adoption of pottery as regional populations assumed more dispersed settlement patterns. In this context, the highly individualistic and differentiated surface treatments of the Stallings and Thoms Creek traditions gave way to the seemingly anonymous simple-stamped decorations of the Refuge tradition. Pottery vessels indicative of serving functions are rare in Refuge assemblages of the Savannah River region, although soapstone bowls, now known to postdate Stallings times in the region (Sassaman 1999a), may have filled this need.

CONCLUSION

Early fiber-tempered pottery in the South Atlantic Slope had a common origin, presumably the coast of south Georgia/northeast Florida. Extant social alliances between communities in the middle Savannah and St. Johns regions appear to have contributed to, if not directly resulted in, the spread of flat-bottomed basin technology. The impetus for adopting this innovation was likely culinary, although social alliances clearly affected the rate and spread of innovations thereafter for reasons other than food-processing efficiency. Divergences in the technology, morphology, decoration, and use of early pottery after about 4000 B.P. are arguably the result of varying levels of social integration and sociopolitical differentiation among regional populations. Demand for serving vessels for feasting at "centers" of social interaction (competitive or otherwise; Hayden 2001) may have led to increased demand for vessels in general and thus been the essential factor in production intensification.

The diversification of cultural expression after 4000 B.P. manifested in the varied choices potters made about shaping, decorating, and using vessels was arguably rooted in the ongoing negotiation of identity and affiliation begun long before pottery was invented. The coexistence of groups using pottery and those eschewing pottery, or the coexistence of groups using pots directly over fire and others maintaining age-old techniques of stone boiling, or the coexistence of groups adding sand to pastes and others adding sponge spicules must be understood as relational phenomena—relational across both the socialized spaces that defined boundaries and alliances and the deep time that naturalized cultural preference. As we can see in many of the chapters of this volume, more nuanced perspectives on the culture histories of early pottery are enabled by expanding our perspective to include technology and function, as well as surface treatment, as active and relevant expressions of cultural choice.

3

Spatial Variation in
Orange Culture Pottery

Interaction and Function

Rebecca Saunders

Orange pottery is a low-fired earthenware tempered with Spanish moss (Simpkins and Allard 1986; Simpkins and Scoville 1981) or palmetto (Brain and Peterson 1971) fibers. The traditional culture history of the type places production of Orange wares between ca. 4000 and 2500 B.P. (Milanich 1994:94). A terminal Transitional period between ca. 2500 and 2000 B.P. has also been recognized. This has been defined, in part, by pastes with both fiber and other inclusions, usually sand, sponge spicules, or both. These mixed pastes have been interpreted as indicating an evolution of the paste toward later types (e.g., Bullen 1959, 1972); however, the reality of this "transition" has been criticized along a number of fronts (see below and Heide 2000; Milanich 1994; Mitchell 1993:52; Shannon 1986, 1987).

Distribution of the ware, and the eponymous culture, extends at least as far north as southern coastal Georgia, where, in some of the literature, it overlaps with Stallings fiber-tempered pottery (e.g., DesJean 1985; Shannon 1987). In other reconstructions, a St. Simons phase and series of types exists on the Georgia coast between the two (see Saunders and Hays, this volume, for a more comprehensive discussion). Orange wares are found south along the Atlantic coast and St. Johns and Indian River drainages to the Glades area and along the Florida Gulf coast in the Tampa Bay region and the panhandle. Although it has a much wider distribution, the heartland of Orange pottery production appears to have been the St. Johns River valley and the adjacent Atlantic coast (Figure 3.1).[1]

The material aspects of Orange culture are well described (e.g., Bullen and Stoltman 1972; see Milanich 1994 for a summary). In addition to fiber-tempered pottery, artifacts of shell and bone, particularly shell hammers and gouges and bone pins, are common. Stone, not locally available in most Orange territory, is uncommon. In coastal areas, by the beginning of the Orange period, adaptation to estuarine resources is total. Subsistence information indicates that small, netable fish and molluscs, primarily oyster, comprised over 95 percent of the diet. The Orange culture adaptation to the estuaries

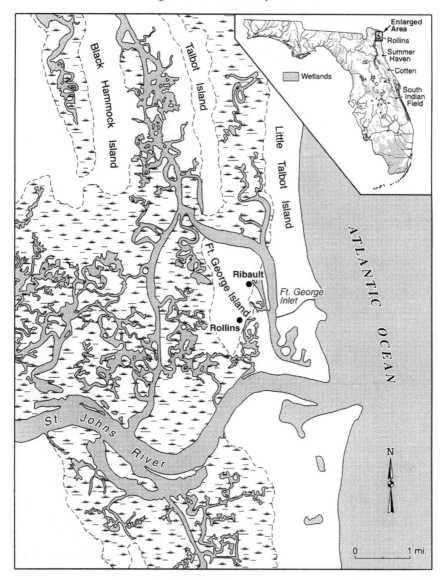

Figure 3.1. Location of sites mentioned in the text.

was so complete that there appears to have been little need to develop extraregional ties through trade—exotic artifacts are rare. Yet, as this study
demonstrates, Orange pottery is extremely cohesive stylistically, indicating
fairly strong interaction over some 302 km (188 miles), the distance from
Ft. George Island, Florida, to South Indian Field (8BR23).

Orange culture pottery from ring contexts at the Rollins Shell Ring site

(8DU7510; also 8DU72, see Russo et al. 1993:101–102) north of Jacksonville, Florida, dates to around 3800–3600 B.P. (corrected) or between 4350 and 3350 2cal B.P. (see below). Bullen's description of the Orange 3 period was based on results from the Summer Haven site (8SJ46). If his single date on shell from that site (3330 ± 200 rcybp) is also corrected for isotopic fractionation and reservoir effect, and calibrated, the result is 2cal 4208 (3644) 3198 B.P. (1cal 3903–3408); the Rollins dates fit well within this range.

In this chapter, I summarize Orange 3 pottery attributes as they are expressed at Rollins and use that information as a basis for exploring intersite differences in Orange culture pottery of 4000–3500 years ago. Three other reasonably well-documented Orange 3 sites provide comparative material for the analysis of Rollins pottery. These include the Summer Haven site (8SJ46), the Cotten site (8VO83), and South Indian Field (8BR23) (Figure 3.1). To anticipate the conclusions, the intersite data suggest that the pottery assemblage at Rollins is stylistically similar to that recovered in quite distant sites but quite different from assemblages at contemporaneous sites in the immediate area. These similarities and differences have implications for interpreting levels of interaction among Orange cultures and for ascribing site function at Rollins.

SITE DESCRIPTIONS

Shell rings are one of three site types recognized for coastal Late Archaic occupations: sheet middens and nonshell sites are the other two settlement types (DePratter 1979). The function of shell ring sites is debated. Many (e.g., Cable 1997; Russo and Heide 2002; Sassaman 1993a; Waring 1968a) consider shell rings ceremonial sites. However, an influential article by Trinkley (1985) argued for a more mundane explanation. Trinkley proposed that rings were the result of day-to-day accretion of meals at egalitarian village sites. Accruing evidence for intentional mounding of massive quantities of food remains at many ring sites (Saunders 2002a, 2002b), including Rollins (Saunders 1999), favors the former hypothesis—that ring construction and use was ceremonial, at least for part of the time. Indeed, one reason for the following comparisons was to examine the differences in pottery assemblages between sheet midden and shell ring sites to determine whether there were significant differences in pottery assemblages between shell rings and the other two site types.

Rollins Shell Ring

At 250 m in diameter and up to 7 m in height, Rollins Shell Ring is one of the larger rings in the Southeast. It is generally horseshoe shaped, but nine smaller rings articulate with the western and northern sides (Figure 3.2). The presence of these "ringlets" alone suggests that something more than a village midden was present at the site. Rollins was tested by Russo and Saunders (1999) as part of a larger research project intended to address the question of shell ring function. Ten 1-×-2-m units were excavated in various areas of the site, including the ring interior, the interior of the ringlets, and the eastern arm of the ring. Additionally, to explore ring formation processes, a 16-×-1-m trench was dug in the western arm, extending from the edge of a ringlet through the ring and into the main ring interior. Profiles of the trench revealed at least three depositional episodes of the main portion of the ring, each consisting of large deposits of loose, whole oyster, along with abundant small fish bone and crab claws; there was little to no soil associated with these deposits. Each of these deposits was capped with a thin (1–3 cm) lens of humic sand or clayey sand. Overlying the whole was a 20-cm-thick midden composed of moderate whole and broken oyster in a dark grayish-brown to brown humic sand. I (Russo and Saunders 1999; Saunders 1999; Saunders and Russo 2000) have speculated that the loose shell and bone were deposited as part of feasting ceremonies accompanying aggregation of the dispersed population of the Fort George Island area.

Studies of zooarchaeological data on seasonality of ring deposition are ongoing. Measurements on Atlantic Croaker (*Micropogonias undulatus*) otoliths from seven different proveniences in the ring indicate that capture was strongly seasonal (Quitmyer 2000); all were taken in the summer. Sectioning and examination of growth rings of all other otoliths large enough to study from the central ring features indicated spring exploitation.[2]

Radiocarbon dates (Table 3.1) on oyster from the western and eastern arms are virtually identical (calibrated intercepts of 3580 ± 70 B.P. and 3620 ± 70 B.P., respectively), indicating that the ring shape was inherent in the site plan at the beginning of ring deposition. Dates from the top and bottom of Feature 1, the main ring deposits exposed in the trench, demonstrate that the ring was built up quickly. It appears that the site saw some later use as well. Dates from the top of the western ring (FS 508) and from a midden or pit feature in the interior of Ringlet I (FS 281) are 1,000 years younger. Though these dates are associated with Orange pottery, these deposits are not considered related to ring use. Deptford and St. Marys pottery were also recovered in small amounts from isolated areas on the site.

As in many ring sites, the center of the ring contained no earth or shell midden and few artifacts; ringlet interiors generally had few artifacts as well, except where later occupations or slopewash occurred. Excavations in the ring were more productive. Orange 3 artifacts from throughout the site

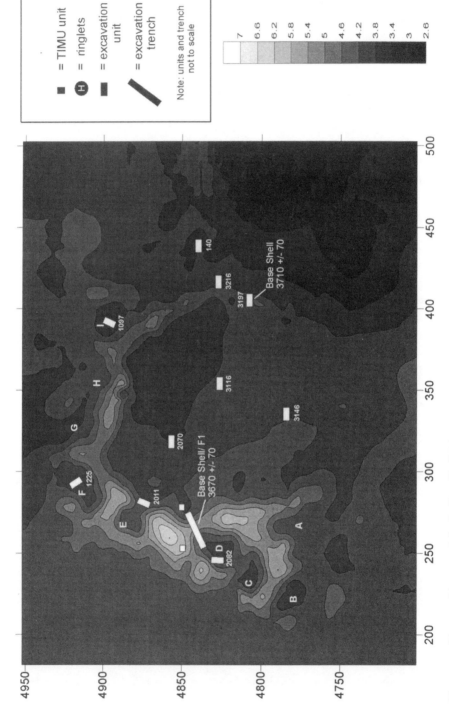

Figure 3.2. Topographic map of the Rollins Shell Ring.

Table 3.1. Radiocarbon dates from the Rollins Shell Ring site.

FS #	Lab #	Description	Sample	Corrected B.P.	2Cal/1Cal (Intercept) 1Cal/2Cal B.P.
281	GX-29516	Unit 1097, 30–40 cmbs, pit feature	Oyster	2460 ± 70[a]	2305/2192 (2110) 2004/1924
467	WK-7433	Unit 3197, 10–20 cmbs, midden	Oyster	2690 ± 60	2610/2460 (2350) 2315/2280
488	WK-7438	Trench 1, Unit 1, Feature 1, top deposit, 33 cmbs	Oyster	3600 ± 60	3640/3570 (3475) 3420/3350
85	Beta-119816	Trench 1, Unit 2, Feature 1, bottom deposit, 90–100 cmbs	Oyster	3670 ± 70	3770/3675 (3580) 3470/3395
508	Beta-119817	Unit 3197, 80–90 cmbs, midden	Oyster	3710 ± 70	3820/3710 (3620) 3545/3440
459	GX-25750	Trench 1, Feature 11, base (initial occupation), 200 cmbs	Bulk carbon	3730 ± 80	4350/4227 (4088) 3932/3842
Russo 1993	Beta-50155	4850N/250E, 60–65 cmbs (Russo 1993)	Oyster	3760 ± 60	3855/3799 (3685) 3620/3540

[a]Calibrated using Calib 4.1.2. Delta R = −5 ± 20. Other calibrations by Beta Analytic.

consisted of pottery, shell tools, bone tools and ornaments, lithic debitage, and ground stone celt fragments (see Saunders 2003). Slightly more than 8,000 Orange sherds were recovered, but only 860 were larger than 3 cm, which were the sherds chosen to conduct the detailed paste and stylistic analysis. Just 10 chert flakes were recovered from the one-quarter-inch screen from all proveniences on the site. Other stone artifacts included 18 small quartz and quartzite fragments, 13 pieces of sandstone, two pieces of chert shatter, one broken chert pebble, one unidentified stone, and a small steatite vessel fragment. Only 10 of these weighed more than 10 g. The two heaviest quartzite artifacts (121.6 g and 93.0 g) were probably celt fragments. Both came from the base of the shell ring in Trench Unit 5. Two whelk shell hammers were recovered from below the shell in Unit 8. The discard of these "heavy-duty" tools indicates a great deal of activity, possibly site preparation, prior to and at the same time as the first shell deposits.

Summer Haven

The closest site to Rollins is the Summer Haven site, 114 km (71 miles) south of Rollins on a barrier island south of Matanzas Inlet. The entire site was never systematically tested or accurately mapped. Ninety-nine percent of this large oyster-shell sheet midden site was already disturbed when a small intact portion in the Route A1A right-of-way was tested by Bullen and Bullen in 1959 (Bullen and Bullen 1961). Bullen and Bullen did note that the site probably originally covered an area of 152 m × 61 m, with the long axis of the site paralleling the shore. The Bullens excavated two adjacent 10-foot-square units in which the minimum depth of the deposit was 1.2 m. The lower portion of this midden was composed primarily of oyster, whereas the upper levels were composed largely of coquina.

More extensive work at Summer Haven was conducted in 1992 by Janus Research (State of Florida 1995). This work was also done to mitigate construction and was restricted to the Highway A1A right-of-way. Janus removed all road fill within the right-of-way, excavated some 30 1-x-2-m units, and then stripped the area to the base of the midden, exposing 142 cultural features. These included postholes that appear to be the remnants of four circular structures. Fourteen human burials were uncovered and analyzed; four of these individuals exhibited artificial cranial deformation. Over 6,000 Orange sherds were analyzed, along with 14 steatite vessel sherds. Eleven silicified limestone flakes were recovered along with three haftable bifaces. Three shell beads, three shell dippers or vessels, and two columnellas were also recovered, along with 73 other shell tools. These included adzes, planes, gouges, and hammers. Bone artifacts were also frequent and included three bone points, 35 bone pins (none of them whole), 14 "miscellaneous" (State of Florida 1995:93, table 15) worked bone fragments, and 21 modified shark teeth. This diverse and abundant artifact assemblage indicated to the researchers that the site represented a village midden. A seasonality study on oysters was abandoned when modern samples from the Matanzas River failed to show differences in growth patterns between the winter and summer months (State of Florida 1995:119–120), so site seasonality is unknown.

Janus's research produced corrected radiocarbon dates of between 4000 and 3700 B.P. and calibrated dates between 4181 and 3613 (Table 3.2), more or less contemporaneous with Rollins. Most important, both Bullen and

Table 3.2. Radiocarbon dates from the Summer Haven site; all dates on shell.

Description	Corrected B.P.	2Cal/1Cal (intercept) 1Cal/2Cal B.P.
S1/2 of Feature 152	3880 ± 70	4063/3949 (3839) 3751/3646
NE1/4 of Feature 101	3840 ± 70	3973/3885 (3811) 3688/3613
NE1/4 of Feature 143	3940 ± 60	4094/3998 (3918) 3836/3759
Burial 10, pit fill	3840 ± 60	3965/3874 (3811) 3696/3630
Column sample 1	4000 ± 70	4181/4089 (3989) 3912/3832

Note: Data from State of Florida 1995. Corrected data calibrated using Calib 4.3, Delta R −5 ± 20. Differences with Table 4.2 are Calib version and reservoir correction value.

Mitchell (1993), who analyzed the Summer Haven pottery for Janus, kept detailed records of designs and motifs on the fiber-tempered sherds.

Cotten Site

The Cotten site was excavated by Griffin and Smith in 1947. This sheet midden, 156.0 km (97.5 miles) from Rollins, paralleled the bank of the Halifax River for some 345 m. The midden ranged between 44 m and 110 m wide (Griffin and Smith 1954), and midden deposits were up to 3.4 m deep. The shell midden was composed primarily of coquina (*Donax variabilis*), though later sites in the area contain oyster. Griffin and Smith suggested that local conditions did not support oyster growth until a rise in sea level backed up the Halifax River and created estuaries.

Griffin and Smith excavated a 7.62-m (25-foot) trench in the densest portion of the midden and four smaller tests in shallower portions of the midden. They recovered 1,513 Orange sherds, 19 steatite sherds (these occurred in the upper levels of the excavations), two bone pins, three incised turtle carapace bones, four shark vertebra beads, two worked antler fragments, and one chert projectile point fragment. Shell artifacts were "not particularly numerous" (Griffin and Smith 1954:48). Only a conch shell adze, a shell disc, and a whelk gouge could be attributed to the Orange period component.

Griffin and Smith did not speculate on site function, nor is there any information on site seasonality. One radiocarbon date is available for Cotten. The assay was run on shell in 1957; the sample was from the middle of the cultural deposits (Bullen 1958:101). The presumably uncorrected date was 3020 ± 200. The corrected and calibrated date is 1cal 3462 (3254) 2961 (2cal 3704–2745). The large sigma makes comparison difficult, but because Bullen included Cotten in his Orange 3 designation, rough contemporaneity with Rollins is assumed. Griffin and Smith also kept good records of designs present, though not as detailed as those from Summer Haven.

South Indian Field

The last site in this comparison is South Indian Field, which Rouse (1951) and Ferguson (1951) investigated in 1944. South Indian Field is on the eastern edge of the marshy terrain surrounding the headwaters of the St. Johns River, 302 km (188 miles) from Rollins. This site, 17.6 km (11 miles) inland, was a 245-X-173-m earth midden, with a maximum depth of around 2.4 m. Rouse profiled amateur excavations done in the 1930s and 1940s by the landowner, A. T. Anderson, and catalogued Anderson's collections. Additional tests, consisting of two 8-X-2-m trenches, were excavated in Middens 1 and 2 (Ferguson 1951).

An extensive earth midden covered the property; the site also contained four elevated areas composed of refuse and patchy shell. What shell there was, according to Rouse (1951) and Russo (personal communication, 2002), was *Unionidea* (freshwater mussel), apple snail (*Pomacea paludosa*), and banded mystery snail (*Viviparus georgianus*). Clam, conch, and oyster were present but rare. A relatively large number of whelk and conch shell tools were present, however, indicating considerable traffic, either physically or in trade, with the coast. Griffin and Smith compared the pottery analysis done by Ferguson (1951) to their results at Cotten, making this site another good candidate for the study of design variability.

ROLLINS POTTERY

In total, 8,331 fiber-tempered sherds were recovered from the test excavations at Rollins. The majority of these were less than 3 cm in surface area and were not subjected to the same level of analysis as the larger sherds—they were simply identified as decorated or plain and counted and weighed. The remaining 800 Orange sherds were examined for a number of technological and stylistic attributes, including type and frequency of inclusions. Frequency of fiber, quartz, and mica was based on Rice (1987:349); Rice's six frequency categories were combined into three: rare (1–3 percent), common (5–10 percent), and abundant (20–30 percent). All observations were made on fresh breaks under 10X magnification. Each fresh break was also examined under 70X magnification for sponge spicules. Construction method, finishing techniques, vessel form, vessel diameter, and design and motif variability were also recorded.

Paste Analysis

The paste analysis indicated that Orange pottery at Rollins was always tempered, usually with "abundant" (71.5 percent of the sherds) to "common"

(27.7 percent) fiber (indicated by the vesicles left by the burned fibers). Less than one percent of the sherds had rare fiber and not a single sherd had no fiber whatsoever. The relatively frequent, charred, examples of fiber remaining in the sherds appear consistent with Spanish moss. Sponge spicules were not present in any of the fiber-tempered sherds, though they did appear in some of the later St. Marys cob- and cord-marked sherds recovered at Rollins. Clays were somewhat micaceous, with rare mica visible in over 50 percent of the sample (much of this was observed on the sherd surface, however; mica was less frequent in the fresh breaks).

Much of the Rollins pottery had inclusions in addition to fiber. Quartz grains were common or abundant in 61 percent of the sherds, rare in 31 percent, and absent in only 8 percent. This sand could be an inclusion in the clay resource. However, much of it is angular to subangular—a characteristic commonly ascribed to added quartz temper (but that does not completely discriminate temper from natural inclusions; Rice 1987:410). Whether natural or intentional, this high incidence of sand in sherds from contexts temporally far removed from anything that could be considered "transitional" (Orange 5) suggests that more rigorous paste analyses from Orange and other early pottery contexts are needed before invoking transitional attributes for pastes with mixed inclusions (see also Cordell, this volume).

Comparative information on paste characteristics of Orange pottery in the literature is hard to assess. Bullen and Bullen (1961:5) mentioned that the paste in sherds from Summer Haven was "normal," although a few sherds had limestone inclusions. Mitchell (1993:51; State of Florida 1995:65) observed "fiber, fiber and sand, sand and fiber, and fiber and shell tempering agents" in his analysis of the Summer Haven sherds recovered in 1992. Mitchell (1993:51) also noted that "pure fiber-tempering was the most common tempering agent identified, and sand and fiber tempering was the least common." However, he added: "It should be noted that even the Orange Period sherds identified and classified as fiber-tempered were found to contain small amounts of sand" (Mitchell 1993:51). Ferguson (1951:17) noted a few "atypical sherds with quartz sand temper" at South Indian Field. Paste at the Cotten site was described only as fiber tempered (Griffin and Smith 1954:33).

Cordell (this volume) provides the first good comparative data on pastes from sites across Florida. Her data indicate that Rollins and Summer Haven share an absence of sponge spicules and a relative abundance of sand inclusions as compared with sherds from the Cotten site and South Indian Field. Cordell's data also demonstrate that there are significant differences in paste characteristics across the Orange production area. As alluded to above, whether these differences reflect actual behavioral choices on the part of the potters—that is, whether sand and other inclusions are true tempers—or whether these differences simply reflect clay resource characteristics (which might also be selected for by potters) cannot be answered at this time.

Other Attributes

Bullen (1972) described Orange 3 vessels as hand modeled, not coiled. However, Ferguson (1951:17) considered all pottery at South Indian Field to be coiled. On the basis of horizontal fiber orientation on fresh breaks, Mitchell (1993:53) suggested the same construction method for the vast majority of Summer Haven vessels. Fiber orientation was not systematically recorded for all sherds in the Rollins assemblage. However, a sample of 31 large sherds from the Rollins Minimum Number of Vessels (MNV) assemblage were inspected for fiber orientation. Twenty-four of these had predominantly horizontal fiber orientations, one had nonhorizontal orientations, and six had roughly equal amounts of horizontal and nonhorizontal orientations.

Whether or not this indicates coil construction is unclear. Experimental data produced by graduate students Steven Fullen and Kelli Ostrom in the Louisiana State University Museum of Natural Science Laboratory of Anthropology[3] indicate no significant difference ($p = .067$) in fiber orientation in vessels produced by the two different construction methods when orientation was broken down into three groups: horizontal orientation (which could include a trace of other orientations); more or less equal or a two-thirds to one-third mix of horizontal and nonhorizontal orientations; and predominantly nonhorizontal with traces of horizontal orientation.

Other data for vessel construction method are also equivocal. No coil breaks were identified in the assemblage. Trinkley (1986), however, has argued that a lack of coil breaks is not sufficient evidence to reject coil construction. He (Trinkley 1986) used radiographic techniques to document the orientation of fiber vesicles in sherds from the Fish Haul (38BU805) site in South Carolina. Our attempt to replicate this analysis failed. X-ray examination of 12 large Orange sherds at varying powers failed to give a clear indication of fiber orientation, nor was any additional thickness or compaction at coil junctions visible.[4]

Additional evidence for hand modeling consists of the presence of laminar splits in vessel bodies. Vertical profiles of 33 sherds indicated a split or separation of the vessel wall, suggesting that at least some vessels were formed of an inner and an outer layer. During construction of our experimental hand-modeled vessel, Fullen (2001) noted that, when he attempted to model a high wall (>8 cm), if the wall was not at least 9 mm thick, the wall buckled outward. Fullen found the most expedient recourse was to fold the wall over on itself and then add additional clay to the top of the

fold to continue to raise the vessel wall. After firing and intentional break-
age, 12 sherds from the experimental hand-modeled vessel displayed laminar
splits identical to those in the Rollins sherds.[5] None of the coiled vessel
sherds displayed similar splitting. Fullen proposed that poor consolidation
of the folding described above created the layering effect.[6]

Once constructed, the vessels at Rollins were frequently well finished.
Ninety percent of vessel interiors were either hard tooled or burnished. Of
these, 20 percent retained the reflective gloss, compacted surface, and thor-
ough hard tooling that defined burnishing for this collection. The remainder of the sherds were simply smoothed with a soft tool such as leather.
Vessel exteriors were treated in the same manner at nearly the same frequencies. Apparently if a vessel interior was hard tooled or burnished, so was
the exterior. This correlation is significant at $p < .0001$.

Finishing may have been finer for Rollins than for South Indian Field.
Ferguson (1951:19) remarked that, for the South Indian Field pottery, "in
some cases the smoothing has brought a thin film of fine paste to the surface partially covering (or rarely, completely covering) the fiber tracks." A
reanalysis of the South Indian Field material would be necessary to quantify
the number of burnished sherds. Data on surface finishing are unavailable
for the other sites under consideration.

Bullen (1972:15) described two vessel forms for the Orange 3 phase. The
first, represented by curved sherds, comprised "fairly large, straight sided,
round mouthed vessels with flat bottoms," called basins, and the second, represented by flat sherds, comprised rectangular, flat-bottomed containers with
rounded corners. Griffin and Smith (1954:33) reported only "flat bottomed,
straight-sided pots" at the Cotten site. While noting the difficulty of recon-
structing form from small sherds, Ferguson (1951:19) commented that the
most typical vessel form at South Indian Field was a simple, large, flat-bottomed bowl with straight, outflaring sides, presumably a basin. According to
Bullen (1972:15), both curved and flat Orange 3 vessels were about 10 cm
deep with walls between 4 mm and 13 mm thick—generally thicker than
the 6–7 mm of the earlier phases. The Rollins MNV assemblage yielded a
mean sherd thickness of 10.6 mm with a range between 5.6 and 18.6 mm.

One hundred thirty-two distinct vessels could be isolated in the Rollins
collection. The MNV was based on sherds with unique incised designs,
along with other rim and body attributes. Despite the relatively high MNV,
and an intensive, though largely unsuccessful effort at cross-mending between proveniences, formal information was difficult to reconstruct because
of small sherd depth. Nevertheless, Rollins seems to have more formal variability than that previously described for Orange 3 vessels. Of the 124 sherds
in the MNV assemblage with form or profile information, 40.3 percent
were curved and derived from shallow vessels, i.e., with walls that broke

Table 3.3. Vessel forms in the Rollins Shell Ring pottery assemblage.

Vessel Form	Vessel Profile									
	Incurved		Straight		Unrestricted		Outslanting		Total	
	Freq	Pct	Freq	Pct	Freq	Pct	Freq	Pct	Freq	Pct
Shallow bowl	13	26.0	1	0.2	13	26.0	23	46.0	50	40.3
Deep bowl/pot	0		0		0		5	100.0	5	4.0
Curved UID[a]	6	14.6	0		22	53.7	14	33.3	42	33.1
Flat, shallow basin	0		0		1	33.3	2	66.6	3	2.4
Flat, UID	0		3	30.0	2	20.0	5	50.0	10	8.1
UID	3	21.4	0		6	42.9	5	35.7	14	11.3
Total	22	17.7	4	3.2	44	35.5	54	34.5	124	100.0

[a]UID = Unidentified.

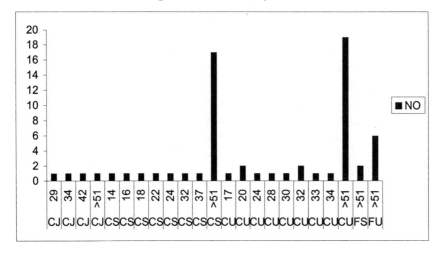

Figure 3.3. Rollins vessel diameters by vessel profile. CJ, Curved jar (>10 cm in depth); CS, curved shallow (<10 cm in depth); CU, curved unidentified; FS, flat shallow; FU, flat unidentified.

toward the base at under 10 cm (Table 3.3).[7] Profiles of these shallow vessels could be incurved, straight, unrestricted, or outslanting. Another large proportion of sherds (33 percent) were curved, but profiles were too small to determine whether they represented shallow or deep (>10 cm in depth) vessels. Five vessels, all with slightly outslanting walls, could be identified as being curved and deeper than 10 cm. All bases in the collection (n = 58) were flat or semiflat.

Thirteen vessels were identified from "flat" sherds with very little to no curvature. These sherds may represent vessels similar to Bullen's rectangular containers with curved corners. Three were flat and shallow with outslanting or unrestricted profiles. Flat unidentified-depth rims ran the gamut of all orientations, with the majority outslanting or straight. Not surprisingly, all of the Rollins flat sherds for which determination of diameters could be attempted indicated orifices greater than 51 cm in diameter (the limit of our chart) (Figure 3.3); however, only about five percent of the projected diameter was present in every case, so these readings may not be valid.

On the basis of vessel diameter, the curved vessels can be broken down into two groups. Forms with diameters between 15 and 42 cm (n = 20), of which there were only one to two examples in each size category, make up one group. Vessels with diameters greater than 51 cm (with the same caveat as above) form a second, more common group (n = 44). The latter group could be Bullen's basins. The smaller curved, shallow vessels cannot be distinguished from what would be identified as bowls in Woodland assemblages (except for their flat bases). Small bowls have not been described for Orange 3 components in the past.

Other aspects of the Rollins pottery assemblage also have not been previously described. Incurving vessel profiles have not been recorded for Orange assemblages,[8] although they are apparently represented in Stallings assemblages. These constitute almost 18 percent of the Rollins sample (Table 3.3). As noted previously, five sherds indicated five distinct containers over 10 cm in depth. These deep forms also have not been described. They are about average in wall thickness (10.8 mm) with respect to the assemblage as a whole, they are both plain and decorated, and all have hard tooled or burnished exteriors, though three have only smoothed interiors. These "pots" have generally simple rims, though one is flanged, and they were found in proveniences throughout the trench; that is, they are not strictly later vessels. Finally, one partially reconstructed vessel with a highly elaborated, flattened rim and careful exterior incising has many characteristics of a brimmed serving vessel, albeit a thick one (Figure 3.4).

Vessel function is obscure. Only one sherd, a body sherd, is sooted. There were no interior residues. For Stallings assemblages, Sassaman (1993a; this volume) has suggested that basins were used for indirect-heat cooking with boiling stones or baked-clay objects; indirect-heat cooking does not result in sooting. However, no boiling stones, soapstone slabs, or baked-clay objects, which would have contributed the necessary heat source inside the pot for indirect-heat cooking, have been recovered from Rollins, so this functional attribution is problematic. However, direct heat on embers also does not result in sooting (Hally 1983). The Rollins basins could have been used directly on coals either for cooking or to keep foods warm. Sassaman (1993a) also noted that some incurved vessels without sooting may have been serving vessels; this is a logical functional attribution for all of the Rollins shallow bowls with small (14–42 cm) diameters (n = 7).

The lack of sooting at Rollins is interesting in another respect. Sassaman (1993a) noted a dramatic increase in sooting on vessels from coastal Stallings sites coeval with Rollins. He interpreted this rise to indicate an increase in direct-heat cooking. Assuming that pressures to adopt direct-heat cooking on the coast would be as compelling to Orange peoples as they were to Stallings peoples, the lack of sooting at Rollins might suggest that these were special-purpose vessels used in conjunction with some ceremonial activity. More information on sooting from a number of different Orange functional contexts is needed before much credence can be placed on this statement, however.

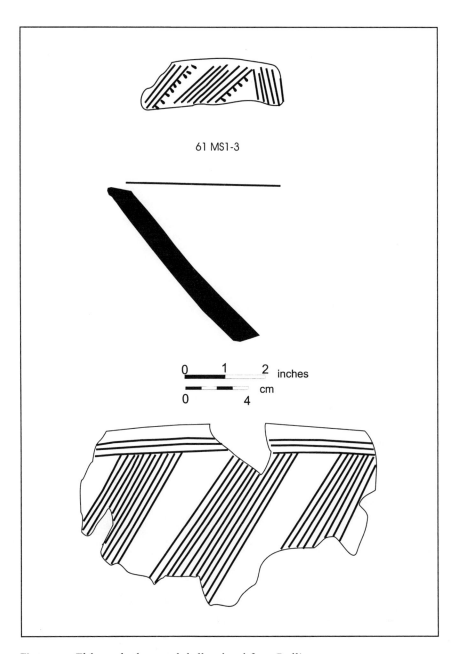

61 MS1-3

0 1 2 inches

cm

0   4

Figure 3.4. Elaborately decorated shallow bowl from Rollins.

DESIGN AND MOTIF VARIABILITY

While similarities and differences in production techniques and vessel forms offer some information on broad areas of practicing traditions, design and motif analyses can give more specific information on interaction through space and time. A stylistic homogeneity is inherent in Bullen's Orange 3 designation; he noted that Orange 3 pottery attributes at Summer Haven, Cotten, and South Indian Field were "remarkably close" (Bullen 1972:15). Griffin and Smith noted that over three-quarters of the motifs from Cotten and South Indian Field could be classified in categories common to both sites, despite the over 100 air miles (160 km) between them. Using concepts from both interaction and agency theory (see, e.g., Carr 1995:184), this close correspondence in design elements and motifs could indicate circulation of potters (as wives?), or of pots, throughout the area. It also suggests a certain symbolic element to the designs themselves, structured to promote intra-group cohesion, to distinguish the group from others, or to do both.

Surface decoration at Rollins supports the previous statements of design homogeneity in Orange 3. However, direct comparison using published data is difficult. Because different analysts have described and combined designs and motifs differently, it is impossible to compare all individual designs directly except in the case of Summer Haven, where both Bullen and Mitchell depicted literally every discrete design, as was done with the Rollins assemblage. For material from South Indian Field, Ferguson assigned a letter designation to a major design group and described several variants for each. Frequencies of designs were reported only by major group. Griffin and Smith presented a more detailed breakdown of design variations and frequencies and then combined some of their categories to compare with Ferguson's four most abundant "design motifs."

The Griffin and Smith analysis and my own comparison of Rollins and Summer Haven designs (incorporating both Bullen's and Mitchell's data) are shown in Table 3.4. At all four sites under discussion, zoned oblique incising was the most common design—to incorporate Ferguson's data, right- and left-slanting oblique must be combined, as well as vertical and zoned vertical incising. Rank order of the rest of the designs is variable, though it is interesting to note that, in terms of the rank order, Cotten and Rollins appear more similar than Rollins and Summer Haven, which are much closer in space. This seems yet another indirect proof of the broad level of interaction between relatively distant Orange 3 communities.

Because of Bullen's and Mitchell's scrupulous design analyses, a more direct comparison can be made between Summer Haven and Rollins. Ten of the 76 recorded designs[9] at Rollins can be directly cross-referenced to one of Bullen's original 15 Summer Haven designs or Mitchell's additional 23.

Table 3.4. Design comparison across four sites.

South Indian Field % Dec (t = 311)	Cotten % Dec (t = 231)	Design/Motif	Summer Haven % Dec (t = 883)	Rollins % Dec (t = 319)
28.6	40.2	Zoned oblique, either direction	45.5	19.7
19.6	8.2	Oblique, no zoning, either direction	5.3	15.0
12.9	5.2	Chevrons, zoned or unzoned	0.6	2.8
1.9	24.6	Vertical or zoned vertical	8.2	18.5

An additional 32 are slight variants (involving number of lines used, orientation, or location of ticking, for instance) or are design fragments that are probably portions of more complex designs within both the Rollins and Summer Haven design assemblages. These account for 29.1 percent of the sherds in the collection. The bulk of the remainder fit well within the design grammar (or how elements and designs may be combined) of any particular category of design. In Figure 3.5, for example, all designs associated with cross-hatching and punctation at Summer Haven and Rollins are depicted. Motifs containing these designs and elements were the most variable in the collection, yet it is clear that fairly strict rules for rotation and combination of elements were followed.

Four designs at Rollins were slightly curvilinear (Figure 3.6). With the exception of Tick Island designs—and the Rollins designs are not curvilinear enough to qualify—all other Orange designs are rectilinear. Curvilinearity notwithstanding, the motifs fit inside the design grammar of the Orange tradition.

SURFACE DECORATION AND SITE VARIABILITY

As discussed above, the design assemblages from South Indian Field, Cotten, Summer Haven, and Rollins are similar. However, the sites differ in terms of the percentage of plain vs. decorated wares. Rollins and Summer Haven site percentages by sherd are quite different, with Rollins at 45.0 percent decorated and Summer Haven at 27.6 percent in Mitchell's sherd analysis[10] (State of Florida 1995:table 11). However, differences with the other assemblages are even more striking. Only 6.8 percent of the sherds at South Indian Field and 4.6 percent of the sherds at the Cotten site were decorated.

Traditionally, such differences might be interpreted as representing change through time, with incised wares increasing in frequency after their introduction in the Orange 2 phase. Data from the Ribault Club site (8DU76) challenge this interpretation.

The Ribault Club site is on Fort George Island, less than 1 km from the Rollins Shell Ring site (Figure 3.1). Systematic subsurface testing by Water and Air Research, Inc., in 1986 defined an extensive oyster-shell sheet midden bordered on the west by a nonshell component (Dickinson and Wayne 1987). The site, which parallels the shore of the Fort George River, is over 400 m in length and 200 m wide. More recently, Johnson (2000) was hired by the state of Florida to mitigate the effects of construction on the site. He dug three 50-x-50-cm shovel tests and three 1-x-2-m tests through shell midden that was between 30 and 40 cm thick. Johnson radiocarbon-dated oyster shell associated with fiber-tempered pottery (some of which contained sponge spicules), and the corrected date was 3700 ± 70 B.P. (Beta

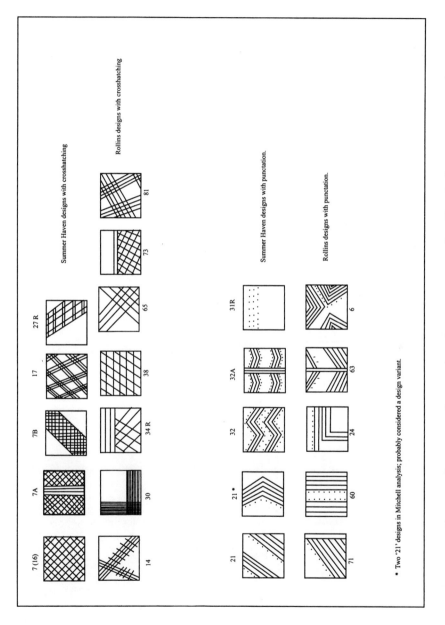

Figure 3.5. Motif variants for two motif groups from Summer Haven and Rollins. Both 27R & 31R are decorations on flanged rims.

Summer Haven designs with crosshatching

Rollins designs with crosshatching

Summer Haven designs with punctation.

Rollins designs with punctation.

7 (16)
7A
7B
17
27 R
14
30
34 R
38
65
73
81

21
21 *
32
32A
31R
71
60
24
63
6

* Two '21' designs in Mitchell analysis; probably considered a design variant.

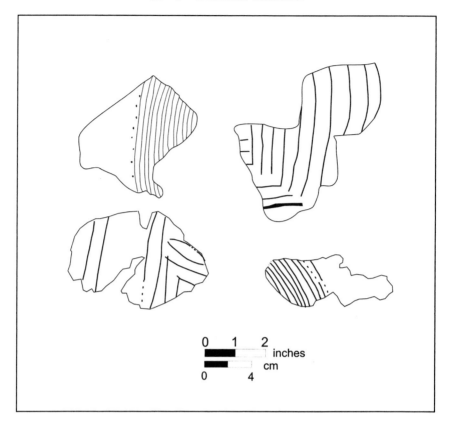

Figure 3.6. Sherds with slightly curvilinear designs. Clockwise from upper left: FS55.12; 60.21 and 60.22 (crossmend); 84.34; 501.01.

144944), virtually identical to two corrected dates from Rollins, one (3670 ± 70 B.P.) from shell at the base of the ring on the west side of the ring and the other (3710 ± 70 B.P.) from the base of the ring on the east side (Table 3.1). Lack of space prohibits a discussion of the spicules,[11] the date, and so-called transitional attributes (but see above and Heide 2000). For this chapter, the important datum is the proportion of plain to decorated wares at a site that is both proximate to and contemporaneous with Rollins but lacks its distinctive shape and size. In Johnson's assemblage from Ribault, 2.6 percent of 155 sherds were decorated (Johnson 2000:87).[12]

A similar paucity of decorated wares in the area is apparent in the results of the Timucuan Preserve survey, executed by Russo et al. (1993). Russo recorded 28 shell midden sites (excluding Rollins) and two artifact scatters in sand with Orange components in the Timucuan Preserve. Rolland (personal communication, 2002) has analyzed the Orange sherds from these sites. Many of the samples are small; 19 sites had sherd counts of less than 10. Of those sites with higher counts—between 10 and 376 sherds—all had between 78 percent and 96 percent plain wares. The sample from Rollins collected during the survey yielded 46 percent plain. This comparison is admittedly flawed because contemporaneity between Rollins and the Timucuan Preserve sites cannot be demonstrated. Nevertheless, one thing is clear—there is far less decorated pottery at sites in the immediate area of Rollins than at Rollins itself.

The data from the "fiber-tempered area" of the Devils Walking Stick site (9CAM177) provide a comparison with the third site type associated with coastal Late Archaic components, a nonshell occupation. The site is 30.5 km (19 miles) north of Rollins Shell Ring on the property of the Kings Bay Naval Submarine Support Base, near St. Marys, Georgia. A single radiocarbon date on charcoal yielded an uncorrected date of 3600 ± 100 B.P. (Beta 3499); corrected and calibrated, the date is 2cal 4231 (3892) 3635 B.P. (1cal 4084–3725), which overlaps with the date range from Rollins. At Devils Walking Stick, a mere 1.8 percent of 322 sherds were decorated (Saunders 1985).

DISCUSSION AND CONCLUSION

The low frequency of decorated pottery at contemporaneous sheet midden and nonshell Orange sites in the St. Marys region, as well as at the contemporaneous shell midden sites of Summer Haven, Cotten, and South Indian Field, suggests that site function may influence the proportion of decorated Orange wares at any given site. I have suggested in the past (Saunders 1999; Saunders and Russo 2000) that the Rollins Shell Ring site and other shell ring sites may have been locations for macrobands or tribes to gather at certain times throughout the year for ceremony, feasting, information exchange, mate selection, and other social activities. One testable implication for this would be a more elaborate, or otherwise formally distinct, vessel assemblage at ring sites.

Russo and Heide (this volume) and Gibson and Melancon (this volume) found only small amounts of pottery in ceremonial sites that date to the adoption of pottery in their respective study areas. Rollins, however, was occupied some 500 years after pottery was first produced along the lower Atlantic coast. At this point, pottery technology in the area had passed from the realm of prestige into a practical technology (Hayden 1998). However, elaborate decorations or time-consuming finishing techniques could increase the cost of production to the extent that a prestige pottery could still exist (Hayden 1998:34). Thus, at this stage in the process, one could easily predict higher frequencies of elaborate pottery at feasting sites than at more strictly utilitarian sites; Michie (1979) offered the same hypothesis with respect to shell rings on the South Carolina coast. Given that the sites compared here are reasonably contemporaneous, and acknowledging the different excavation techniques used at all these sites, the large differences in the proportion of plain to decorated wares between Rollins on the one hand and Ribault, Devils Walking Stick, Summer Haven, Cotten, and South Indian Field on the other do suggest a more elaborate vessel assemblage at Rollins. Other pottery attributes at Rollins, such as the abundance of sand in much of the ware (though this may be a natural inclusion, it could represent clay resource selection), the preponderance of hard tooling and burnishing, the lack of sooting, and unusual vessel forms, may also indicate that vessels functioned differently at Rollins than at sheet midden and nonshell sites.

The expectation of a more elaborate vessel assemblage at ceremonial/ feasting sites and other contexts where intragroup and intergroup relations were played out is consistent with style theory (e.g., Carr 1995; Wobst 1977), worldwide ethnographic and archaeological data (e.g., DeBoer and Moore 1982; Hayden 1996a, 1996b), and archaeological data from post-Archaic sites in the Southeast (e.g., Cordell 1984; Fuller and Fuller 1987),[13] though the data indicate more complexity than the mound/midden, sacred/secular pottery dichotomy Sears (1973) proposed some time ago (Cordell 1984:197; Smith and Williams 1994:34). For Late Archaic manifestations, Sassaman (1995b:233) has argued that the large (>40 cm in diameter) vessels with unique vessel forms (carinated bowls) and elaborate incised and punctated designs recovered from the Stallings Island and Lake Springs (9CB22) sites had a "public context for their use." These vessels, along with the "immense accumulation of food refuse, including much shellfish, [are] suggestive, if not convincing, evidence for public feasting" at both those massive shell sheet midden sites (Sassaman 1995b:233). It would be surprising if the same were not true for coastal ring sites. More information is needed from well-dated sites of the three different occupational types—sheet midden, nonmidden, and ring—with good seasonality information to conclude that Rollins and other shell rings contain a distinctive pottery assemblage. However, the evidence to date suggests that this is a hypothesis worth pursuing.

ACKNOWLEDGMENTS

The fieldwork undertaken to produce these data was supported by a grant from the National Geographic Foundation. Kelli Ostrom did the primary analysis of the sherds. Thanks to Greg Heide, Mike Russo, and Vicki Rolland for input on earlier drafts of this chapter.

4

Paste Variability and Possible Manufacturing Origins of Late Archaic Fiber-Tempered Pottery from Selected Sites in Peninsular Florida

Ann S. Cordell

Late Archaic period fiber-tempered pottery from Florida has been variously called Orange (Bullen 1972; Griffin 1945b), semifiber tempered (Bullen and Bullen 1953), Norwood (Bullen 1969; Phelps 1965), and simply fiber tempered. The relationships of the various fiber-tempered wares found in different parts of Florida—and of the peoples who made them—are poorly understood. In this chapter, paste variability in fiber-tempered pottery from several peninsular Florida sites is investigated. The primary focus is on southwest Florida sites and Orange culture sites in east Florida, but the study includes sites from the central peninsular Gulf Coast and Okeechobee areas. Pottery samples are compared in terms of aplastic composition and other physical properties to document interregional similarities and differences. These data are then used to suggest possible manufacturing origins for different paste categories and to explore the possibility of interaction between east Florida and Gulf coastal populations. The results will show that paste analysis will be essential in resolving patterns of interregional interactions.

POTTERY SAMPLES

Selection of samples from southwest Florida and adjacent areas was guided by Widmer's 1988 summary of sites with fiber-tempered pottery (Widmer 1988:68–73). Selection of east Florida samples was based on collections available at the Florida Museum of Natural History (FLMNH). Site numbers are presented in Table 4.1.

The southwest Florida sample of 170 sherds is from 15 sites in coastal Lee, Charlotte, and Collier Counties, including six sites on Marco Island (Figure 4.1 and Table 4.1). The central peninsular Gulf Coast area to the north is represented by 30 sherds from the Palmer, Canton Street, and Perico Island sites. The Askew site from the northern peninsular Gulf Coast area is represented by 14 sherds. For convenience, this site is grouped with central pen-

Table 4.1. List of sites, samples, and sampling proportions.

Geographic Area	Location or Site Name	Site #[a]	References	Culture Period	Total Sherds Sampled	Total Sample (MNV)
East Florida n = 7 sites n = 61 sherds MNV = 50	Summer Haven	8SJ46	Bullen and Bullen 1961; State of Florida 1995; Mitchell 1993	Orange 3	10 (1%)	10
	Bluffton	8VO22	Bullen 1955	Orange 1-2	10 (1%)	10
	Tick Island	8VO24	Jahn and Bullen 1978	Orange 3	10 (3%)	10
	Blue Spring	8VO43	Sassaman 2003b	Orange 1	3	2
	Cotten	8VO83	Griffin and Smith 1954	Orange 3	11 (1%)	10
	South Indian Field	8BR23	Ferguson 1951	Orange 3	5 (38%)	5
	Mount Elizabeth	8MT30	Janus Research 1998; Russo and Heide 2002	Orange 1	12 (16%)[b]	3
Central Peninsular Gulf Coast n = 4 sites n = 44 sherds MNV = 38	Askew[c]	8CI46	Bullen and Askew 1965	Orange 5	14 (100%)	13
	Perico Island	8MA6	Willey 1949a	NA	1 (100%)	1
	Canton Street	8PI55	Bullen et al. 1978	Orange 5	2 (100%)	1
	Palmer	8SO2A	Bullen and Bullen 1976	Orange 1-4	27 (44%)	23

Okeechobee	Fort Center	8GL13	Sears 1982	Orange 5	46 (25%)	33
n = 1 site						
n = 46 sherds						
MNV = 33						
Southwest Florida	Turtle Bay II	8CH37	Bullen and Bullen 1956	Pre-Glades	2 (100%)	2
n = 15 sites	Cash Mound	8CH38	Bullen and Bullen 1956	NA	2 (100%)	2
n = 170 sherds	Dunwody[d]	8CH61/8	Luer 1999	Pre-Glades	4 (100%)	4
MNV = 132	Brit Army	8LL no#	FLMNH	Pre-Glades III (Orange 3–4)	7 (100%)	6
	Howard Mound[e]	8LL44/45	Luer 1989	Pre-Glades	1 (100%)	1
	Useppa Island	8LL51	Marquardt 1999	Pre-Glades III (Orange 3–4)	4 (67%)	4
	Wightman	8LL54	Fradkin 1976	NA	8 (38%)	5
	Marco Island	8CR107x1	Cockrell 1970a, 1970b; Morrell 1969; Widmer 1974	Pre-Glades III (Orange 3–4)	75 (38%)[b]	64
		8CR108		Pre-Glades	11 (13%)[b]	8
		8CR110		Pre-Glades I Late (Orange 1)	29 (11%)[b]	17
		8CR111			1 (17%)[b]	1
		8CR112			17 (20%)[b]	12
		8CR153		Pre-Glades	3 (20%)[b]	3

Continued on the next page.

Table 4.1. *Continued*

Geographic Area	Location or Site Name	Site #[a]	References	Culture Period	Total Sherds Sampled	Total Sample (MNV)
	Horrs Island	8CR696	Russo 1991	Pre-Glades	2 (100%)	2
		8CR no#	McMichael 1982	Pre-Glades	4 (100%)	1
Total					321	253

[a]Curation facilities: Florida Museum of Natural History, Gainesville, for all southwest Florida sites (except Marco Island sites), all central peninsular Gulf Coast and Okeechobee area sites, and all east Florida sites except 8VO43 and 8MT30; Florida Bureau of Archaeological Research, Division of Historical Resources, Tallahassee, for all Marco Island sites; University of Florida Department of Anthropology (Kenneth E. Sassaman), Gainesville, for 8VO43; and Martin County and the Southeast Florida Archaeological Society chapter of the Florida Anthropological Society (Sonja Gray and Sally McKeige) for 8MT30.

[b]Sampling proportion closer to 100 percent in terms of sherds large enough for minor destructive ceramic technological analysis.

[c]The Askew site is located in the northern peninsular Gulf Coast area (after Milanich and Fairbanks 1980:22).

[d]Luer believes these sherds are listed incorrectly in FLMNH accession records and are actually from the nearby Cedar Point Shell Heap site, 8CH8 (see Luer 1999:46).

[e]Luer believes these sherds are listed incorrectly in FLMNH accession records and are actually from the nearby Calusa Island midden, 8LL45 (see Luer 1989:251–253).

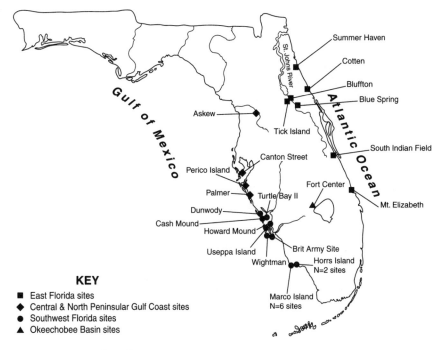

Figure 4.1. Map of site locations.

insular Gulf Coast sites in Table 4.1 and subsequent tables. The Okeechobee area to the east is represented by 46 sherds from the Fort Center site. All samples with the exception of those from Marco Island in Collier County are from collections housed at FLMNH. The Marco Island samples are from the Bureau of Archaeological Research in Tallahassee.

The comparative sample from Orange sites in east Florida consists of grab samples of five to 11 sherds each from Summer Haven in St. Johns County; Bluffton, the Cotten site, and Tick Island in Volusia County; and South Indian Field in Brevard County. These samples are from FLMNH collections. Samples were also obtained from Blue Spring in Volusia County and from the Mount Elizabeth site in Martin County.

The total sherd sample is 321, but cross-mending reduced the sample size to 253 including 189 plain and 61 incised sherds, plus three sherds with scored surface treatment. Most of the sherds from southwest Florida had been categorized as Orange, semifiber tempered, or simply fiber tempered as determined from FLMNH catalog cards and site reports (Cockrell 1970b; Widmer 1974). The central and northern peninsular Gulf Coast sherds had been categorized as Orange, semifiber tempered, Norwood, and "semi-Pasco-semi-Orange," according to FLMNH catalog cards. Most of the Fort Center sherds had been categorized as semifiber tempered and most of the east Florida sherds had been categorized as Orange, according to FLMNH catalog cards. An exact provenience listing by sample number is on file at the FLMNH Ceramic Technology Laboratory (FLMNH-CTL).

Radiocarbon dates are fairly comparable for the different geographic areas (Table 4.2). Conventional dates ranging from about 4000 to 3000 B.P. have been obtained for sites on Useppa, Marco, and Horrs Islands in coastal southwest Florida. Dates for the central peninsular Gulf Coast come from the Palmer site and range from about 4000 to 3500 B.P. Dates from the Summer Haven, Cotten, Bluffton, Blue Spring, Tick Island, and Mount Elizabeth sites in east Florida range from about 4000 to 3500 B.P. A date of 2400 B.P. was obtained from Fort Center, but this is thought to postdate the fiber-tempered pottery.

PASTE ANALYSIS

For purposes of this study, paste was defined in terms of kind, size, and relative abundance of aplastics and/or temper constituents. A binocular microscope with magnifications ranging from 10× to 70× was used to identify aplastics and to estimate particle size (Wentworth scale) and relative abundance. All observations were made on fresh breaks and/or on edges that had been freshly cut with a rock saw, as textural integrity was remarkably preserved after sawing in many cases. Other physical properties also were recorded, including surface and core color, thickness (in millimeters), and weight (in grams). Fragments of larger sherds were refired in an electric furnace for 15 minutes at a temperature of 700° C to assess clay differences in terms of relative iron content. Munsell soil color charts were used to record original and refired colors.

Thirty sherds were thin-sectioned and examined with a polarizing microscope. The petrographic analysis was conducted to evaluate homogeneity and differences within and between paste categories, and point counts were made for quantifying relative abundance of inclusions. The point-counting procedure generally followed recommendations by Stoltman (1989, 1991, 2001). A counting interval of 1 mm by 1 mm was used with 10× (100) magnification. Each point or stop of the mechanical stage was assigned to one of the following categories: clay matrix, void (nonfiber-temper voids such as channel voids, closed pores, and micropores [Rice 1987:350]), fiber-temper voids, charred fibers, silt particles, sponge spicules, and very fine through very coarse aplastics of varying compositions (primarily quartz). The point-count data include a finer breakdown of particle size than is usually specified (e.g., Stoltman 1989:149, 1991:108, 2001:314). A "sand size"

Table 4.2. List of radiocarbon dates.

Site Name, #	Provenience	Lab #[a]	Sample	Conventional Date B.P.	Calibrated Ranges[b] B.P. 2Cal/1Cal (Intercept) 1Cal/2Cal	References
East Florida						
Summer Haven, 8SJ46	S 1/2 feature 152	Beta	Oyster	3880 ± 70	3977/3883 (3812) 3689/3619	State of Florida 1995:38
	NE 1/4 feature 101			3840 ± 70	3942/3833 (3725) 3639/3563	
	NE 1/4 feature 143			3940 ± 60	4061/3959 (3868) 3810/3695	
	Burial 10 fill			3840 ± 60	3898/3826 (3725) 3662/3584	
	Column sample 1			4000 ± 60	4134/4058 (3956) 3864/3807	
Bluffton, 8VO22	Sq. A-5, level 13	RL-32	*Strombus* celt	4061 ± 110	4363/4201 (4055) 3880/3722	Bullen 1972:11
Tick Island, 8VO24	Narrow sand zone associated with preceramic burials	M-1264	Charcoal	5450 ± 303[c]	6891/6537 (6217) 5912/5592	Jahn and Bullen 1978:22; Sassaman 2003a
		M-1265	Charcoal	5320 ± 204[c]	6497/6300 (6085) 5906/5613	
		M-1268	Charcoal	5450 ± 184[c]	6656/6408 (6217) 5992/5766	
		M-1270	Marine shell	5431 ± 200[c]	5851/5784 (5742) 5720/5693	
	FLMNH 99921.21	B-166675	Soot	3630 ± 40	4080/3980 (3920) 3880/3840	
	FLMNH 99921.1	B-166676	Soot	3740 ± 40	4230/4150 (4090) 4000/3980	
	FLMNH A20111.252	B-166677	Soot	3930 ± 40	4500/4420 (4410) 4300/4250	

Continued on the next page.

Table 4.2. Continued.

Site Name, #	Provenience	Lab #[a]	Sample	Conventional Date B.P.	Calibrated Ranges[b] B.P. 2Cal/1Cal (Intercept) 1Cal/2Cal	References
Blue Spring, 8VO43	TU2-level E	B-145694	Nutshell	3510 ± 70	3970/3870 (3820) 3690/3620	Sassaman 2003b
	TU2-level K	B-145695	Charcoal	3730 ± 40	4215/4145 (4085) 3990/3970	
	TU4-feature 7	B-164962	Charcoal	3780 ± 50	4290/4240 (4150) 4090/3990	
Cotten, 8VO83	Sq. 15R1, level 16	M-215	*Fasciolaria*	3421 ± 200	3704/3462 (3254) 2961/2745	Bullen 1958a:101
Mount Elizabeth, 8MT30	TU-A, level 11	B-116551	*Busycon*	3950 ± 70	4141/4059 (3928) 3837/3729	Janus Research 1998; Russo (this volume)
		B-116550	*Mercenaria*	3970 ± 50	4124/4060 (3965) 3886/3824	
Central Peninsular Gulf Coast						
Palmer, 8SO2A	Test A, 1 foot	G-596	*Busycon*	3751 ± 120	3940/3806 (3629) 3467/3351	Bullen and Bullen 1976:13
	Test A, 2–2 1/2 feet	G-597	*Venus*	3626 ± 120	3802/3626 (3464) 3347/3206	
	Test A, 4 feet	G-598	*Busycon*	3976 ± 120	4254/4084 (3912) 3762/3613	
	Test A, 8 feet	G-599	*Busycon*	4451 ± 125[c]	4856/4788 (4548) 4405/4231	
	Test A, 11 feet	G-600	*Busycon*	4501 ± 120[c]	4945/4816 (4627) 4444/4299	
Okeechobee						
Fort Center, 8GL13	Fill, midden from circle junctions near river	I-3356	Charcoal	2400 ± 112[d]	2751/2711 (2357) 2335/2150	Sears 1982:116

Southwest Florida

Useppa Island, 8LL51	Test A–4, level 3	B-17336	*Mercenaria*	3891 ± 80	4047/3908 (3819) 3689/3604	Marquardt 1992:11, 1999:79
Marco Island, 8CR107x1	Test 2, Sq. 100, level 7	I-4570	Wood charcoal	3060 ± 112	3544/3382 (3301) 3079/2947	Cockrell 1970b
	Test 2, Sq. 100, level 4	I-4569		3155 ± 108	3632/3470 (3376) 3264/3077	
	Test 3, Sq. 109, level 3	I-4572		3315 ± 112	3831/3687 (3553) 3401/3271	
	Test 3, Sq. 109, level 4	I-4571		3375 ± 112	3892/3813 (3613) 3470/3363	
	Test 3, Sq. 109, level 4	I-4573		3400 ± 108	3956/3826 (3673) 3475/3385	
Marco Island, 8CR112	Lowest cultural strata	I-6650	Wood charcoal?	4965 ± 108[c]	5926/5887 (5660) 5595/5474	Widmer 1974, 1988:71
Horrs Island, 8CR696	FS. 562	B-40277	Oyster	3201 ± 70	3158/3054 (2942) 2849/2767	Russo 1991:424

[a]B = Beta Analytic, Inc.; G = Göteborg, Sweden; I = Isotopes, Inc.; M = University of Michigan; RL = Radiocarbon, Ltd.

[b]For measured radiocarbon dates (all except Blue Spring, Mount Elizabeth, and Summer Haven), conventional dates have been calculated using Calib 4.1.2 (Stuiver, Reimer, Bard, et al. 1998) with isotopic fractionations of 0 ± 0 for shell, 25 ± 5 for carbon, and Delta R = 36.0 ± 14.

[c]Thought to date the preceramic midden.

[d]Pottery predates this date.

index for each thin section was calculated following Stoltman (2001:314). Further details about the point-counting procedure and analysis of point-count data are on file at FLMNH-CTL. All analyses were conducted in the FLMNH-CTL.

DESCRIPTION OF FIBER-TEMPERED PASTE VARIABILITY

Three principal tempers or aplastic constituents were identified in the analysis: plant fibers, represented by casts or voids; quartz sand; and sponge spicules. Other constituents noted for a few sherds included limestone, shell, unidentified (UID) whitish noncarbonate inclusions, rounded clay lumps, ferric concretions, and mica.

Fiber tempering is represented by extensive channel voids, left over when the fiber temper, presumably Spanish moss or palmetto fibers, burned out during firing (Figure 4.2a). The charred remnants of actual fibers are present in several cases (Figure 4.2b) and appear consistent with Spanish moss.

Quartz sand in varying sizes and abundance occurs in all sherds in the sample. Its status as an added temper or a naturally occurring constituent, or some combination of both, is uncertain. Quartz aplastics falling into silt and very fine particle sizes are considered more likely to be naturally occurring constituents of the clay source (Rice 1987:411; also see Stoltman 1989:149–150, 1991:109–111). Angular as opposed to rounded quartz particle shapes may be indicative of tempers, as are coarser particle sizes (Rice 1987:411; Stoltman 1989:149, 1991:109–111). In the present sample, the very fine grains tend to be subangular, while the coarser grains tend to be more subrounded, even within individual sherds. Angularity of the very fine quartz might argue in favor of the temper attribution. However, the co-occurrence of subangular very fine quartz with larger, subrounded quartz within individual sherds in the present sample indicates that the very fine quartz may be naturally occurring constituents of the clay source(s). This pattern is also observed in thin sections of other sherds with abundant quartz inclusions from Florida sites and in thin sections of clay samples (e.g., Cordell 2001, 2002, 2003; Cordell and Koski 2003:table 3; samples stored in FLMNH-CTL).

The status of sponge spicules as added temper or naturally occurring constituents is also uncertain. For the past 25 years or so, it has been assumed that sponge spicules are naturally abundant in some Florida clays (Borremans and Shaak 1986). The validity of this assumption is currently being questioned by some Florida researchers, who are investigating whether sponges were collected and processed for spicule temper, a practice still fol-

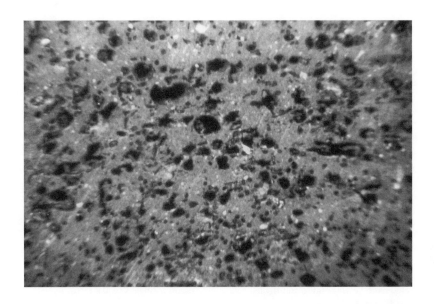

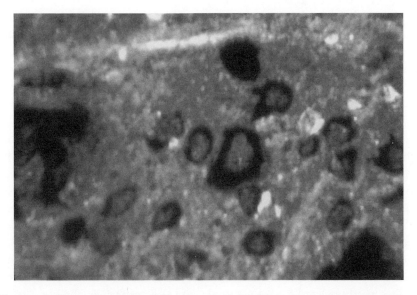

Figure 4.2. Photomicrographs of fiber-tempered sherd from Summer Haven (sample #286). a, Cross section showing fiber temper voids (width of image approximately 15 mm); b, close-up of voids with charred fibers (width of image approximately 2 mm).

Table 4.3. Description of gross paste categories.

Gross Paste Categories	# of Cases	Sponge Spicule Frequency	Mean Sherd Density[a]	# of Paste Categories
Chalky "St. Johns"	66 (28%)	Abundant	0.83 g/cm^3	3
Nonchalky	130 (54%)	Absent or rare	1.15 g/cm^3	6
Intermediate Spiculate	43 (18%)	Occasional to frequent	1.09 g/cm^3	3
Other[b]	14	Variable	Not calculated	6

[a]Sherd density was estimated by calculating grams per cubic centimeter from sherd weight (g), thickness (cm), and estimated sherd size or area (cm^2); the differences in mean density between chalky and nonchalky pastes ($t = 11.1787$, $df = 188$) and between chalky and intermediate spiculate pastes ($t = 6.3632$, $df = 101$) are statistically significant at $p < .0001$; the difference between nonchalky and intermediate spiculate pastes is not statistically significant.
[b]Deleted from sample and from total used in calculating percentages of chalky, nonchalky, and intermediate spiculate cases.

lowed in Amazonia today (Heckenberger et al. 1999; Rolland and Bond 2003; cf. Cordell and Koski 2003).

One other category of inclusion should be mentioned. Lenticular voids were observed in addition to fiber voids in one sample. These lenticular voids range in size from very fine to very coarse but are very difficult to distinguish except in thin section. It is uncertain at this time whether these voids represent the dissolution of inclusions such as shell fragments or gypsum crystals or the addition of fiber temper using a plant species other than Spanish moss.

Three gross paste categories for fiber-tempered pottery were identified in the analysis (Table 4.3). One has so-called chalky St. Johns–like paste, containing abundant sponge spicules, accounting for 28 percent of the cases. Another category has a nonchalky paste, generally lacking sponge spicules; this category comprises 54 percent of the cases. The third is an "intermediate" spiculate category, with frequent sponge spicules, accounting for 18 percent of the sample. A fourth "other" grouping consists of 14 sherds that had been identified as semifiber tempered by previous researchers but that turned out to be sand-tempered plain and a few other types. These sherds were subsequently deleted from the sample, and this resulted in the elimination of the Wightman and Cash Mound sites from the southwest Florida sample and Perico Island from the central peninsular Gulf Coast sample.

The chalky fiber-tempered sherds can be fairly easily distinguished from

Table 4.4. Comparison of traditional vs. gross paste categories.

Traditional Categories	Gross Paste Categories				Total
	Chalky	Nonchalky	Intermediate Spiculate	Other[a]	
Orange	64 (40%)	75 (47%)	19 (12%)	1 (1%)	159
Orange (w/limestone)	—	2 (100%)	—	—	2
Fiber	1 (3%)	26 (79%)	6 (18%)	—	33
Semifiber	—	19 (40%)	16 (34%)	12 (26%)	47
Semi-Pasco/ semi-Orange	—	1 (100%)	—	—	1
Norwood	—	3 (75%)	—	1 (25%)	4
FBT1[b]	1 (50%)	—	1 (50%)	—	2
FBT2[b]	—	4 (80%)	1 (20%)	—	5
Total	66	130	43	14	253

[a]Seven sand-tempered plain, three Pineland Plain, one Belle Glade Plain, two St. Johns Plain, and one Goodland Plain all misidentified as having fiber temper.
[b]FBT1 and FBT2 represent an earlier attempt to distinguish gross paste differences within traditional fiber-tempered categories (Cordell 1985:119, 1992:108, 113).

most nonchalky fiber-tempered sherds with the unaided eye. Chalky tactual quality applies to many of the chalky paste sherds. In addition, most chalky fiber-tempered sherds are noticeably "lightweight" and are in fact lower in density than nonchalky and intermediate spiculate sherds (Table 4.3). Intermediate spiculate and nonchalky fiber-tempered sherds are not distinguishable without the aid of a microscope. Postdepositional alteration of some sherds, especially some from the Fort Center site, made recognizing the presence of sponge spicules difficult, even with magnification higher than 70×. Data on file at FLMNH indicate that original classifications, including those done by Bullen, are inconsistent with obvious temper differences. Table 4.4 shows that most cases categorized as Orange fall into the chalky and nonchalky gross paste categories. Most cases categorized as semifiber tempered occur in the nonchalky and intermediate spiculate categories. Most of the sherds categorized as simply fiber tempered and as Norwood occur in the nonchalky category. Conversely, most of the sherds in the chalky paste grouping had been categorized as Orange. Nonchalky and intermediate spiculate categories are more diverse, especially the nonchalky sample, with sherds categorized as Orange, just fiber tempered, semifiber tempered, and Norwood. Of the 14 sherds that had been misidentified as semifiber tempered, most turned out to be sand-tempered plain, but they included examples of Belle Glade Plain, St. Johns Plain, and Goodland Plain.

Description of Fiber-Tempered Paste Categories

Each gross paste category was subdivided into three or more categories on the basis of relative abundance of one or more of the following: fiber voids, sponge spicules, quartz sand and other constituents, and particle size of quartz sand constituents.

Chalky Paste

Three chalky fiber-tempered paste categories (C1–C3) were distinguished on the basis of differences in abundance and particle size of quartz sand constituents (Table 4.5). Most of the sherds in these categories are otherwise characterized by common to abundant fiber voids and sponge spicules. Quartz particle size and frequency are smallest and lowest, respectively, in category C1 and largest and greatest, respectively, in category C3. The very fine quartz sand of category C1 very likely represents natural constituents of the clays. The status as temper vs. natural constituents of the larger quartz sand in C3 is less certain. Point-count data corroborate that categories C1 and C3 differ primarily in terms of sand abundance and size range (see Table 4.5 for mean sand size indexes). Category C2 is intermediate between C1 and C3, but no thin sections were included for corroboration. The petrographic analysis revealed that quartz grain shape is predominantly angular to subangular in C1 and subrounded in C3, although very fine quartz grains in C3 tend also to be subangular. Point-count data within C1 and C3 categories indicate within-group homogeneity with respect to most of the attributes considered.

Refired colors of chalky fiber-tempered sherds indicate that at least three broad categories of clay resources, presumably spiculate clay resources, are represented. One has relatively low iron content, characterized by very pale brown refired colors (10YR Munsell hues). The second has moderate iron content, with brown to strong brown colors (primarily 7.5YR hues). The third has higher iron content, with light reddish brown to red colors (primarily 2.5YR and 5YR hues). There is some degree of overlap between the moderate and moderate to high iron colors. The low iron clay or clays are common in paste category C1, rare in C3, and absent in C2. The moderate iron clay or clays are common in C1 and modal in C2 and C3. The higher iron clay(s) category is modal in C1, common in C3, and absent in C2.

Table 4.5. Description of chalky fiber-tempered paste categories.

	Fiber Void Frequency	Quartz Frequency & Size	Sponge Spicule Frequency	Other Constituents	Mean Sand Size Index[a]	Refired Color/Iron Content	Comments[c]
C1 n = 32 (n = 4)	Common to abundant (21%–31%)	Frequent to common; very fine to fine (3%–10%)	Abundant (18%–34%)[b]	Rare ferric concretions in n = 3	1.035	Very low to moderate-high	Frothy cross section from fiber voids; tactually slightly chalky to chalky; very lightweight
C2 n = 3	Abundant	Common to abundant; very fine to fine	Frequent to common	NA	NA	Moderate	
C3 n = 31 (n = 4)	Common to abundant (18%–30%)	Frequent to common; fine to medium (16%–25%)	Common to abundant (13%–21%)	Rare ferric concretions in n = 8	1.502	Very low to moderate-high	compared to nonchalky and intermediate spiculate sherds

Sample numbers in parentheses refer to number of thin sections; percentages listed in parentheses are based on point-count data.

[a]"Sand size index" was calculated following Stoltman (2000:314).

[b]Low value of 18 percent for sample number 41 is attributed to the orientation of the thin section, which was cut perpendicular to the long axis of the sponge spicules, exposing spicules in spherical cross section instead of longitudinal section, thereby reducing the chance of their being counted during point-count analysis.

[c]Comments apply to all three paste categories.

Intermediate Spiculate Paste

Three categories of intermediate spiculate paste (IS1–IS3) were distinguished on the basis of differences in fiber void frequency and particle size of quartz sand (Table 4.6). Fiber void frequency is highest in IS1, lowest in IS2, and intermediate in IS3. Quartz sand is generally finer in IS1 and IS2 than in IS3. Most sherds in these categories are otherwise characterized by occasional to frequent sponge spicules. Categories IS1 and IS2 differ primarily in relative abundance of fiber temper. IS1 and IS2 differ from IS3 primarily in terms of range of quartz sand sizes. Point-count data indicate overlap between IS1 and IS2 in many attributes. However, this is based on only two thin sections from IS1 and one from IS2. Point-count data corroborate the sand-size differences between IS1–IS2 vs. IS3 (see Table 4.6 for mean sand size indexes).

Refired colors of intermediate spiculate sherds indicate that at least three clay sources, presumably spiculate, may be represented (Table 4.6). One is characterized by moderate iron content and is common in IS1 and IS2 categories. Two are characterized by moderate to high iron content, one of which occurs in IS2 and the other in IS3.

Chalky and intermediate spiculate categories appear to be unrelated in terms of clay resources. The intermediate spiculate grouping may be more closely related to south Florida spiculate pastes such as Belle Glade and a recently defined category referred to as Pineland paste (Cordell 2005).

Nonchalky Paste

Six nonchalky fiber-tempered paste categories were defined (NC1–NC6). The first four (NC1–NC4) represent points along a continuum of fiber void and quartz sand size and frequency (Table 4.7). Fiber void frequency is highest in the first category (NC1) and lowest in the fourth (NC4). Quartz frequency is lowest in the first category and highest in the third and fourth categories. Quartz particle size is generally smallest in the NC1 category and larger in the other categories (Table 4.7). The fifth category (NC5) is slightly micaceous but is otherwise similar to the first (NC1). The very fine quartz sand of categories NC1 and NC5 very likely represents natural constituents of the clays. The quartz sand in most of the other nonchalky categories is generally larger and its status as temper vs. natural constituents is less certain.

Point-count data (on file, FLMNH) corroborate the distinctions between NC1 and NC2 and the other categories on the basis of most of the attributes considered. The differences between NC2 and NC3 and NC4 are corroborated by point-count data related to frequency of fiber voids, total

Table 4.6. Description of intermediate spiculate fiber-tempered paste categories.

	Fiber Void Frequency	Quartz Frequency & Size	Sponge Spicule Frequency	Other Constituents	Mean Sand Size Index[a]	Refired Color/Iron Content	Comments
IS1 n = 16 (n = 2)	Common to abundant (21%–30%)	Common to abundant; fine to medium (26%–30%)	Occasional to frequent (3%–5%)[b]	Rare ferric concretions in n = 1	1.175	Moderate	Frothy cross-section from fiber voids; sandy texture
IS2 n = 13 (n = 1)	Frequent (22%)	Abundant; fine to medium (34%)	Occasional to frequent (3%–5%)[b]	NA	1.180	Moderate to moderate–high	Sandy texture; similar to I1, but fewer fiber voids
IS3 n = 14 (n = 1)	Frequent to common (18%)	Frequent to common; fine to medium (35%)	Occasional to frequent (3%–5%)[b]	Rare ferric concretions in n = 7	1.600	Moderate to moderate–high	Dense, sandy/gritty texture; not frothy

Sample numbers in parentheses refer to number of thin sections; percentages listed in parentheses are based on point-count data.

[a]"Sand size index" was calculated following Stoltman (2000:314).

[b]Percentages estimated with reference to a comparison chart (Rice 1987:349).

Table 4.7. Description of nonchalky fiber-tempered paste categories.

	Fiber Void Frequency	Quartz Frequency & Size	Sponge Spicule Frequency	Other Constituents	Mean Sand Size Index[a]	Refired Color/Iron Content	Comments
NC1 n = 12 (n = 5)[b]	Common to abundant (27%–37%)	Occasional to frequent; very fine to fine (13%–21%)	Rare to occasional for n = 4	None	1.046	Moderate to moderate–high[c]	Frothy cross section from fiber voids; heterogeneous quartz sizes
NC2 n = 57 (n = 8)	Common to abundant (20%–35%)	Common to abundant; fine to medium (20%–38%)	Rare to occasional for n = 15	Rare ferric concretions in n = 3	1.401	Moderate to moderate–high[c]	Frothy cross section from fiber voids; sandy texture
NC3 n = 30 (n = 3)[d]	Frequent (14%–25%)	Abundant; fine (27%–43%)	Rare to occasional for n = 7	Rare ferric concretions in n = 6	1.227	Moderate to moderate–high[c]	Slightly frothy from fiber voids; sandy texture
NC4 n = 8 (n = 2)	Occasional to frequent (11%–21%)	Abundant; fine to medium (37%–49%)	Rare for n = 3	Rare ferric concretions in n = 2	1.370	Moderate to moderate–high[c]	Sandy texture; not frothy
NC5 n = 8 (n = 1)[e]	Common to abundant (34%)	Frequent; very fine to fine (13%)	Rare (in thin section only)	Occasional mica & ferric concretions	1.000	Moderate	Micaceous clay source; otherwise like NC1
NC6a n = 4	Abundant to occasional	Common to abundant; fine to medium (27% for #168)	None	UID whitish noncarbonate lumps	NA	Moderate[c]	n = 2 similar to NC2; n = 1 similar to NC3; n = 1 similar to NC4

NC6b n = 3 (n = 1)[f]	Frequent (18% for #168)	Common to abundant; fine to medium (27% for #168)	None	Limestone lumps	1.140 for #168	Moderate to moderate to high[c]	n = 2 similar to NC3; n = 1 similar to NC4
NC6c n = 3 (n = 1)[e]	Abundant (37% for #276)	Occasional to frequent; very fine to fine (18% for #276)	None	Shell, limestone (decomposed shell) (3% for #276)	1.000 for #276	Moderate[c]	Otherwise like NC1
NC6d n = 1	Occasional to frequent	Abundant	None	Ferric concretions	NA	NA	Otherwise like NC3 or NC4
NC6e n = 2	Common	Common to abundant; fine	None	Limestone, w/calcareous matrix	NA	Very low	Calcareous clay source
NC6f n = 2	Frequent	Common; fine to medium	None	Rounded clay lumps	NA	Moderate to high	Pinellas–like paste (unique clay source?) with fiber temper

Sample numbers in parentheses refer to number of thin sections; percentages listed in parentheses are based on point-count data.

[a] "Sand size index" was calculated following Stoltman (2000:314).

[b] Point-count data for one case representing NC5 and one of NC6c are included with NC1.

[c] Minimum number of clays represented by NC1–NC4 and most cases in NC6 is three.

[d] Point-count data for one thin section representing NC6b are included with NC3.

[e] Point-count data also included with NC1.

[f] Point-count data also included with NC3.

quartz sand, and amounts of fine and very fine quartz. Point-count data indicate that the differences between NC3 and NC4 may not be sufficient to warrant separate categories. However, this is based on only three thin sections for NC3 and two for NC4. Point counts within category NC2 indicate within-group heterogeneity along geographic lines with respect to most of the attributes considered. Petrographic data indicate that quartz grain shape is predominantly angular to subangular for very fine and some fine sizes, while medium and coarser sizes tend to be subrounded.

The sixth category (NC6) is a catchall grouping that is extremely heterogeneous, characterized by occasional to frequent inclusions of varying compositions (Table 4.7). These include limestone, shell, whitish noncarbonate inclusions, ferric concretions, and subrounded clay lumps. Eleven of the 15 sherds otherwise conform to properties of the first four categories. In some cases, the occurrence of these other constituents is such that they could represent fortuitous or accidental inclusions. The relative frequency of the whitish noncarbonate inclusions and limestone inclusions in NC6a and NC6b, respectively, is occasional and the distribution of these constituents is not homogeneous throughout the sherd body. In fact, limestone inclusions were not present in the thin section representing this category. It is thus likely that these constituents represent accidental additions to the clay(s) or incidental inclusions that were naturally occurring in the clay source(s). This explanation is supported by the presence of rare shell and limestone in two thin sections representing NC2 paste and in another representing NC1 paste. Sherds with NC6a paste are otherwise similar to categories NC2 (n = 2), NC3 (n = 1), and NC4 (n = 1). Sherds with NC6b paste are otherwise similar to categories NC3 (n = 2) and NC4 (n = 1). The relative frequency of the shell and limestone (decomposed shell) inclusions in NC6c is occasional to frequent and the distribution is fairly homogeneous. Thus it is more likely that these constituents represent temper rather than accidental additions, although it is possible that such inclusions could be natural constituents of the clay source(s). Category NC6c sherds are otherwise similar to those in the NC1 paste category. Occasional to frequent ferric concretions occur in one sherd (NC6d). The composition is otherwise similar to sherds of categories NC3 and NC4. These ferric concretions were probably naturally present in the clay. This is supported by the presence of rare to occasional ferric concretions in many sherds in NC3 and NC4.

Four of the 15 sherds have paste characteristics that distinguish them from the other NC6 sherds. Two sherds have frequent limestone inclusions (NC6e) but also have a calcareous matrix. The limestone inclusions are probably natural to the clay source, but in this case, the clay source is itself calcareous. Two other sherds have subrounded clay lumps (NC6f) and, except for the fiber tempering, are reminiscent of the paste of the late prehistoric type Pinellas Plain (Cordell 2005).

Refired colors of nonchalky fiber-tempered sherds indicate that at least three broad categories of nonspiculate clay resources are represented within NC1, NC2, NC3/4, and most of the NC6 categories. Within each paste category, one clay source has moderate iron content and is modal in most of the categories. Two clay sources have moderate to high iron content and are modal in NC3 and NC6f. Very low iron clay is represented by category NC6e, with the calcareous matrix.

Diversity in Aplastics

At first glance, it appears that the present sample shows more diversity in aplastic composition than is traditionally considered for fiber-tempered pottery in Florida (e.g., Griffin 1945b:219). However, a review of the literature indicates that some of this diversity has been documented (Table 4.8). Quartz sand is well known as a constituent, especially of semifiber-tempered (e.g., Bullen 1972:24; Sears 1982:24) and Norwood series (Phelps 1965) pottery. It is also frequently mentioned as a constituent of Orange pottery, although in quantities that are "not appreciable" (e.g., Bullen 1969:28, 1972:10, 15, 17; Ferguson 1951:17).

Although sponge spicules have never been mentioned explicitly in descriptions of Orange paste characteristics (e.g., Griffin 1945b; Sears and Griffin 1950), their presence can be inferred from pottery categorized by Bullen as "fiber-tempered St. Johns Plain" from late Orange/early St. Johns contexts at the Sunday Bluff site in Marion County (Bullen 1969:29, 45). Bullen also noted one such sherd from a collection from Poverty Point (Bullen 1971:67). Goggin mentioned a late Orange "hybrid chalky-fiber-tempered ware" (Goggin 1949:24, 1952:97) and suggested it may have led to the development of St. Johns pottery ware (Goggin 1952:101; see also Bullen 1969:45). Crusoe mentioned a fiber-tempered St. Johns paste, although sponge spicules were misidentified as diatoms (Crusoe 1971b). Chalky fiber-tempered sherds also occur at Tick Island, according Jahn and Bullen (1978:13) and FLMNH catalog cards, although none so designated were included in the present sample.

Bullen noted mica in fiber-tempered pottery from Jackson County in northwest Florida (Bullen 1958b:338). Saunders observed mica in over 50 percent of fiber-tempered sherds from the Rollins site in Nassau County, Florida (Saunders, this volume). Limestone was mentioned as a constituent of one fiber-tempered sherd from the Askew site in Citrus County, categorized as "semi-Pasco-semi-Orange" (Bullen and Askew 1965:206). One percent of the Orange sherds from Summer Haven were described as hav-

Table 4.8. Occurrence of nonfiber aplastics in fiber-tempered pottery

Aplastic or Temper	Designation	Site, Region, or Context	Reference
Quartz	Semifiber-tempered	Late Orange/Transitional	Bullen 1972:24, also 1971:64
		Fort Center, 8GL13	Sears 1982:24
	Norwood series	Gulf Coast	Phelps 1965
	"Fiber-tempered St. Johns"	Sunday Bluff, 8MR13	Bullen 1969:29, 45
	"Hybrid chalky fiber-tempered ware"	Northern St. Johns area	Goggin 1949:24, also 1952:97, 101
	"Chalky, like very early St. Johns"	Poverty Point, Louisiana	Bullen 1971:67
Sponge Spicules	"Fiber-tempered chalky paste"	St. Johns pottery from Florida	Crusoe 1971b:31
	"Semi-fiber-tempered St. Johns"		Jahn and Bullen 1978:13
	"Fiber-tempered chalky" "Semi-fiber, semi-chalky" "Chalky fiber-tempered"	Tick Island, 8VO24	FLMNH catalog nos. 103272, 103528, A–348
Limestone	Orange Plain w/limestone inclusions	Summer Haven, 8SJ46	Bullen and Bullen 1961:4–5
	"Semi-Pasco-semi-Orange"	Askew, 8CI46	Bullen and Askew 1965:206
Mica	"Orange Plain with micaceous material"	Chattahoochee River #1, 8JA8	Bullen 1958b:338, also 1972:18
	"Fiber-tempered"	Rollins, 8DU7510	Saunders, this volume

ing fine limestone inclusions (Bullen and Bullen 1961:4). The other inclusions observed in the present sample, UID noncarbonate inclusions, shell, ferric concretions, and clay lumps, were not mentioned in any of the references that were consulted. However, the fine limestone inclusions in the Summer Haven sherds are actually fragments of shell and decomposed shell.

GEOGRAPHIC VARIABILITY IN PASTE

In comparing the distribution of gross paste categories by geographic area, some interesting trends are readily apparent (Table 4.9 and Figure 4.3). For example, chalky paste sherds are absent in the Okeechobee/Fort Center sample, and pottery of intermediate spiculate paste is absent in the east Florida sample. But all three gross paste categories are well represented in the southwest Florida and central peninsular Gulf Coast samples.

East Florida Sample

For the east Florida sample, chalky paste, fiber-tempered sherds are common only in the Tick Island, Bluffton, and South Indian Field samples (Table 4.9). Nonchalky fiber-tempered sherds are most common in the Summer Haven, Cotten, Blue Spring, and Mount Elizabeth samples. Intermediate spiculate paste sherds are absent in samples from all of the sites and chalky fiber-tempered sherds are absent in the samples from the Summer Haven, Blue Spring, and Mount Elizabeth sites. The observed distribution may, however, be attributed to small sample size, at least for some sites. The sampling proportion for the east Florida sites with respect to the curated collections was only 1 percent to 3 percent (see Table 4.1). Thus the east Florida sample is not likely to be representative of the full range of variability at these sites, nor, perhaps, of the predominant or modal categories.

The Summer Haven sample may be representative of the modal paste categories on the basis of paste descriptions by Mitchell (1993:18, 51). The absence of chalky fiber-tempered pottery at this site is supported by its absence in another northern St. Johns–area site, Rollins (Saunders, this volume). The Bluffton sample, with 80 percent nonchalky and 20 percent chalky fiber-tempered paste, might be representative of gross modal categories on the basis of a study of a larger sample by Shannon (1986:55, 56, 59, 60) in which sponge spicules are not listed as constituents of the pottery. The representativeness of the present samples from the Cotten, South Indian Field, and Tick Island sites is uncertain. The FLMNH holdings from South Indian Field consist of only two small surface collections. (The collection studied by Ferguson [1951] is curated at the Yale Peabody Museum

Table 4.9. Geographic distribution of gross paste categories.

Geographic Area	Site Name	Site #	Gross Paste Categories			Total
			Chalky	Nonchalky	Intermediate Spiculate	
East Florida n = 50	Summer Haven	8SJ46	—	10 (100%)	—	10
	Bluffton	8VO22	4 (40%)	6 (60%)	—	10
	Tick Island	8VO24	9 (90%)	1 (10%)	—	10
	Cotten	8VO83	2 (20%)	8 (80%)	—	10
	Blue Spring	8VO43	—	2 (100%)	—	2
	South Indian Field	8BR23	3 (60%)	2 (40%)	—	5
	Mount Elizabeth	8MT30	—	3 (100%)	—	3
Central Peninsular	Askew	8CI46	—	12 (92%)	1 (8%)	13
Gulf Coast n = 36	Canton Street	8PI55	1 (100%)	—	—	1
	Palmer	8SO2A	7 (32%)	12 (54%)	3 (14%)	22
Okeechobee n = 29	Fort Center	8GL13	—	14 (48%)	15 (52%)	29
Southwest Florida n = 124	Turtle Bay II	8CH37	—	1 (50%)	1 (50%)	2
	Dunwody[a]	8CH61/8	—	3 (100%)	—	3
	Brit Army	8LL no#	4 (67%)	2 (33%)	—	6
	Howard Mound[b]	8LL44/45	—	1 (100%)	—	1
	Useppa Island	8LL51	1 (25%)	2 (50%)	1 (25%)	4

Marco Island	8CR107x1	30 (47%)	23 (36%)	11 (17%)	64
	8CR108	—	3 (38%)	5 (62%)	8
	8CR110	—	17 (100%)	—	17
	8CR111	1 (100%)	—	—	1
	8CR112	4 (33%)	3 (25%)	5 (42%)	12
	8CR153	—	3 (100%)	—	3
Horrs Island	8CR696	—	1 (50%)	1 (50%)	2
	8CR no#	—	1 (100%)	—	1
Total		66	130	43	239

[a]Luer believes these sherds are listed incorrectly in FLMNH accession records and are actually from the nearby Cedar Point Shell Heap site, 8CH8 (see Luer 1999:46).
[b]Luer believes these sherds are listed incorrectly in FLMNH accession records and are actually from the nearby Calusa Island midden, 8LL45 (see Luer 1989:251–253).

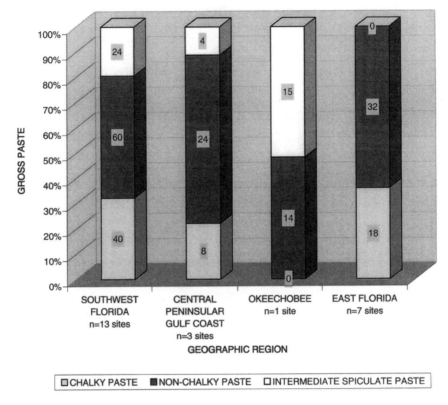

Figure 4.3. Bar chart of geographic distribution of gross paste categories.

of Natural History.) The present Tick Island sample consists primarily of chalky fiber-tempered sherds. Although previously reported at Tick Island, this paste is not considered to be common in the assemblage (Jahn and Bullen 1978:13). The high proportion of chalky fiber-tempered sherds in the present sample is surprising considering that, according to FLMNH catalog cards, no sherds included in the sample were classified as chalky fiber tempered. Although the sample sizes are small, the Blue Spring and Mount Elizabeth samples are representative with respect to their larger excavated assemblages (see Table 4.1).

Among the chalky fiber-tempered sherds from east Florida sites, very fine C1 paste is most common, especially at Tick Island and the Cotten site (Table 4.10). Category C3 paste, with more quartz sand and larger sand sizes, occurs in the Bluffton and South Indian Field samples. Category C2 also occurs in the Bluffton sample. Among the nonchalky paste sherds, categories NC1, NC2, and NC5 are most common (Table 4.11). NC1 and NC5 are

Table 4.10. Geographic distribution of chalky fiber-tempered paste.

Geographic Area[a]	Site Name	Site #	Chalky Paste			Total
			C1	C2	C3	
East Florida[b]	Bluffton	8VO22	—	2	2	4
n = 18	Tick Island	8VO24	9	—	—	9
	Cotten	8VO83	2	—	—	2
	South Indian Field	8BR23	1	—	2	3
Central Peninsular	Canton Street	8PI55	—	—	1	1
Gulf Coast[c]	Palmer	8SO2A	1	—	6	7
n = 8						
Southwest Florida[d]	Brit Army	8LL no#	3	1	—	4
n = 40	Useppa Island	8LL51	—	—	1	1
	Marco Island	8CR107x1	16	—	14	30
		8CR111	—	—	1	1
		8CR112	—	—	4	4
Total			32	3	31	66

[a]Chalky fiber-tempered paste was absent in the Okeechobee area Fort Center sample.
[b]Absent in the Summer Haven, Blue Spring, and Mount Elizabeth samples.
[c]Absent in the Askew sample.
[d]Absent in the samples from 8CH37, 8CH61/8, 8LL44/45, 8CR108, 8CR110, 8CR153, 8CR696, and 8CR no#.

the finest paste categories in terms of quantity and sizes of quartz constituents. All of the sherds with shell and limestone inclusions, excluding those with calcareous paste (NC6e), are also otherwise similar to NC1/NC5 in terms of quartz sand size and frequency. Sandier categories NC3 and NC4 are rare (n = 1 for NC3) and absent, respectively, in this area. It is interesting to note that category NC2 is the only nonchalky category that occurs with regularity in all of the study areas (Table 4.11). However, point-count data indicate that NC2 sherds from east Florida sites (n = 4 thin sections) are characterized by finer particle sizes than NC2 sherds from southwest Florida (n = 3 thin sections) and the central peninsular Gulf Coast (n = 1 thin section).

Central Peninsular Gulf Coast Sample

In the central peninsular Gulf Coast sample, chalky fiber-tempered sherds occur in samples from two of the three sites, Palmer and Canton Street

Table 4.11. Geographic distribution of nonchalky fiber-tempered paste.

Geographic Area	Site Name	Site #	Nonchalky Paste						Total
			NC1	NC2	NC3	NC4	NC5	NC6	
East Florida	Summer Haven	8SJ46	—	—	—	—	8	2[a]	10
n = 32	Bluffton	8VO22	2	4	—	—	—	—	6
	Tick Island	8VO24	—	1	—	—	—	—	1
	Cotten	8VO83	4	2	—	—	—	2[b]	8
	Blue Spring	8VO43	1	—	—	—	—	1[a]	2
	South Indian Field	8BR23	2	—	—	—	—	—	2
	Mount Elizabeth	8MT30	1	1	1	—	—	—	3
Central Peninsular Gulf Coast[c]	Askew	8CI46	—	2	3	1	—	6[d]	12
n = 24	Palmer	8SO2A	1	6	1	2	—	2[e]	12
Okeechobee	Fort Center	8GL13	—	6	8	—	—	—	14
n = 14									
Southwest Florida[f]	Turtle Bay II	8CH37	—	1	—	—	—	—	1
n = 60	Dunwody[g]	8CH61/8	—	2	—	1	—	—	3
	Brit Army	8LL no#	—	—	—	—	—	2[h]	2
	Howard Mound[i]	8LL44/45	1	—	—	—	—	—	1
	Useppa Island	8LL51	—	1	1	—	—	—	2
	Marco Island	8CR107x1	—	14	7	2	—	—	23
		8CR108	—	2	1	—	—	—	3

	8CR110	—	12	5	—	—	17
	8CR112	—	1	1	1	—	3
	8CR153	—	2	1	—	—	3
Horrs Island	8CR696	—	—	—	1	—	1
	8CR no#	—	—	1	—	—	1
Total		12	57	30	8	15	130

[a]NC6c (with limestone and shell; sherds otherwise similar to NC1 paste).

[b]NC6e (calcareous paste with limestone and shell).

[c]Nonchalky fiber-tempered paste was absent in Canton Street sample.

[d]Two NC6a (with UID noncarbonate inclusions; otherwise similar to NC3 or NC4 pastes), three NC6b (with limestone; otherwise similar to NC3 and NC4 pastes), one NC6d (with ferric concretions; otherwise similar to NC3 or NC4 pastes).

[e]NC6f (with clay lumps—Pinellas-like paste).

[f]Absent in 8CR111 sample.

[g]Luer believes these sherds are listed incorrectly in FLMNH accession records and are actually from the nearby Cedar Point Shell Heap site, 8CH8 (see Luer 1999:46).

[h]NC6a (with UID whitish inclusions; otherwise similar to NC2 paste).

[i]Luer believes these sherds are listed incorrectly in FLMNH accession records and are actually from the nearby Calusa Island midden, 8LL45 (see Luer 1989:251–253).

(Table 4.9). Nonchalky paste occurs and is prominent in samples from two of the three sites, Askew and Palmer. Intermediate spiculate paste is rare in the Askew sample, a minority category at Palmer, and absent in the Canton Street sample. Although the sample sizes are small, they are considered representative at least for the Askew and Palmer sites. The sampling proportions, with respect to FLMNH catalog records, are 100 percent for the Askew site and 44 percent for Palmer. In terms of sherds large enough for technological analysis, however, the proportion for the Palmer site is considerably higher than 44 percent. The present sample of one (one MNV) from the Canton Street site has chalky paste. This sample is undoubtedly not representative of variability in the excavated collection (see Bullen et al. 1978:6), which is apparently curated in Pinellas County.

For the two sites with chalky fiber-tempered pottery, category C3 is most common (Table 4.10). For nonchalky fiber-tempered paste, the modal categories are NC2 and NC3; NC4 also occurs (Table 4.11). Finer NC1 paste is rare in this subarea (n = 1). Micaceous NC5 paste is absent. The sherds with occasional other constituents (limestone, noncarbonate, and ferric concretions) are otherwise similar to sherds with NC3 and NC4 pastes. The sherds with clay lumps that are otherwise similar to Pinellas paste (NC6f) occur only in the central peninsular Gulf Coast sample. For the two sites with pottery of intermediate spiculate paste, category IS1 is the only category observed (Table 4.12).

Okeechobee Area—Fort Center Sample

The Okeechobee area Fort Center sample consists of approximately equal proportions of nonchalky and intermediate spiculate fiber-tempered pastes (Table 4.9). Chalky fiber-tempered paste is absent. The sample is considered reasonably representative, with a 25 percent sampling proportion of the FLMNH collection. In terms of sherds large enough for technological analysis, however, the sampling proportion is probably considerably higher. For nonchalky paste, categories NC3 and NC2 are present to the exclusion of the other nonchalky categories (Table 4.11). Category IS3 of sherds with intermediate spiculate paste, with the largest particle sizes of quartz constituents, is most common; the other two categories occur, but are rare (Table 4.12).

Southwest Florida Sample

For the southwest Florida sample, chalky paste fiber-tempered sherds are present in samples from five of the 13 sites, but common only in two Marco Island samples and one sample from Lee County (Brit Army site) (Table 4.9). Nonchalky fiber-tempered sherds are present in all site samples but one

Table 4.12. Geographic distribution of intermediate spiculate fiber-tempered paste.

Geographic Area[a]	Site Name	Site #	Intermediate Spiculate Paste			Total
			IS1	IS2	IS3	
Central	Askew	8CI46	1	—	—	1
Peninsular	Palmer	8SO2A	3	—	—	3
Gulf Coast[b]						
n = 4						
Okeechobee	Fort Center	8GL13	1	1	13	15
n = 15						
Southwest	Turtle Bay II	8CH37	—	1	—	1
Florida[c]	Useppa Island	8LL51	1	—	—	1
n = 24	Marco Island	8CR107x1	5	5	1	11
		8CR108	1	4	—	5
		8CR112	4	1	—	5
	Horrs Island	8CR696	—	1	—	1
Total			16	13	14	43

[a]Intermediate spiculate fiber-tempered paste was absent in the east Florida samples.
[b]Absent in the Canton Street sample.
[c]Absent in samples from 8CH61/8, 8LL no#, 8LL44/45, 8CR110, 8CR111, 8CR153, and 8CR no#.

and are prominent in samples from three sites, two on Marco Island and one in Charlotte County. Fiber-tempered sherds with intermediate spiculate paste are present in samples from six sites but are common only in three from Marco Island. The observed distribution may, however, be attributed to small sample size for some sites. Most of the sites (excluding Marco Island sites) are represented by small surface collections. Although sample sizes are small, the sampling proportion for most of these sites is 100 percent. The sampling proportions for excavated Marco Island sites, which have larger sample sizes, range from 11 percent to 38 percent. In terms of sherds large enough for technological analysis, however, the sampling proportions are considerably higher and the representativeness of these samples is not in doubt.

Among the five sites with chalky fiber-tempered pottery, category C1 paste occurs in samples from two (Table 4.10). Category C3 occurs in samples from four of the five sites, and C2 is rare in the area (n = 1), occurring at only one site. Category C1 is the modal paste in the 8CR107x1 and Brit Army site samples. Categories C1 and C3 occur in approximately equal abundance in the 8CR107x1 sample. Category C3 is the modal paste in the 8CR112 sample.

For nonchalky fiber-tempered paste, the modal categories are NC2 and NC3; NC4 also occurs in the samples from a few sites (Table 4.11). NC1, with the finest texture, is rare in this subarea (n = 1), occurring at only one site. Micaceous NC5 is absent. Two sherds with occasional noncarbonate inclusions from the Brit Army site in Lee County are otherwise similar to sherds of NC2 paste. Among the six sites with pottery of intermediate spiculate paste, categories IS1 and IS2, which are closely related according to point-count data, are the modal categories (Table 4.12). IS3 is rare (n = 1), occurring at only one site.

TEMPORAL DIMENSION OF PASTE VARIABILITY

Sassaman (2003a) recently outlined data that contradict Bullen's unilineal chronology for fiber-tempered pottery. Sassaman's data from east Florida middle St. Johns sites demonstrate contemporaneity of sites traditionally considered Orange 1 (on the basis of the absence of decorated pottery) and Orange 3 (on the basis of incised designs) (Sassaman 2003a; see also Saunders, this volume). His work also calls into question the traditionally considered late temporal position of chalky fiber-tempered pottery and semifiber-tempered pottery with abundant quartz sand (Sassaman 2003a). The samples and data from the present study corroborate Sassaman's observations on all counts.

The traditional chronological positions of sites in the sample are included in Table 4.1. Orange 1 pottery samples in the present study are from the Bluffton, Blue Spring, and Mount Elizabeth sites in east Florida; the Palmer site (lower levels) in central peninsular Florida; and 8CR110–112 in southwest Florida. The Bluffton site was dated to the Orange 1–2 periods on the basis of superposition of plain and incised fiber-tempered pottery (Bullen 1955, 1972:11). Blue Spring and Mount Elizabeth were considered Orange 1 on the basis of the absence of incised fiber-tempered pottery (Janus Research 1998; Sassaman 2003a, 2003b). At the Palmer site, an early Orange (Orange 1 or 2; Bullen 1972:13; Bullen and Bullen 1976:9) designation was assigned to the lower levels that contained only plain fiber-tempered pottery. Three Marco Island sites, 8CR110, 8CR111, and 8CR112, which yielded only plain fiber-tempered pottery, were assigned to the Pre-Glades I Late subperiod, the temporal equivalent of Orange 1 (Widmer 1988:69,

71–72). Excavated sherds from the other Marco Island sites and 8CR696 on Horrs Island and surface collections from the remaining southwest Florida sites also yielded only plain fiber-tempered pottery. Whether these other sites represent time frames equivalent to the Orange 1 period is uncertain.

The Orange 3 samples are from Summer Haven, the Cotten site, South Indian Field, and Tick Island in east Florida and from 8CR107x1, 8LL51, and the Brit Army site in southwest Florida. Of the east Florida sites, Summer Haven, Cotten, and South Indian Field were considered contemporaneous Orange 3 period sites on the basis of similar design elements on incised fiber-tempered pottery (Bullen 1972:14, 15; Griffin and Smith 1954:43; Saunders, this volume) (see Table 4.1). The Tick Island sample is also considered Orange 3 on the basis of Orange 3–style incised designs, including flat, wide rims with incised lips, although curated collections also contain earlier preceramic Archaic and later St. Johns materials (Jahn and Bullen 1978).

Among the southwest Florida sites, the assemblage from 8CR107x1 on Marco Island was assigned to the Pre-Glades III subperiod, the temporal equivalent of Orange 3–4 (Widmer 1988:72). The pottery includes Orange 3–style designs on incised sherds, including flat, wide rims with incised lips. The collections from 8LL51 on Useppa Island and the Brit Army site on Sanibel Island appear to be contemporaneous to 8CR107x1 on the basis of similar incised designs.

For the central peninsular Gulf Coast sample, the fiber-tempered pottery from both the Askew and Canton Street sites is thought to date to the Orange 5 period (Milanich 1994:94), formerly known as the Transitional period (Bullen 1971; Bullen and Askew 1965:212–213; Bullen et al. 1978:22–23). An Orange 4 or Orange 5 designation may also be assigned to the upper levels of the Palmer site (Bullen and Bullen 1976:9). Bullen described the incised fiber-tempered sherds at the Palmer site as having simple incised designs and greater amounts of quartz sand than the earlier or lower plain pottery (Bullen and Bullen 1976:10).

For the Okeechobee area Fort Center site, Sears (1982:185) estimated a time frame of 1000–800 B.C. (2950–2750 B.P.) for this semifiber-tempered component, the temporal equivalent of Orange 5 (Milanich 1994:94).

Most of the conventional radiocarbon dates (Table 4.2) contradict the chronological distinction between the Orange 1 and Orange 3 sites, however. For the east Florida Orange 1 sites, the radiocarbon dates include 4061 ± 110 B.P. from Bluffton (Bullen 1972:11), 3780 ± 50 B.P. to 3510 ± 70 B.P. from Blue Spring (Sassaman 2003a, 2003b), and 3970 ± 50 to 3950 ± 70 B.P. from Mount Elizabeth (Janus Research 1998; Russo and Heide 2002). These dates overlap with dates from Orange 3 sites: 3840 ± 60 B.P. from Summer Haven (State of Florida 1995), 3421 ± 200 B.P. from the Cotten site (Bullen

1958a:101), and 3930 ± 40 B.P. to 3630 ± 40 B.P. from Tick Island (Sassaman 2003a:8). No dates are available for South Indian Field, and the other dates from Tick Island (Table 4.2) are from prepottery contexts.

The only site in the present sample that demonstrates the stratigraphic sequence of plain and decorated, besides Bluffton, is the Palmer site. The early vs. later temporal interpretation for the plain vs. incised pottery based on superposition seems to be corroborated by radiocarbon dates that range from 3976 ± 120 B.P. for the lower, plain fiber-tempered component to 3626 ± 120 B.P. for the upper, incised levels (Bullen and Bullen 1976:13).

This summary corroborates Sassaman's (2003a) data contradicting the temporal distinction between Orange 1 and 3 culture periods. In addition, this contradicts the accepted chronological significance of plain vs. incised fiber-tempered pottery (also see Saunders, this volume). Table 4.2 also shows that some of the radiocarbon dates from southwest Florida and central peninsular Gulf Coast sites are as early as dates from east Florida. This may indicate contemporaneity of fiber-tempered pottery manufacture over a wide geographic area. When gross paste is considered, other interesting contradictions of accepted chronological indicators become evident.

The consensus among some Florida archaeologists is that chalky fiber-tempered paste occurs late in the sequence of Orange pottery. This understanding is based on observations by Bullen (1969:45, 1971:67) and Goggin (1949:24, 1952:97, 101; see also Sassaman 2003a). The spiculate character of chalky fiber-tempered sherds in the present sample was apparently overlooked by previous researchers in both the east Florida and Gulf coastal areas. In the present sample, chalky fiber-tempered pottery occurs in both "early" and "later" contexts. In the east Florida sample, chalky fiber-tempered paste is present in the Bluffton sample, one of the "early" Orange sites. Chalky fiber-tempered paste is present in three of the four Orange 3 samples, being absent only in the Summer Haven sample. In the central peninsular Gulf Coast sample, chalky fiber-tempered paste is present in the hypothesized Orange 1 levels at the Palmer site but absent in the later Orange upper levels. Chalky fiber-tempered paste is present in the Orange 5 period Canton Street sample but absent in the Askew sample. In the southwest Florida sample, chalky fiber-tempered paste is present in samples from 8CR111 and 8CR112, two of the three Pre-Glades I Late/Orange 1 sites. Chalky fiber-tempered paste is present in samples from 8CR107x1, 8LL51, and the Brit Army site, all three possible Pre-Glades III/Orange 3 sites. Chalky fiber-tempered paste is absent in the samples from all seven of the southwest Florida sites of unspecified Pre-Glades temporal position.

Thus the occurrence of chalky fiber-tempered pottery at sites in the present sample contradicts its alleged status as an indicator of late Orange occupations. Accordingly, its presumed late temporal significance needs to be reconsidered. There may be instead a geographic component to its occurrence. Chalky fiber-tempered pottery may be more common in east Florida sites along the middle St. Johns than in the northern St. Johns area. This is supported by its absence in fiber-tempered assemblages of the northern St. Johns Summer Haven and Rollins sites (Mitchell 1993:51; Sassaman 2003a:7; Saunders, this volume).

There is also a relationship between surface treatment and chalky fiber-tempered paste in the present sample. Over 50 percent of chalky fiber-tempered sherds in the sample are incised. Sassaman (2003a:7) also discussed the co-occurrence of incising and chalky fiber-tempered paste. There is, additionally, a tendency for incising to occur more frequently on chalky fiber-tempered sherds with finer pastes. Here, most of the incised sherds occur on very fine chalky C1 paste, while most of the plain sherds have sandier C3 paste. Seventy-eight percent of C1 sherds are incised vs. 32 percent for C3 paste, and the difference is statistically significant ($\chi^2 = 11.579$, df = 1, $p < .001$).

The presence of semifiber-tempered pottery, i.e., fiber-tempered pottery with considerable quantities of quartz sand in an otherwise fiber-tempered paste, has also been considered an indicator of Orange 4 and Orange 5 contexts (Milanich 1994:94). In the present sample, quartz sand is present in fiber-tempered pottery regardless of temporal position. The occurrence of quartz sand in pre–Orange 4 fiber-tempered pottery is corroborated by Mitchell (1993:51) for Summer Haven and by Saunders (this volume) for the Rollins Shell Ring site. The explicit absence of quartz sand in many published descriptions (e.g., Bullen et al. 1978:9; Bullen and Bullen 1976:10; Griffin 1945b:219) or lack of any mention of quartz sand as a constituent (e.g., Bullen 1955:7; Bullen and Bullen 1961:5; Ferguson 1951:17; Griffin and Smith 1954:33) may simply be attributed to low quartz frequency and/or particle sizes too small to be seen with the unaided eye. In the present sample, the sandiest paste categories, NC3 and NC4, occur in most of the sites, "early" and "later," with the exception of most of the east Florida sites. Here, the sandiest categories were observed only in the southernmost Mount Elizabeth sample. This pattern may reflect geographic differences in tempering practices or geographic differences in the relative sandiness of clay resources. The paucity of Orange 4–5 sites in the present sample precludes evaluation of the increase in sandiness through time, however.

Tempering practices or resource availability may also impact surface treatment. Within the nonchalky sample, there is a tendency for incising to occur less frequently on fiber-tempered sherds with sandier pastes, although the pattern is not as marked as it was for the chalky fiber-tempered sample.

Only 8 percent of the fiber-tempered sample with NC3 and NC4 pastes (combined) have incised decorations vs. 30 percent of the sample with NC1, NC2, and NC5 pastes (combined). The difference is statistically significant ($\chi^2 = 7.022$, df $= 1$, $p < .01$).

INTERREGIONAL COMPARISONS AND PROVISIONAL MANUFACTURING ORIGINS

Interregional differences in the distribution of fiber-tempered pastes are now considered in order to suggest provisional manufacturing origins for the paste categories. It should be mentioned that statewide manufacture of fiber-tempered pottery was possible on the basis of the statewide occurrence of Spanish moss (*Tillandsia usneoides*) (Wunderlin 1998:195). As discussed previously, chalky fiber-tempered pottery is present at five of the 13 southwest Florida sites in the sample, three sites from Marco Island and two from coastal Lee County, and at two of the three central peninsular Gulf Coast sites, Palmer and Canton Street (Table 4.10). The chalky C1 paste sherds in the present sample from southwest Florida are especially similar to C1 paste sherds from the east Florida sites of Tick Island and the Cotten site. The similarities are based on composition, refired colors, and point-count data. Orange 3–style incised designs are also similar between east Florida and southwest Florida samples (Figure 4.4). For example, a sherd from 8CR107x1 (Figure 4.4, top row, left) is quite similar to a sherd from the Cotten site (Figure 4.4, middle row, left). Other incised sherds from southwest Florida (Figure 4.4, top row, middle and right) are more similar to sherds from Tick Island (Figure 4.4 [middle row, center and right]; see Marquardt 1999:83 [FLMNH A20387] for other examples of incised sherds with chalky fiber-tempered paste; see Bullen and Bullen [1961:7–9]; Ferguson [1951:plates 2 and 3]; Griffin and Smith [1954:plate I]; Jahn and Bullen [1978:figs. 7 and 8] for other similar east Florida examples, which may or may not have chalky paste).

The Gulf coastal samples with category C3 paste are more similar to C3 paste sherds from the east Florida sites of Bluffton and South Indian Fields in terms of paste characteristics. Most of the incised C3 sherds from the Gulf coastal samples are too small to reconstruct designs for comparison with the east Florida samples.

It is provisionally suggested that the chalky paste, fiber-tempered pottery found in southwest Florida and central peninsular Gulf Coast sites may have east Florida manufacturing origins (Table 4.13). This is based not only on the similarities outlined above but also on the relative abundance of chalky pottery in general, which is much greater in east Florida than in Gulf

Figure 4.4. Incised chalky fiber-tempered sherds (top row left and middle sherds from Marco Island [8Cr107]; top row right sherd from Brit Army site; middle row left sherd from Cotten site; middle row center and right sherds from Tick Island; bottom center sherd from South Indian Field).

coastal Florida. The radiocarbon dates and newly established contemporaneity of Orange 1 and 3 sites support the plausibility of the hypothetical relationships between the southwest Florida and east Florida sites. This indicates interaction or exchange between east Florida and Gulf coastal populations.

Nonchalky fiber-tempered paste is present at most of the sites in the sample, in all geographic regions (Table 4.9). Differences become apparent when individual paste categories are considered, however (Table 4.11). The first category, NC1, with very fine texture, occurs mainly in the east Florida sample, at five of the seven sites. It is also the modal nonchalky category in the east Florida sample. The fifth category, NC5, is a slightly micaceous version of NC1 and occurs only in the east Florida sample. The second category, NC2, with greater quartz sand size and frequency, occurs with some regularity in all the geographic areas and most of the sites in the sample. The sandier category NC3 occurs mainly in the southwest Florida, central peninsular Gulf Coast, and Fort Center areas. Only one NC3 sherd is present in the east Florida sample, from Mount Elizabeth, the southernmost site in the east Florida sample. The fourth category, NC4, which is most similar to NC3 paste, is present only in the southwest Florida and central peninsular Gulf Coast samples.

Table 4.13. Provisional manufacturing origins of fiber-tempered paste categories.

Gross Paste	Paste Category	Provisional Manufacturing Origins		
		East Florida	Gulf Coastal Florida	Okeechobee (Fort Center)
Chalky Paste	C1	X	—	—
	C2	X	—	—
	C3	X	—	—
Nonchalky Paste	NC1	X	—	—
	NC2	X	X	X
	NC3	X?	X	X
	NC4	—	X	—
	NC5	X	—	—
	NC6	X (6c, e)	X (6a, b, d, f)	—
Intermediate	IS1	—	X	—
Spiculate Paste	IS2	—	X	—
	IS3	—	—	X

From these distributional data, the first nonchalky category, NC1, probably has east Florida manufacturing origins (Table 4.13), as does category NC5. The NC1 paste sherd in the Palmer sample from Sarasota County and the sherd from a Lee County site are particularly similar in paste characteristics to sherds from the east Florida sites of Bluffton and Cotten, respectively. The hypothetical relationship between the Palmer site and Bluffton is plausible on the basis of radiocarbon dates (Table 4.2). The temporal position of the Lee County sherd is unknown, so it is difficult to evaluate the plausibility of its hypothetical relationship to the Cotten site.

For nonchalky categories NC2 and NC3, multiple manufacturing origins, including east Florida, Gulf Coast, and Fort Center areas, are suggested provisionally. The suggestion of multiple manufacturing origins for NC2 and NC3 categories is supported by refired color data indicating that a variety of clay sources may be represented. Point-count data also support multiple manufacturing origins for NC2 paste pottery. Thin sections representing east Florida samples (n = 4) are consistently finer in terms of sand size index and percentages of fine through coarse quartz than thin sections of Gulf Coast (n = 4) sherds. Southwest Florida and central peninsular Gulf

Figure 4.5. Incised nonchalky fiber-tempered sherds (top row left and middle two sherds from Marco Island [8Cr107]; top row right sherd from Brit Army site; second row left sherd from Palmer; second row middle and right sherds from Askew; third row left and center sherds from Cotten; third row right sherd from Tick Island; bottom row sherds from Summer Haven).

Coast samples are not differentiated in this interpretation, because of similarities in physical properties and incised designs (see Figure 4.5) that may indicate common manufacturing origins. Pottery of the fourth category, NC4, was probably also made in the Gulf coastal region.

The heterogeneous sixth category, NC6, has mixed manufacturing origins (Table 4.13). The subcategories with noncarbonate white inclusions (NC6a), limestone (NC6b), and ferric concretions (NC6d) probably were made in the central peninsular Gulf Coast region owing to the absence of these categories in the east Florida and Okeechobee samples and rarity in the southwest Florida sample. Sherds of these categories were observed almost exclusively in the sample from the Askew site. It is uncertain whether the two sherds with UID noncarbonate inclusions in the southwest Florida sample represent a local ware or evidence of interaction with the central peninsular Gulf Coast area. There are noncarbonate white inclusions in fiber-tempered pottery from the Rollins site as well (Rebecca Saunders, personal communication, 2001). It is uncertain how similar these Rollins inclusions are to the noncarbonate inclusions of category NC6a. In any case, if the sherds from Rollins are comparable to the Summer Haven sample and other east Florida samples in terms of abundance and particle size of quartz constituents, then the Rollins site would not be a likely source for the NC6a sherds from central peninsular Florida.

The subcategory with rounded clay lumps (NC6f) may also have central peninsular Gulf Coast manufacturing origins on the basis of its similarity to the presumed local Pinellas paste. This paste was only observed at the Palmer site in the central peninsular Gulf Coast sample. The subcategories with shell temper (NC6c) and calcareous paste (NC6e) have east Florida manufacturing origins on the basis of their absence in the Gulf coastal and Okeechobee areas. The sherds with shell inclusions occur only at Summer Haven and Blue Spring in the east Florida sample, and the sherds with a calcareous paste occur only at the Cotten site in the east Florida sample (Table 4.11).

Fiber-tempered sherds with intermediate spiculate paste are present at six of the 13 southwest Florida sites, two of the three central peninsular Gulf Coast sites, and at Fort Center (Table 4.12). Sherds of the first category (IS1) are found mainly on Marco Island and the Palmer site in southwest Florida and the central peninsular Gulf Coast, respectively. Sherds of the second category (IS2) are found mainly on Marco Island and are absent in the central peninsular Gulf Coast sample. However, the first two categories appear closely related to each other in terms of physical properties and point-count data, indicating similar clays may be represented. Sherds of the third category (IS3) are found almost exclusively at Fort Center. Intermediate spiculate paste sherds are absent in the east Florida sample, although this could be an artifact of small sample size.

For now, until larger samples can be examined, it is provisionally suggested that there were Gulf coastal manufacturing origins for the first two categories of fiber-tempered pottery with intermediate spiculate paste and Okeechobee/Fort Center area manufacturing origins for the third category (Table 4.13). This is supported by differences in refired colors between the Gulf Coast and Fort Center samples.

INTERPRETATIONS AND RECOMMENDATIONS

These suggestions regarding manufacturing origins point to interregional exchange or interaction between east Florida and Gulf coastal populations, especially for the chalky fiber-tempered wares and at least one category of nonchalky paste. Interaction within the Gulf coastal region, between people living in southwest Florida and the central peninsular Gulf Coast, may be indicated on the basis of general similarity in physical properties of the nonchalky pottery. Particular similarities in simple incised designs might also indicate interaction between Gulf coastal people, although such designs are not unique to the Gulf coastal area. The Fort Center sample shows the least evidence of interaction with adjacent regions on the basis of paste categories and refired colors. However, interaction between Fort Center and southwest Florida populations may be indicated on the basis of the distribution of a few sherds of intermediate spiculate paste.

Some of these interpretations are specified as "provisional." This is so for a number of reasons. The interpretations regarding manufacturing origins are essentially based on the presence and relative abundance vs. absence of certain paste categories across the geographic regions. Some interpretations may be questionable owing to small sample size, especially for the east Florida sites. Examination of larger samples, especially from east Florida Orange sites, will be essential to gain a better understanding of variability in fiber-tempered pottery from this area. The results of such a study could impact interpretations presented here. The study and comparison of clay sources from the different regions would be useful in resolving manufacturing origins, but this was beyond the scope of this particular project.

The possible temporal dimension to fiber-tempered paste differences also warrants further investigation. The present data contradict popular assumptions regarding the temporal significance of chalky fiber-tempered pottery and fiber-tempered pottery with abundant quartz sand. However, fiber-tempered sherds from Orange 4 and later sites are poorly represented in the sample. Resolving this issue will require consideration of more sherds from a variety of well-dated contexts.

This study also raises typological issues. Orange and Norwood series have been defined to refer to fiber-tempered pottery from east Florida and Gulf coastal Florida, respectively (Griffin 1945b; Phelps 1965). But these categories do not account for the paste variability documented in this study and would, therefore, mask potential evidence for interregional interactions and potential temporal differences. It seems inappropriate to refer to both chalky and nonchalky fiber-tempered sherds from east Florida as Orange, as they clearly have been in the past. Bullen considered chalky fiber-tempered pottery to be rare (Bullen 1969:29), but the present sample indicates it may be more common than previously thought. Surely the fiber-tempered pottery typology should be revised to take gross paste differences as well as geographic differences into account. Clearly, there is still much to be considered to improve our understanding of Late Archaic pottery in Florida.

ACKNOWLEDGMENTS

Special thanks are given to Rebecca Saunders and Chris Hays for providing the instigation for this study with their invitation to participate in the SAA symposium "Early Pottery in the Lower Southeast: Stylistic and Technological Approaches to Function and Interaction" (New Orleans, April 21, 2001). I am grateful to Scott Mitchell/FLMNH, Gainesville; Dave Dickel/ Bureau of Archaeological Resources, Tallahassee; Ken Sassaman/University of Florida Anthropology Department; and Martin County/Southeast Florida Archaeological Society for loan of fiber-tempered sherds used in this study. Sonja Gray and Sally McKeige of the Southeast Florida Archaeological Society were instrumental in making the Martin County sherds available for study. Special thanks are due to Jerald Milanich and William Marquardt for providing funding for the thin sections. Earlier versions of this chapter benefited from constructive criticisms by Jerald Milanich, Kenneth Sassaman, Michael Russo, and Karen Jo Walker, for which I am very appreciative. The present version has benefited from further scrutiny by Jerald Milanich, Kenneth Sassaman, Rebecca Saunders, and reviewers of this volume.

5

The Emergence of Pottery in South Florida

Michael Russo and Gregory Heide

Relatively few discussions exist on the causes of the early adoption of pottery in Florida. Those few discussions that do exist are generally concerned with early fiber-tempered wares and include theories of spread or migration from coastal Georgia (Milanich 1994:86; Sassaman, this volume) or South America (Crusoe 1971a; Ford 1969; Reichel-Dolmatoff 1972; cf. Stoltman 1972b). Some suggest that the first pottery in Florida may have been locally manufactured (e.g., Milanich 1994:86), but most suggest that the first pottery "developed" (Bense 1994:88; Carr and Beriault 1984:2) or was "added" (Widmer 1988:67) without specifying the how or why. Appropriately, archaeologists studying early pottery in Florida have been and continue to be strongly involved in developing pottery chronologies, identifying styles and technological attributes, and associating regional archaeological expressions through pottery types. Not typically considered are the conditions under which pottery was adopted. Certainly, nothing so formal as a model has been developed to account for the invention or acceptance of this remarkable innovation.

We present a model for the adoption of early pottery at one site, the Joseph Reed Shell Ring (8MT13) (Figure 5.1), and in one area, the East Okeechobee region of south Florida (Figure 5.2). The unexpected discovery of sand-tempered and spiculate[1] wares dating between 3500 and 3000 B.P.[2] offers a look at what may be the first intensive use of pottery in south Florida. We link the adoption of this pottery to theories of prestige technology and feasting (Clark and Blake 1994; Hayden 1995a, 1995b, 1998, 2001; Rice 1999). We suggest that pottery was adopted in an otherwise nonpottery-producing region of Florida because it represented a novel, prestigious technology by which entrepreneurs (aggrandizers, *sensu* Clark and Blake 1994; Hayden 1998) could gain and/or display their status through their ability to obtain rare and socially valued innovative technologies. In addition, the uniqueness of the pottery was used to distinguish the Joseph Reed cultural group from the fiber-tempered pottery producers to their north.

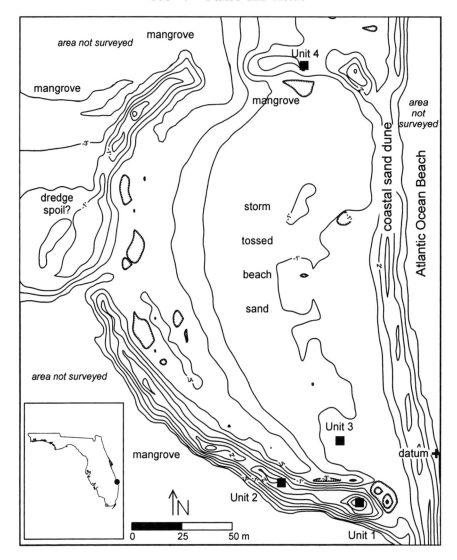

Figure 5.1. The Joseph Reed Shell Ring (after Kennedy 1980).

POTTERY AS PRESTIGE TECHNOLOGY

Function/adaptation proponents argue that pottery was introduced and accepted to serve technological needs. Under conditions of environmental stress, for example, hunter-gatherers adopted pottery to increase the efficiency of storing, preparing, and extending the nutritional values of scarce foods (Hoopes 1995:195; Lowe 1971:213 [as cited in Clark and Gosser 1995]; O'Shea 1981; Rice 1999:31). If only for a few days, watertight vessels may

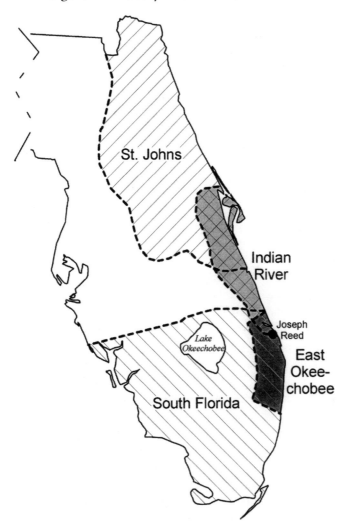

Figure 5.2. Culture regions of Florida described in the text.

extend the shelf life of food through pickling or fermentation. Vermin-proof vessels enhance long-term seed storage (Vitelli 1989:26). Through the production of soups, pottery may extend the nutritional value of foods that include protein sources that would otherwise go underutilized (e.g., mammal toe and backbone sections, small snails), as well as facilitate the softening of food for consumption by the very young and old. Pottery may facilitate the rehydration of dried and smoked foods (Hoopes 1995:192). In short, function/adaptation arguments view the introduction of pottery as filling and/or expanding subsistence needs that old technologies (e.g., roasting, drying, stone boiling) no longer met. As such, pottery was first used in quotidian subsistence contexts.

In contrast, prestige technologists argue that initial pottery was found in ceremonial and public contexts. It arose not because old technology failed but because, as new technology, it was novel and rare and hence contained inherent economic value and assignable social value. Self-motivated individuals wishing to display their power and prestige would obtain pottery as they would other rare and valued technology such as metals, feathers, or exotic stones—that is, through trade, bride wealth, gifts, and repayment. In hunter-gatherer societies, the primary medium of value is food. Ever perishable, food is gifted, in part, because it cannot be stored or can only be stored at cost to the owner. As such, items and obligations of more durable value are sought in place of food: promises of reciprocal food gifts, alliances in war, brides, and rare and otherwise valued objects. Gifting obligates recipients into reciprocal economic and social repayments at least equal in value to, but usually more valued than, the food given away.

In this setting, self-aggrandizing individuals will seek to better their economic and social standing to the greatest degree the society will allow. Objects received in payment for gifting food or hosting a feast symbolize the individual's accumulatory prowess and raise his/her social status. Those who give more, receive more in prestige, status, and power. Accumulators may seek not only greater quantities of valued objects in recompense for their food giveaways but will often seek rare and otherwise valued objects in a public forum. Exchanges of food for valued objects, promised returns of food, and other social obligations are always matters of public display in hunter-gatherer societies. Where sharing is the dominant ethic, deviations from equal distributions of food and gifts must occur in special, public, ritual settings to justify and sanctify the fact that society is allowing certain individuals under certain, special circumstances to receive more than others in an otherwise egalitarian society.

In hunter-gatherer societies, items obtain economic and social value in a number of ways. Association with specific historical events or persons may add value to an object. Or items may be rare and useful and thus have inherent economic value, for instance, workable lithics in a stoneless environment. Regardless of functional utility, items such as feathers, animal parts, and exotic stones can be valued if they are unusual in appearance or contain cultural significance. Value is conveyed to such items through their display in public ritual. Rare or visually unusual pottery may be viewed as socioeconomically important under similar settings.

As a plastic medium, pottery is uniquely suited to display symbolic and social meaning through temper (Rodríguez 1995:145; cf. Vitelli 1995:61), form (Sassaman, this volume), and surface decoration (e.g., Hally 1986; Rice 1999; Saunders, this volume). It is the visual and symbolic aspects of pottery that enhance its specialness and social value and promote its initial development. It can be molded into particular forms, decorated, and continuously modified to facilitate changing social meaning placed within it. In nonpottery-producing societies, the introduction of pottery can be used to reflect social and economic values.

Critical to the social acceptance of pottery into nonpottery-producing societies is the community's natural environment and social organization. Initially, pottery may be adopted only in areas of resource abundance (Hayden 1995a; Rice 1999). Archaeologically, it is known that the adoption of many first regional potteries occurred among societies dependent on riverine and coastal resources. Faunal remains associated with these sites have suggested to some that initial pottery was designed to facilitate the processing of those resources (Aikens 1995:19; Arroyo 1995:206; Cooke 1995:180; Goodyear 1988; Meggers et al. 1965; Roosevelt 1995:129; Sassaman 1993a:81–82; Stoltman 1974:233). However, under prestige-technology models, pottery is not a necessary precursor to fisheries exploitation or to the exploitation of any abundant resource sufficient to support large-scale feasting (Hayden 1995a:260). In many cases, intensive use of aquatic resources preceded the adoption of pottery by hundreds or thousands of years (Clark and Gosser 1995:216; Dickel 1992; Russo 1991, 1992; Sassaman 1993a).

Specific kinds of resources are not essential for the adoption of pottery. For example, initial occurrences of pottery are also found among cultures dependent on different, albeit abundant, resources such as tree products like oil, fruit, and starch (Hoopes 1995:194–195), starchy root crops (Hoopes 1995:194), and horticultural and agricultural grain crops (Crown and Wills 1995:249; Gebauer 1995:108; Manson 1995:74; Moore 1995:48). Rather, it is the stability and the predictability of abundant resources, regardless of kind, that is the key to the adoption of pottery under prestige-enhancing circumstances (Hayden 1995a, 1995b, 1998). These resources are directly linked to the development of economic surpluses that allow for the rise of transegalitarian (incipiently complex) social organizations. Hayden argues that it is only the transegalitarian communities among hunter-gatherers that can permit competitive and reciprocal feasts. In such public ceremonies, individuals are freed from the sharing ethic, ubiquitous among generalized hunter-gatherers, which levies social proscriptions on hoarding and trading for personal gain. Individuals are allowed to obtain and use surpluses to accumulate other valued goods and social debts. While pottery is not a necessary concomitant of such societies, if pottery is introduced, aggrandizing individuals will use the rare item to facilitate their prestige-seeking ventures. Pottery, then, will arise first in those areas of resource abundance among social formations that allow private ownership and/or other forms of socioeconomic inequalities to arise (Hayden 1998:13).

As a new material item, pottery is economically valuable as a result of its relative rarity, a rarity that can be controlled and enhanced through the manipulation of its form, decoration, and socially imbued meaning (Hayden 1995a). However, as the novelty of the medium wears off, as improvements in and knowledge of manufacturing techniques expand to greater numbers of the populace, and/or as pottery becomes otherwise more accessible, it may shift from a prestige to a practical, utilitarian technology. Hayden (1995a:260–261) warns that the change from prestige to practical may be rapid (and thus, we assume, may render the first occurrences of prestige pottery archaeologically invisible). Ways of obtaining prestige are ever-evolving, and prestige-seeking individuals may choose either to change the appearance of pottery to distinguish prestige from utilitarian pottery or to abandon it altogether as a marker of status (Armit and Finlayson 1995:272; Bradley 1984:272; Hayden 1995a:263).

POTTERY AND FEASTING AT SHELL RINGS

Woodburn (1981:439–440) has noted that "in the absence of other valuables, possession or control of food is singularly important as a means of differentiating one member of the community from another and as a source of power." It is not incongruent that shell rings occur adjacent to estuaries and marshes, environments with some of the highest biomass production on the planet. Among the first permanent coastal settlements in the Southeast are shell rings (Russo 1991, 1996b; Russo and Heide 2001). And shell rings are among the sites where the earliest pottery is found in North America (Sassaman 1993a; Trinkley 1985; Waring and Larson 1968). We suggest that the bountiful environments allowed for the development of sedentary communities in and around shell rings with a consequent increase in social complexity. In certain cases this led to the acceptance of pottery as a prestige technology (Russo and Heide 2002).

Having suggested it, we find that supporting the idea that shell rings represent places where incipient social complexity arose presents unique problems. By definition, transegalitarian communities permit displays of inequality, despite lingering egalitarian tendencies to maintain a level social playing field (Hayden 1996b; Woodburn 1981). And it is egalitarian social leveling mechanisms that may disguise the rise of sociopolitical hierarchies in the archaeological record of shell rings.

Archaeologists have long assumed that the builders of Late Archaic shell rings (ca. 5000–3000 B.P.) were socially egalitarian. The individual families among these hunter-gatherer-fisher folk lived equally spaced in small circles of domiciles, discarding their daily subsistence refuse (primarily shell and fish bone) beneath and behind their homes. This discard incidentally resulted in the shell rings we see today. The symmetrical shape of the ring, along with a material record that is depauperate in exotic artifacts, prestige objects, and burials (let alone burials with status items), has been seen as evidence of social equality (Trinkley 1985).

In contrast, we suggest that, far from representing small, symmetrical circles, shell rings vary widely in shape and size and that asymmetries within the rings may reflect social inequalities among the builders (Russo 2004; Russo and Heide 2001). Russo (2004) has suggested for further testing that Late Archaic shell rings functioned as permanent or temporary village-sized occupations in which incipiently hierarchical (read transegalitarian, intermediate, heterarchical) societies held large- and small-scale ceremonies during which feasting occurred as either primary or ancillary activities. At shell-ring feasting ceremonies, all individuals and their accouterments are open to public review. Higher-status individuals and groups held specific places that were most visually dominant either on top of or within the ring, positions from which they were viewed by the community and, in turn, could view and participate in public ceremonies within the central plaza.

During and/or after the close of ceremonies, individuals deposited the refuse (shell, bone, artifacts) of their subsistence and feasting activities at their occupied/used location at the ring. As Woodburn (1981:439–440) has noted, possession and control of food is the principal source of power in societies lacking other valued materials. Russo (2004) has offered a methodology to test the idea that those individuals with greater acquisitive abilities amassed more shell and material objects reflective of their greater power, prestige, and/or reciprocal obligations over other members of society (Hayden 1995a). With this approach, the relative socioeconomic status of an individual or kin group is tied to amounts of food refuse they left behind. In addition, other kinds of valued material objects, such as pottery, may be differentially deposited in the ring, with positions of high status holding the greatest numbers and diversity of pottery and other prestige goods.

EARLY POTTERY AT
THE JOSEPH REED SHELL RING

Recently we completed a brief investigation of the Joseph Reed Shell Ring (8MT13) in the East Okeechobee region of south Florida (Figures 5.1 and 5.2). Most shell rings in the southeastern United States date to the Late

Archaic period (ca. 5000–3000 B.P.), and archaeologists have long suspected that the Joseph Reed ring was an Orange period (Late Archaic, 4300–3000 B.P.) manifestation (Fryman et al. 1980). With six radiocarbon dates (Table 5.1), we confirmed that the ring was constructed around 3300 B.P., with the earliest date being 3455 B.P. (Russo and Heide 2002), well within the range of the Late Archaic Orange period. Unexpectedly, however, pottery from the ring was not the typical Orange fiber-tempered ware found at other Florida Late Archaic pottery-bearing shell rings (e.g., Saunders, this volume). Rather, it consisted of sand-tempered and spiculate ("chalky") wares, pottery types thought not to have been introduced to south Florida until approximately 2500 and 1200 years ago, respectively, well into the Woodland period (Carr and Beriault 1984; Milanich and Fairbanks 1980; Russo and Heide 2002).

The presence of spiculate pottery, particularly at such early dates, is puzzling. Archaeologists have traditionally linked the origins of spiculate, or St. Johns, pottery to peoples of the St. Johns region (otherwise referred to as East and Central Florida [Milanich and Fairbanks 1980:22]) ca. 2000 B.P. The Joseph Reed Shell Ring actually lies outside this region, some 80 miles south (Figure 5.2), and is much earlier. Although St. Johns wares have previously been identified in East Okeechobee (Pepe 1999), they have not been dated as early as the spiculate wares from Joseph Reed and are typically considered to be more recent and rare trade items.

Finding sand-tempered wares at Joseph Reed at such early dates is equally puzzling. Although regional pottery traditions would later come to be dominated by sand tempering, the manufacture of sand-tempered vessels is typically thought to have begun around 2500 B.P. (Carr and Beriault 1984), although some authors cite dates as early as 2800–2600 B.P. (Pepe 1999; Widmer 1988). In East Okeechobee, and south Florida in general, it has long been assumed either that pottery production had not been adopted or that only fiber-tempered pottery was in (limited) use as early as 3300 B.P.

SPICULATE AND SAND-TEMPERED PLAIN WARES IN SOUTH FLORIDA

St. Johns wares have been described as a temperless, soft-paste, "chalky" pottery most abundant along the entire length of the St. Johns River basin and the adjacent Atlantic coastline (St. Johns region in Figure 5.2). They are found in less abundance throughout the rest of Florida and are occasionally found in locations as distant as Louisiana (Hays and Weinstein, this volume; Stoltman, this volume; cf. Gibson and Melancon, this volume). At one time, the chalky pottery in south Florida was distinguished as Biscayne ware (Goggin 1939), but this type name has since been subsumed under the St.

Table 5.1. Radiocarbon dates from the Joseph Reed Shell Ring.

Provenience (cmbd)	Lab #	Material	Measured Age B.P.	Conventional Age	^{13}C	2Cal/1Cal (Intercept) 1Cal/2Cal B.P.[a]
Unit 1, Feature 2	GX-26118	Charcoal	2880 ± 130	2850 ± 130	-26.6	3354/3206 (2951) 2784/2746
Unit 1, Feature 3	WK-7435	Oyster	2868 ± 58	3280 ± 60	-0.2	3306/3208 (3131) 3022/2933
Unit 1 (80–190)	GX-25976	Oyster	3060 ± 80	3455 ± 80	-0.6	3527/3426 (3340) 3245/3139
Unit 2 (48)	GX-25977	Oyster	3010 ± 75	3425 ± 75	+0.3	3464/3379 (3318) 3210/3103
Unit 2 (155)	WK-7436	Oyster	2935 ± 55	3340 ± 60	-0.6	3351/3298 (3205) 3116/3014
Unit 4 (0–20)	GX-26119	Oyster	2880 ± 80	3280 ± 80	-0.7	3335/3232 (3131) 2989/2875

[a]All calibrated ages were determined with Calib 4.3 (Stuiver and Reimer 1993); calibration data are found in Stuiver, Reimer, and Braziunas 1998 and Stuiver, Reimer, Bard, et al. 1998.

Johns rubric (Bullen 1968; Willey 1949a:408). Other pottery types with similar paste characteristics in Florida include Little Manatee, Papys Bayou, and Sarasota Incised on the Gulf Coast (Willey 1949a) and Tomoka wares near Daytona Beach (Griffin and Smith 1949), but these types have limited distributions, and their numbers and type names have not been widely accepted. In general, when archaeologists identify chalky pottery in Florida outside the St. Johns River region, it is called St. Johns ware and often, but not always, is assumed to have originated from the St. Johns region.

As for sand-tempered pottery, most chronologies identify sand-tempered plain as the first ware indigenous to south Florida. Common type names that have been applied to sand-tempered plain pottery near the Joseph Reed Shell Ring in south Florida and the adjacent Indian River area include Glades Gritty Ware (Ferguson 1951; Goggin 1939, 1940, 1947, 1949; Willey 1949a) and smooth plain or residual plain (Willey 1949a). However, Glades is the most common type name used in south Florida for nonspiculate, sandy wares. Unlike spiculate wares, however, sandy or sand-tempered wares in south Florida are usually seen as indigenous rather than trade wares. Glades wares, particularly plain wares, cover a wide temporal range, from at least 2500 (some say 2800) to 500 B.P.

Clay and sand occur throughout south Florida and would have been available to locals interested in manufacturing sand-tempered pottery throughout the Holocene. At present, it is unclear whether spicules were natural inclusions or added temper (Cordell and Koski 2003; Rolland and Bond 2003). In either case, the subsequent indigenous development of Belle Glade (sand- and spicule-containing) pottery suggests that local potters knew of and used either sponges or spicule-bearing clays to make pastes at least 2,000 years ago. In lieu of evidence to the contrary, we suggest that similar environmental conditions were in place at least 3,500 years ago that would allow for freshwater sponge growth and/or mining of spiculate clays for the autochthonous production of spiculate wares. While the pottery found at Joseph Reed may, indeed, represent trade from outside the region, this is not a necessary condition to explain the appearance of the wares at the site.

THE JOSEPH REED POTTERY IN DETAIL

In the 1960s, William Sears recovered three St. Johns sherds and one sand-tempered sherd from the surface of the Joseph Reed Shell Ring (Kennedy and Wheeler 1998:2). One St. Johns sherd was recovered from a shallow test at Joseph Reed Shell Ring (Fryman et al. 1980). Prior to our excavations, this was the only pottery reported from the site. Even with our excavations, however, the number of sherds from Joseph Reed is small. We recovered only 63 additional sherds from three 1-×-1-m units placed in the shell ring (Figure 5.3; Table 5.2). We examined all sherds macroscopically for general observations on inclusions (Russo and Heide 2000). Cordell (2000) examined the sherds microscopically under 45× magnification along fresh breaks and other longitudinal sections to identify the presence of sponge spicules, sand, and other temper or inclusions. Observations on the size and abundance of spicules and sand were made, along with occasional measures of spicule size (Cordell 2000).

Two types of pottery were identified. One is St. Johns Plain (n = 44), characterized by the presence of abundant sponge spicules. The second is a sand-tempered plain ware (n = 19), which in the East Okeechobee region is typically called Glades Plain. Glades Plain is characterized by abundant fine to medium-sized sand particles. None of the chalky wares contain sufficient sand of a coarseness to be classified under the type name Belle Glade as described by Cordell (1992).

In Units 1 and 2, and to a lesser extent Unit 4, only chalky wares were found in the lower levels, while both chalky and sand-tempered wares were found in the upper levels (Figure 5.3). In all three units, strata with no pottery were found beneath the pottery-bearing strata (Figure 5.3). Because of the small size of both the excavations and the pottery assemblage, it is unclear whether the site was first occupied by preceramic or aceramic peoples or whether St. Johns production preceded sand-tempered production at the site (Russo and Heide 2000, 2002).

Only three rims and two bases were recovered. The bases are chalky plain sherds from Unit 2. Both are relatively thick (ranging between 13 and 16 mm; Figure 5.4d depicts the largest base fragment). In form and thickness, the bases are similar to Late Archaic period fiber-tempered, flat-bottomed vessels (Bullen 1955:7, 1958b:338, 1972:15; Milanich 1994:94; Sassaman 1993a:fig. 22) and to vessels associated with the Transitional period (Bullen 1959:45, 1971:67). One chalky plain rim sherd with a flat lip and little to no wall curvature (Figure 5.4a), suggestive of the straight-sided, deep vessels also found in the Late Archaic or Transitional period (Bullen 1955:7, 1959:45, 1971:67), was also found. Of the other rims, one is flat lipped and spiculate (Figure 5.4b) and one is round lipped and sand tempered (Figure 5.4c). Both were too small to determine vessel form or size.

RADIOCARBON DATES AND POTTERY

Six radiocarbon assays on midden oyster and charcoal from the Joseph Reed Shell Ring yielded conventional dates between 3455 B.P. and 2850 B.P. with a mean of 3272 years B.P. (Table 5.1). A date from the deepest provenience

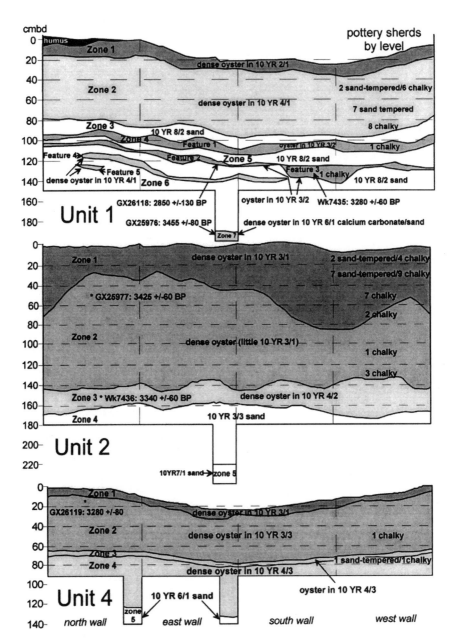

Figure 5.3. Profiles of Joseph Reed Units 1, 2, and 4.

Table 5.2. Pottery by unit and level from the Joseph Reed Shell Ring.

cmbd	Unit 1	Unit 2	Unit 4
0–20		2 sand-tempered; 4 spiculate	
20–40		7 sand-tempered; 9 spiculate	
40–60	2 sand-tempered; 6 spiculate	7 spiculate	1 spiculate
60–80	7 sand-tempered	2 spiculate	1 sand-tempered; 1 spiculate
80–100	8 spiculate		
100–120	1 spiculate	1 spiculate	
120–140	1 spiculate	3 spiculate	

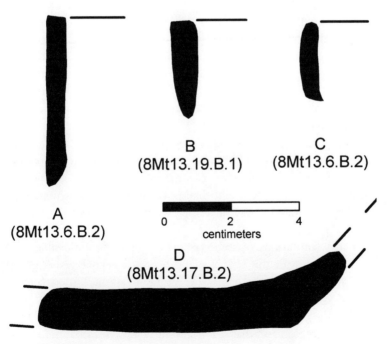

B
(8Mt13.19.B.1)

C
(8Mt13.6.B.2)

A
(8Mt13.6.B.2)

0   2   4
   centimeters

D
(8Mt13.17.B.2)

Figure 5.4. Rim and base profiles, Joseph Reed pottery.

in Unit 1 came from oyster shell recovered at 190 cm below datum (cmbd; datum = highest ground surface in the unit). This provenience lacked pottery and yielded a conventional date of 3455 ± 80 B.P. The uppermost date came from oyster in Unit 4 between 0 and 20 cmbd and yielded an age of 3280 ± 80 B.P. This level also lacked pottery; however, both chalky and sand-tempered plain wares were recovered from underlying strata. An oyster sample associated with a feature containing a chalky sherd in Unit 1 (Feature 3) yielded an identical date of 3280 B.P. One date on oyster from Unit 2, which was associated with seven chalky sherds, produced an age of 3425 ± 75 B.P., while another date on oyster a meter below the former yielded an age of 3340 ± 60 B.P. The Unit 2 dates overlap in age at two standard deviations between 3460 and 3275 B.P., indicating, despite the appearance of the two statistical means, that the stratigraphic relationship of the oyster from which the dates were obtained is not necessarily out of order.

In the profile of Unit 1, Feature 2 is stratigraphically linked with the adjacent Feature 3, suggesting contemporaneity (Figure 5.3). However, when compared to the date of 3280 B.P. obtained from Feature 3, the conventional age from Feature 2 seems early at 2850 B.P.; the dates are some 430 years apart. Again, at two standard deviations, the conventional ages suggest near contemporaneity. If we use the more precise calibrated measure of age, the ranges actually overlap between 3306 and 2933 2cal B.P. (Table 5.1).[3]

In summary, the radiocarbon dates from Joseph Reed Shell Ring are stratigraphically consistent within each unit. Across the site, too, they are coherent, suggesting a period of occupation of perhaps as little as a few hundred years. We accept all dates as derived from secure, undisturbed contexts and provide the reader with the profiles (Figure 5.3) and descriptions for independent assessment. For the purposes of this study we assume that shell and charcoal dates are directly comparable to each other only when corrected for $^{13}C/^{12}C$ fractionation. Shell dates are more accurate when they are corrected for reservoir effect, and both charcoal and shell dates are most accurate when calibrated. However, our goal is to compare the radiocarbon dates from the shell ring to established pottery chronologies, none of which are based on calibrated dates. Therefore, we use conventional ages for comparison.

Given the limitations of radiocarbon dating, it is impossible to determine precise dates for the arrival of pottery at Joseph Reed (e.g., Barnett 1995:84) regardless of which measure of radiocarbon is used. Such precision, however, is not required to investigate the use of pottery at Joseph Reed. That the pottery at the site represents the earliest nonfiber-tempered pottery in the region and that it is contemporary with fiber-tempered pottery found elsewhere in the state is sufficient to discuss the case we present.

THE PLACE OF THE JOSEPH REED POTTERY IN THE OKEECHOBEE POTTERY CHRONOLOGY

Two aspects of the Joseph Reed pottery run counter to existing views on pottery in Florida. One, the pottery at Joseph Reed consists of both sand-tempered and chalky wares at a time when most archaeologists believed these wares were unknown in Florida. Two, chalky wares seem to precede or at least coexist with the production of sand-tempered wares prior to 2800 B.P. This contradicts the idea (Carr and Beriault 1984; Griffin 1974, 1988:127; cf. Milanich and Fairbanks 1980) that sand-tempered pottery was the first locally produced ware in south Florida. Of course, pottery chronologies are geared to present syntheses, not exceptions. By design, they overlook anomalies to temporal trends in order to arrive at generalized patterns (e.g., Milanich 1994:86; Milanich and Fairbanks 1980:27, 61). As such, rare pottery types and types apparently out of sequence have been excluded from consideration in most generalized Florida chronologies. In this light, early sandy and chalky wares at Joseph Reed may not be as anomalous as they first appear.

In the following discussion note that only conventional (corrected) radiocarbon ages derived from shell are directly comparable to either measured (uncorrected) or conventional ages derived from charcoal. Thus, shell dates not originally reported as corrected are corrected below, while uncorrected charcoal dates have not been corrected. (Stuiver and Polach [1977:358] discuss the method to facilitate the corrections, which has been followed here.)

At Caxambas (8CR107x1) on the southwest Florida Gulf Coast, three charcoal samples from a shell midden yielded uncorrected ages of 3400 ± 108 B.P., 3375 ± 112 B.P., and 3155 ± 108 B.P. (Buckley and Willis 1972). Sand-tempered plain and fiber-tempered wares were associated with the dated material. To the north of Caxambas, at Mulberry Midden (8CR697), Lee et al. (1993) dated two shell samples associated with sand-tempered plain sherds that yielded uncorrected dates of 3000 ± 80 B.P. and 2990 ± 70 B.P. (corrected ages equal 3430 ± 80 B.P. and 3391 ± 70 B.P., respectively; Russo and Heide 2002).

At the Palmer/Hill Cottage site (8SO2), Bullen and Bullen (1976) described two levels in the large shell midden as containing Orange, St. Johns, and sand-tempered wares. Radiocarbon assays on shell from these levels yielded uncorrected dates of 3350 ± 120 B.P. and 3225 ± 120 B.P. (corrected ages equal 3750 ± 120 B.P. and 3625 ± 120 B.P., respectively; Russo and Heide 2002). At the J-5 site (8JA8) in the panhandle, Bullen (1958b) identified St. Johns associated with Orange wares in a context with charcoal that yielded an uncorrected age of 3150 ± 250 B.P. (Russo and Heide 2002).

The reader should view with caution the contexts from which the pottery and dates were derived (Russo and Heide 2002). The data do suggest, however, that Joseph Reed occupants may not have been alone in Florida in the use of nonfiber-tempered pottery prior to 3,000 years ago, despite regional chronologies that suggest only fiber-tempered wares were manufactured during this period. Indeed, the absence of these dominant wares at Joseph Reed is as surprising as the presence of the nonfiber-tempered wares. This, in part, may be due to the specific time the site was occupied. We know that potters in the East Okeechobee region were producing or using fiber-tempered pottery ca. 4000 to 3800 B.P. (Janus Research 1998; Pepe and Jester 1995). However, no fiber-tempered pottery with associated radiocarbon dates has been identified in the region between 3800 B.P. and 3000 B.P., the latter date being the accepted end date of the production of Orange/Norwood pottery elsewhere in Florida (Milanich 1994). Joseph Reed seems to be the only site in the region with conventional radiocarbon dates and pottery dating between 3500 and 2800 B.P., and, as stated, that assemblage lacks fiber-tempered wares. This, of course, may simply be the result of a small sample size—few sites in the region of this period have been radiocarbon dated. But with this caveat in mind, we can offer a tentative pottery chronology for the region.

Taking Pepe and Jester's (1995) coastal culture-area concept and utilizing radiocarbon dates from Joseph Reed, Mount Elizabeth (8MT30; Janus Research 1998), and Scheurich Midden (8PB9261; Wheeler et al. 1997), an early pottery chronology (conventional ages) for the region is described (Figure 5.5). No fiber-tempered sites postdating 3800 B.P. have yet been identified in East Okeechobee (Russo and Heide 2002). Sometime between 3425 and 3280 B.P., the first chalky wares appear at Joseph Reed (Unit 2 and Feature 3 in Unit 1). They are also found above Feature 2, which dates to 2850 B.P. The range, then, for the use of chalky wares at Joseph Reed, and tentatively for the region, is placed between 3400 and 2850 B.P. This date is as much as 2,200 years earlier than the suggested entry of spiculate wares in the region (Pepe and Jester 1995) and as much as 900 years earlier than the widely accepted entry of spiculate wares into the St. Johns and Indian River regions to the north (Milanich 1994; Rouse 1951).

According to Pepe and Jester (1995:19), sand-tempered pottery made its first appearance in the region around 2700 B.P. (about 100 years later than attributed to the wider south Florida region by Carr and Beriault [1984]), although no dates from East Okeechobee have yet been obtained to confirm these ages (cf. Pepe [1999], who cited 2500 B.P. as the initial introduction). At Joseph Reed, sand-tempered wares are found above Feature 2 (Unit 1), which dates to 2850 B.P. This is only slightly older than is suggested by

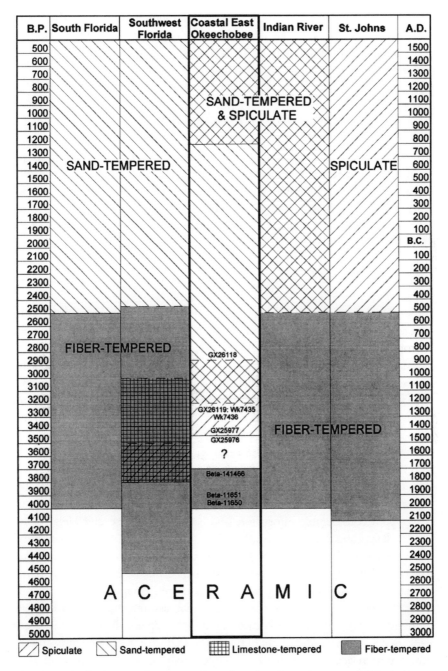

Figure 5.5. Preliminary early pottery chronology based upon tempers and inclusions for coastal East Okeechobee (based on Joseph Reed dates; Janus Research 1998; Pepe and Jester 1995; and Beta-141466 from Scheurich Midden). Other chronologies adapted from Widmer (1988) for southwest Florida, Carr and Beriault (1984) for south Florida, and Milanich (1994) for the Indian River and St. Johns regions.

the Pepe and Jester chronology. But sand-tempered pottery is also found below the date of 3280 B.P. from Unit 4. The tentative introduction for sand-tempered plain pottery in the region, then, is placed at 3280 B.P. (Figure 5.5).

THE EMERGENCE OF POTTERY AT THE JOSEPH REED SHELL RING

In diameter, Joseph Reed is the largest shell ring yet identified in the southeastern United States. It is the largest site, and the only pottery-bearing site, of its time in East Okeechobee. Thus, the location, size, and material constituents of Joseph Reed set it apart from all other sites in the region. To understand the emergence of pottery at the site, we need to understand the environmental and social setting under which the site itself developed.

Comparing Joseph Reed Pottery to Traditional Models of Pottery Origin

First, we recognize that the pottery from Joseph Reed is associated with radiocarbon dates that do not neatly fit accepted chronologies. One reviewer of early work on the site suggested that the entire site may have been contaminated somehow, thus affecting the accuracy of the radiocarbon dates. This is a possibility and certainly the easiest way out of the dilemma. But we are stymied as to what possible contamination could have occurred over the entire site. We note also that radiocarbon ages from surrounding sites (e.g., Janus Research 1998; Wheeler et al. 1997) do not seem to have suffered from any large-scale contamination.

Obtaining radiocarbon dates from small units is always problematic—functions of features remain unknown, strata are not always decipherable, and shell and artifacts may trickle in from superior contexts. That is why we have spent considerable effort here and elsewhere (Russo and Heide 2000, 2002) describing the contextual integrity of strata and features and interpretations of radiocarbon ages. Such discussion does not necessarily refute the possibility of contamination or disturbance, but we hope it does provide archaeologists with data they need to make their own assessments of contexts. In lieu of evidence to the contrary, we assume the dates are uncontaminated and from sound contexts, contexts apparently more secure and recorded in greater detail than those for many of the radiocarbon dates upon which accepted Florida chronologies have been constructed (e.g., Bullen 1958b, 1961; Widmer 1988; see Heide 2000 for an extended discussion of the context of early St. Johns pottery and radiocarbon dates).

To identify the early, and possibly initial, use of nonfiber-tempered wares in the East Okeechobee region, we need to briefly assess the theoretical models that have been used to describe the origins of pottery in the region. Joseph Reed presents problems to both models of migration/diffusion and technofunctional models related to efficiency. In terms of migration/diffusion, the pottery from Joseph Reed has nowhere to migrate from. It is not tempered with fiber as is the pottery of the site's nearest contemporaneous pottery-producing neighbors to the north. Thus, a direct connection cannot be made with those neighbors in terms of paste and temper (design and form, however, cannot be ruled out until more data are obtained). In addition, the presence of initial nonfiber-tempered pottery in south Florida presents problems for any theory positing northern South American origins of early pottery in the southeastern United States (Crusoe 1971a; Ford 1969; Reichel-Dolmatoff 1972). The pottery from Joseph Reed effectively places between the two continents two distinct pottery types that need to be explained away. While contemporary sand-tempered wares are found in Georgia and South Carolina, allowing for the possibility of diffusion of the tempering idea, the idea would have had to jump over a great distance, three to five hundred miles. In terms of a functional explanation for the adoption of pottery, in the region and nearby, the same types of food (e.g., shellfish, fish), in equal or greater amounts, were being prepared prior to and after the adoption of pottery (e.g., Cumbaa 1976; Janus Research 1998; Russo 1991; Russo et al. 1993; Wheeler et al. 1997). Any increased efficiency of food processing brought about by the advent of pottery remains to be demonstrated. That is, no evidence of environmental stress (e.g., changes in diet breadth, average size of prey, reduction in settlement size, or alteration in settlement pattern) is apparent in prepottery and subsequent pottery-producing cultures that would have compelled a search for more efficient cooking technologies. Of course, given the fact that there seem to be no contemporary sites in the East Okeechobee region, one could argue that a large settlement-pattern shift did occur at Joseph Reed—a shift requiring the adoption of pottery to process a new food resource, shellfish. This is an arguable contention, however, since at other shell rings and large shellfish middens, cultures thrived without pottery (Dickel 1992; Russo 1991; Russo and Saunders 1999). The need for pottery to process shellfish at all, or to process it more efficiently, is a dubious hypothesis given the myriad of prepottery shellfish deposits found throughout Florida and the greater southeastern United States.

We have previously suggested that Joseph Reed and other shell ring sites were situated along marsh/beach ecotones, which provided abundant and varied resources to feed large numbers of people for extended periods and greater numbers of people for periodic feasts (Russo 2004; Russo and Heide

2000). Under these conditions, aggrandizers facilitated the accumulation of great quantities of food sufficient to host ceremonies for invited guests. In social payment for their efforts, symbols of prestige, including pottery, were allowed to be displayed and were, perhaps, gifted. While some shell rings were built prior to the regional adoption of pottery, most shell rings were constructed during times when early pottery was regionally abundant, not only at shell rings but at many types of sites. At Joseph Reed, however, another situation obtained—it seems to be the only site in the East Okeechobee region with pottery at the time of its occupation.

Joseph Reed Pottery—Local Production vs. Trade

Where did the pottery come from if no other sites in the region were producing it and virtually no center for the production and distribution of sand-tempered or spiculate wares was anywhere to be found in Florida? The pottery could still be exogenous. Trade with southwest Florida and/or the panhandle is indicated by the lithics found at the site (Iceland 2000). Both of those areas have yielded early sand-tempered and spiculate pottery (Bullen 1958b; Heide 2000; Widmer 1988). The assumption that otherwise aceramic peoples of East Okeechobee would import pottery for ritual, and not adopt or begin their own production, is certainly supportable by the transegalitarian ethnographic record. To keep alliances ongoing, groups may specialize in the production of certain goods (e.g., food, weapons) while allowing partners to produce other goods (e.g., pottery). This relationship may obtain even under conditions in which each partner is capable of the other's specialization. Such alliances may be maintained to support peace, war, marriage avenues, trade, or other social needs. By maintaining what appear to be unwarranted economic relations, social interchange is facilitated. Ethnographically, self-imposed exclusion from pottery production and reliance on pottery trade among transegalitarian groups is well known (e.g., Chagnon 1968:100–101; Heckenberger 1998:640).

Relative to the Joseph Reed pottery, problems with the idea of pottery coming from such external sources include the fact that no centers of production of either sand-tempered or spiculate wares are known (only isolated occurrences of pottery at sites have been identified); contemporaneous sites containing sand-tempered pottery are quite distant; and specific pottery types have not been identified at Joseph Reed that link that site to outside sources (only gross similarities in temper and paste have been identified).

Alternatively, the pottery could be indigenous. Peoples in southern Florida, if not East Okeechobee, were well aware of pottery technology, as demonstrated by the sporadic distribution of fiber-tempered sherds (presumably trade wares) found throughout the region. In East Okeechobee, we know that pottery with similar pastes and tempers was produced after the Joseph Reed Shell Ring was abandoned. This indicates that appropriate clay resources were abundant, while the presence of pottery itself at the site indicates that the idea of pottery was present, as was the initiative to make or at least obtain it. Given the limited state of the archaeological record at Joseph Reed and in East Okeechobee, we cannot dismiss the possibility that the pottery was of local manufacture, but we cannot present evidence of where it may have been made—was it made at the site or elsewhere in the region?

Why Sand-Tempered and Spiculate Wares in a Fiber-Tempered World?

Early shell rings exist in South Florida, and these were built by people who did not manufacture or use pottery (Dickel 1992; Houck 1996; Russo 1991). Why then was pottery used at Joseph Reed? The answer may be linked to the kinds of pottery produced. The dominant pottery type in Florida at the time Joseph Reed was occupied was fiber tempered. In fact, fiber-tempered pottery is the dominant pottery obtained from the large shell midden/ village site of Mount Elizabeth (8MT30) only 16 km (10 miles) north of Joseph Reed. Although radiocarbon dates place the Orange occupation of the site at least 500 years earlier than Joseph Reed, the possibility exists that some portion of the occupation there was contemporaneous with Joseph Reed. (Only two, nearly contemporaneous, radiocarbon dates from the site have been obtained, one from 45 cmbd and one from 165 cmbd. Thus, undated material above could be younger; sand-tempered and spiculate sherds were recovered mostly from the upper 40 cm of the site [Janus Research 1998:29].)

Whether or not Mount Elizabeth was wholly or partly occupied at the same time as the Joseph Reed Shell Ring, numerous fiber-tempered sites exist in the Indian River region that borders Joseph Reed, and the juxtaposition of the sand-tempered/spiculate pottery producers at Joseph Reed with the fiber-tempered pottery producers from the Indian River region (Figure 5.2) suggests that Joseph Reed lay within or adjacent to a frontier zone occupied by groups using (or not using) different wares north and south of a shifting line somewhere near the St. Lucie inlet, i.e., near the Indian River and East Okeechobee regional border (Figure 5.2). Certainly, shifting political alliances characterized the region in protohistoric times (e.g., Rouse 1951:43–45); Pepe (1999), in fact, suggests that continuously shifting borders (based on pottery distributions) characterized the East Okeechobee region prehistorically. Incursions of north Florida pottery types fluctuated with traditional south Florida pottery back and forth throughout prehistory.

Of course, Pepe (1999) did not have the pottery from Joseph Reed, and his observations were limited to post-2500 B.P. times. However, we suggest that the long regional history of shifting alliances, cultural boundaries, and waxing and waning of pottery types probably extended back beyond 2500 B.P. Given its large size, the Joseph Reed Shell Ring likely served the greater East Okeechobee region as the preeminent ceremonial center. We suggest that occupants at Joseph Reed used their site to invite guests to ceremonies in order to build or strengthen alliances, exchange marriage partners, or trade goods. As evidenced by the paucity of Orange pottery in the region, and lack of Orange pottery at the site in particular, absent among these guests were fiber-tempered pottery users. At the time Joseph Reed was occupied, the Orange cultures were apparently not in good graces with the East Okeechobee people at the shell ring site. As such, the aggrandizer(s) who hosted the ceremonies at the site did not receive, make, or use fiber-tempered pottery. Nonfiber-tempered wares were used not only to display status (as a rare item, pottery was imbued with economic and social value) but also to reaffirm the occupants' ethnic distinction from their neighbors to the north. However, given a prehistory replete with shifting affiliations and concomitant changes in pottery boundaries, we would not be surprised if future excavations at the site yielded fiber-tempered pottery also.

THE EMERGENCE OF POTTERY IN EAST OKEECHOBEE

We have presented here a model for the adoption of pottery in a particular circumstance in which the social landscape was otherwise devoid of pottery. In one way, the social situation under which the archaeological site was formed is fortunate. Apparently, the initial acceptance of sand-tempered and spiculate pottery was short lived and restricted. Pottery at most other sites in and near East Okeechobee does not appear again for hundreds of years or is so infrequently used that it is archaeologically undetectable. This rare historical circumstance allows for the possibility of identifying the first occurrence of pottery in the region. The situation to the north presents a contrast. In the Indian River and St. Johns regions, hundreds of sites with fiber-tempered pottery have been found. Given the inaccuracy and vagaries of radiocarbon dating, the chances of identifying the first occurrence of pottery in those regions, and determining whether Orange pottery first arose in ceremonial or domestic contexts, may be far more difficult.

Hayden (1995a) suggests that once pottery is adopted for prestige functions into ceremony, it may quickly and widely become adopted for practical purposes. The wide and rapid dispersal of Orange pottery in the St.

Johns River valley, both in ceremonial and domestic contexts, certainly seems to support such a case—a case that, curiously, did not obtain in South Florida, at least with the rapidity evidenced to the north. Perhaps we can hold unstable social relations responsible. As Sassaman (1993a) has pointed out, however useful pottery may be, contradictions in social relations may prevent its full adoption until those contradictions are resolved. Certainly, in far-flung South Florida, potters were exempt from the influence of the soapstone traders that Sassaman suggests slowed the rapid adoption of fiber-tempered pottery across much of the Southeast. But other social impediments in the frontier zone of East Okeechobee may have persisted.

Because prestige associated with first occurrences of pottery may rapidly disappear, prestige seekers are continually seeking new ways to display their status (Hayden 1995a). Pottery is ideally suited for change. Modifications in tempers, designs, and forms can easily be applied to new social requirements. At Joseph Reed, the sample of pottery is small, but changes from spiculate to sand-tempered wares may have occurred through time. This change may be viewed functionally—perhaps sand-tempered pottery was technologically superior to spiculate wares. However, since both pottery types were later used for thousands of years by neighboring cultures processing largely identical foods, we doubt that increased functional efficiency accounts for any change in ware use.

Rather, we see the appearance of the two distinct wares as reflective of sociohistoric circumstances. What those circumstances may have been can only be speculated upon. Since tempering is one of the more resistant traits (as opposed to style or form, for example) adopted by potters (Rice 1987:464), it is possible that at least two groups made or traded in the two distinct wares at the site. This would suggest that some degree of unincorporated occupation was present. That is, either divisional factions (e.g., moieties, other kin groups, or sodalities) lived at the site, or groups who brought pottery to the site were not fully integrated with the rest of the community (e.g., guests, traders, new brides) and these groups made/used pottery distinct from that made/used by other occupants.

Under these social conditions, aggrandizers could use the site as an arena and use the various pottery types to promote their own self-interests. Aggrandizers at large feasting sites typically used pottery as "a tool, designed or appropriated as an active agent of change in an economic context of abundance and a social context of competition and differentiation" (Rice 1999:46). The self-interest of individual promoters at Joseph Reed, which functioned as a large ceremonial feasting site, may have been related to any of the separate pottery-making groups or individuals, but not necessarily. That is, pottery groups may have had their related promoters, or a promoter may have used the pottery from any group for his/her self-aggrandizing purposes. The goal of aggrandizing in large-scale feasts is to obtain social and economic debt from the community members and affiliates. To this end, sand-tempered and spiculate pottery, unique and novel technologies in East Okeechobee, were used not only to impress feast participants but also to maintain social distinctions from those in debt to the aggrandizer, i.e., those of lower status.

Of course, the degree of status differentiation among Joseph Reed occupants was probably limited. Given that South Florida groups outside of ceremonial contexts functioned as largely equal members of societies, persons using pottery at Joseph Reed to gain prestige were likely restricted as to the level to which they were allowed to distinguish themselves. Such social leveling mechanisms are common in transegalitarian settings and may help explain the lack of decoration or other elaboration in pottery at the site. In fact, in all of Florida, the earliest regional wares are undecorated. This contrasts with at least some prestige model predictions, as well as case studies, in which initial pottery is elaborated (e.g., Clark and Gosser 1995:216; Hayden 1995a:260–261; Hoopes 1995:196; Oyuela-Caycedo 1995:135; Roosevelt 1995:129), demonstrating that the degree to which any new prestige-enhancing technology is accepted is subject to specific, and perhaps unpredictable, sociohistoric influences.

Because our samples are so small, it is not clear whether promoters of sand-tempered wares won out over promoters of spiculate wares at Joseph Reed or whether the two wares continued to be used throughout the history of the site. Ultimately, however, sand-tempered plain pottery became widely adopted in South Florida nonceremonial contexts shortly after Joseph Reed was occupied, as the prestige model would predict (Hayden 1995a; Rice 1999). In South Florida, the earliest pottery seems to have emerged under a sociohistoric setting imposing restrictive conditions on pottery producers as to tempers and styles of local wares.

6

Fiber-Tempered Pottery and Cultural Interaction on the Northwest Florida Gulf Coast

L. Janice Campbell, Prentice M. Thomas, Jr., and James H. Mathews

When Gordon Willey (1949b) published his mid-twentieth-century land-mark volume *Archeology of the Florida Gulf Coast,* only a few sherds of fiber-tempered pottery had been found at sites in northwest Florida, and their characteristics were given little more than passing mention. Even up until the early 1960s, fiber-tempered pottery identified in the Florida panhandle remained poorly defined, being variously classed as Stallings, St. Simons, or Orange. None of these classifications, however, were wholly adequate be-cause this area appeared to have at least two varieties of fiber-tempered pottery, one exhibiting exclusively fiber inclusions and the other with both fiber and sand and/or grit inclusions. Further, sites such as Alligator Lake (8WL29) (Lazarus 1965) yielded fiber-tempered pottery in association with Alexander series types, which demanded that the Wheeler fiber-tempered series (from Alabama) also be considered as part of the fiber-tempered as-semblage in the Florida panhandle.

Phelps (1966:22) attempted to clarify the situation by defining the Nor-wood series, a type that occurs tempered only with fiber or as a semifiber-tempered ware; surface treatment was either plain or simple stamped. Al-though the Norwood series appeared applicable to the western panhandle, Phelps's definition restricted its distribution geographically to between the Suwannee and Apalachicola Rivers. As a result, local researchers, such as Lazarus (1965:102–104), were reluctant to adopt the Norwood appellation[1] or to classify fiber-tempered pottery recovered in the Florida panhandle as one of the named series for fear they would be implying widespread diffu-sion or even movement of peoples. Tesar (1980:53) attempted to circumvent the problem by the creation of the "Unnamed Plain" variety on the Gulf Coast west of the Apalachicola River. A sentiment similar to that of Lazarus was echoed by Kimbrough (1990) in her analysis of fiber-tempered pottery from sites in the Apalachicola National Forest. She stated the collections were typical of the Norwood series but advised that application of the term

Norwood to fiber-tempered sherds in the Apalachicola National Forest region did not imply that the cultures operating there were identical to contemporaneous manufacturers of Norwood pottery in other areas.

The quandary over what "type" of fiber-tempered sherds were present in northwest Florida was complicated further by controversy over their chronological placement. Willey (1949b) noted that fiber-tempered pottery in northwest Florida was usually found in contexts that also produced other early pottery types, such as Deptford. However, Tesar (1980) referenced a personal communication from Bense that she had recovered fiber-tempered pottery in stratigraphic contexts underlying an Early Deptford component at the McFadden site (8BY104) in Bay County, Florida. Fiber-tempered pottery was reported in quantity along with some semifiber-tempered sherds by Lazarus (1965) in Elliotts Point deposits at the Alligator Lake site on the Gulf. Chronologically, then, fiber-tempered pottery in northwest Florida has been placed in the Gulf Formational Elliotts Point complex on the one hand and within the Deptford cultural sphere on the other.

In the 1980s, we began intensive and extensive investigations on the Florida panhandle (Figure 6.1), which have generated a substantial body of data on fiber-tempered pottery that can be used to examine the implications of its appearance and manufacture on cultural interaction and developments among the local prehistoric population. In this study, "local" refers specifically to an area that comprises all of Eglin Air Force Base (approximately 464,000 acres) and surrounding areas, extending from the Gulf of Mexico on the south, north to approximately Interstate 10, west to the eastern shore of East Bay, and east to Highway 331 (Figure 6.1). This large area encompasses the southern half of eastern Santa Rosa County, the southern half of Okaloosa County, and the southern half of western Walton County, an area about 44.8 km (28 miles) north-south by just over 80 km (50 miles) east-west.

These data have substantively addressed questions about what type of fiber-tempered pottery is present in the local area, as well as its chronological placement. Most of the fiber-tempered sherds have paste attributes very similar to those of the Norwood series reported by Phelps (1965) and those of the Wheeler types found in south Alabama. Sherds are thick bodied, averaging 1–2 cm thick. The collection is predominantly plain. To date, only one sherd with dentate stamping, classified as Wheeler Dentate Stamped, has been found, and no examples of Norwood Simple Stamped pottery have been reported. Judging from the few rims and larger sherds, the primary vessel form appears to be globular, round-bottomed pots or deep bowls with straight rims and rounded lips; vessel diameters are between 25 and 30 cm. As with both Norwood and Wheeler type descriptions, the frequency of

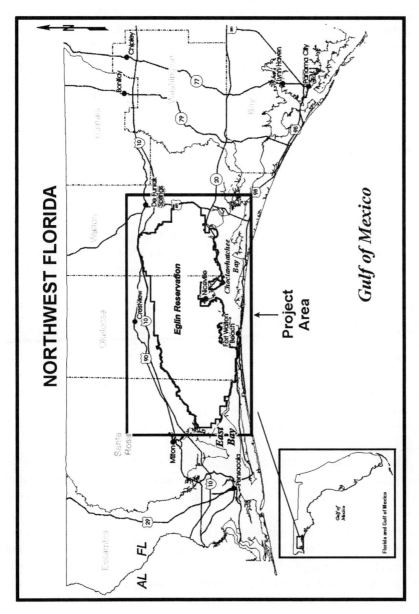

Figure 6.1. Map showing the Florida panhandle and study area.

sand inclusions in the temper varies. According to our examination of fiber-tempered sherds from the study area, roughly 80 percent have moderate amounts of fiber casts, with the remaining 20 percent divided rather evenly between those with sparse and those with abundant fiber casts. The fiber cavities are about 1 mm in diameter, range in length between 1 and 4 cm, and are visible on both the exterior and interior surfaces. The type of fiber has not been definitively identified, but some short branches or filaments typical of Spanish moss have been observed. Surface colors are brown to strong brown with darker cores. A minority have gray, dark gray, or pale brown surfaces.

While the pottery is perhaps similar to Norwood, we concur with Kimbrough's (1990) hesitation in applying this label to the study area. In her recent discussion of sites in the Apalachicola–lower Chattahoochee Valley, White (2003) suggests that the appellation Norwood should be thrown out altogether. She offers instead the use of generic type names like fiber-tempered plain or fiber-tempered simple stamped or even a return to Orange. We agree with White's first suggestion. The issue of what "type" of fiber-tempered sherds are found in the study area has been largely resolved in terms of ware characteristics but not insofar as identifying them with an established type name. In the interim, we will continue to use a generic reference until there is a good basis for naming a local pottery series or for application of one borrowed from another region.

The issue of chronology has been effectively resolved by excavations, a notable example of which was at Pirate's Bay (8OK183) on Santa Rosa Sound (Thomas and Campbell 1985, 1993). Fiber-tempered pottery was recovered from Pirate's Bay in contexts stratigraphically underlying Deptford pottery. The fiber-tempered pottery series, therefore, represents the first instance of pottery in the area, but not the first evidence of heightened cultural interaction.

The first manifestations of heightened cultural interaction that can be clearly demonstrated by the archaeological record occurred sometime around 4450 rcybp. Interaction is embodied by the rise of the Elliotts Point complex, a Gulf Formational cultural relative of the Poverty Point complex centered in the Lower Mississippi Valley (Lazarus 1958). In fact, fiber-tempered pottery is a late addition to assemblages of Elliotts Point sites (Thomas and Campbell 1993); therefore any discussion of the influence of pottery production upon local cultures has to include consideration of this complex prior to the introduction of pottery.

Lazarus found the first evidence of what would be called the Elliotts Point complex in 1953, the same year that Ford looked at an aerial photograph and realized that the Poverty Point site in West Carroll Parish, Louisiana, was a gigantic geometric earthwork. Conferring with Poverty Point scholars, such as Clarence Webb and William Haag, Lazarus (1958) based his definition of the Elliotts Point complex on remains at the Elliotts Point site (8OK10) and the West Choctomar site (8OK13), two sites in Okaloosa County that demonstrated far-flung connections of people on the northwest Gulf coast of Florida with contemporaries to the west.

Found some 560 km (350 miles) as the crow flies from the Poverty Point site and about 105 km (175 miles) from the Claiborne site (22HA501), a regional center on the Mississippi coast, the Elliotts Point assemblage exhibits a commonality of traits with both sites, marked foremost by Elliotts Point Objects. These well-formed baked-clay objects, named for their similarity to Poverty Point Objects, are quite numerous at some sites; e.g., 4,400 were recovered from the Kelly Trust site (8OK877) in Destin, Florida (Thomas and Campbell 1993). They are commonly amorphous; however, spheroid and melon-, biscuit-, and tabular-shaped objects, some with longitudinal grooves and pointed ends, have also been recovered in the study area. All of these traits are shared with their Lower Valley counterparts.

Microliths, some finely executed, are found in Elliotts Point components, and Jaketown perforators, a hallmark of the Poverty Point culture (Webb 1982), are relatively frequent. Florida Archaic Stemmed points are the common projectile points. Gagliano and Webb (1970) observed that the Levy and Putnam points in Elliotts Point sites are directly comparable to some found at the Cedarland (22HA506) and Claiborne (22HA501) sites in Mississippi, as well as to nine "Group F" points from the Poverty Point site. The Levy and Putnam points are also much like Gary Typical and Large, and the large examples would be comparable to Hale points. Motley points occur in minor quantities at Elliotts Point sites, and some could pass muster as part of an assemblage from the type site itself. A distinctive point is the Destin point, which has sloping shoulders and a concave base. To date, this point has been exclusively associated with Elliotts Point sites (Thomas and Campbell 1993). Raw materials are varied, including Tallahatta quartzite and various cherts such as Flint River, Fort Payne, Two Egg, and Coastal Plains, along with minor occurrences of novaculite and chalcedony.

Another item in the Elliotts Point assemblage that heralds cultural interaction is steatite, which occurs in northwest Florida as whole vessels, miniature vessels, sherds, and boatstones. Other nonlocal or exotic materials found include jasper, hematite, granite, and galena. Tools and beads of shell and bone also characterize Elliotts Point assemblages, along with sparse occurrences of lapidary items, plummets, and gorgets. Overall, Elliotts Point artifacts mirror those of the Poverty Point culture and usher in a time of clearly identifiable cultural interaction.

The settings of Elliotts Point sites confirm a preference for settlement along the coast (Figure 6.2). There are few sites in the study area located more than 1.5 km (0.9 mile) from the shore of the bays and bayous. Sites also exhibit a marked trend to cluster in various locations, including the shores of East Bay, Rocky Bayou, the Narrows of Santa Rosa Sound, and on a peninsula of land known as Fourmile Peninsula on the south shore of Choctawhatchee Bay.

Associated middens are dominated by shellfish, including *Mercenaria* sp. (quahog), *Aequipecten irradians* (bay scallop), and *Crassostrea virginica* (oyster). The contents are noteworthy because bay scallops and quahog never occur in major quantities in any prehistoric middens in the study area after Elliotts Point, a fact that appears to be attributable to the formation of Moreno Point, the barrier spit at the current location of Destin, Florida. In a study of Choctawhatchee Bay, Victor Goldsmith (1966) concluded that there were differences between the present sedimentary environment and the one previously occupying the area. A sharp change in the physical, chemical, and biological conditions in the bay began to occur around 7000 B.P., when the westward longshore drift system began to form Moreno Point, which greatly reduced the opening of Choctawhatchee Bay to the Gulf of Mexico after around 3000 B.P. The restriction of water interchange between Choctawhatchee Bay and the Gulf had several effects. The most pertinent to our discussion was the sharp decrease in quahog and bay scallop. Not only are these species consistently found in Elliotts Point shell middens, but they are among the major components of Elliotts Point shell mounds, the most notable of which is the Buck Bayou Mound (8WL90) at Fourmile Peninsula. Again, quahog and bay scallops *never* occur in quantity in prehistoric shell middens in the region after the Elliotts Point era.

Fourmile Peninsula in Walton County appears to have been a hub of Elliotts Point activity (Figure 6.3). The peninsula contains the Buck Bayou Mound, an accretional shell mound surpassed in size only by 8OK6, a Mississippian platform mound in downtown Fort Walton Beach. Although exotic items are found at many Elliotts Point sites in the study area, the most compelling evidence for affiliation with the Poverty Point trade network is derived from Fourmile Peninsula sites, including the Buck Bayou Mound and others. Data from one site, 8WL87 (the site has no name), which were examined by Clarence Webb and David Reichelt (unpublished findings), reveal it to have been a lithic workshop, characterized by finished points, side scrapers, denticulates, utilized flakes, flaking debris, lamellar pieces including a core, drills and blades, hammerstones, one loaf-shaped mano, galena, baked-clay objects, and a jasper gorget and one possible jasper saw, among other items. Also found were over 50 steatite vessel fragments that Gagliano

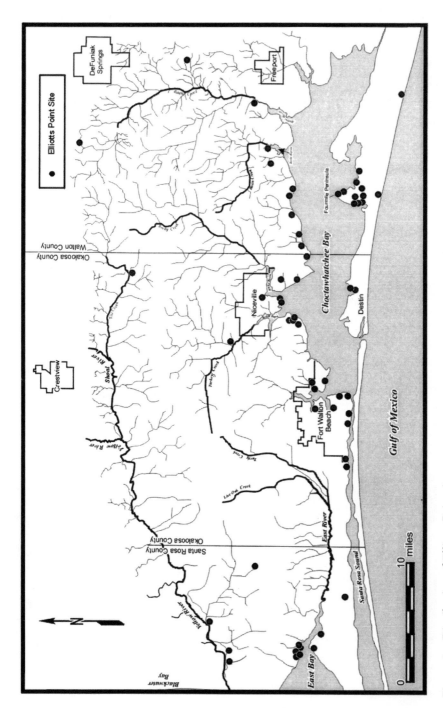

Figure 6.2. Distribution of Elliotts Point sites.

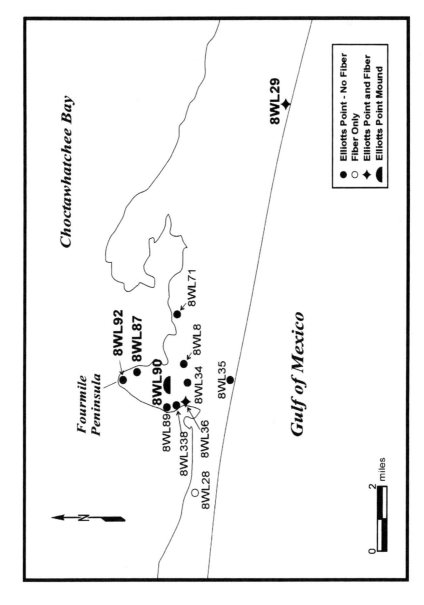

Figure 6.3. Map of Fourmile Peninsula showing location of Elliotts Point sites.

and Webb (1970) believe to represent at least five vessels. The separation of the lithic workshop from the mound is reminiscent of the community patterning at Poverty Point. Another specialized activity area is the Fourmile Drill site (8WL92) on the east side of Fourmile Peninsula, north of both 8WL87 and the Buck Bayou Mound. The collection from this site consists almost exclusively of Jaketown perforators and other microliths (Don Sharon, personal communication, 1985).

East of Fourmile Peninsula, on the Gulf of Mexico, is the aforementioned Alligator Lake site. With its array of exotic items, Alligator Lake is one of the richest Elliotts Point sites in the area (Lazarus 1965). Clear evidence of trade is documented by the recovery of three copper beads fashioned from small ingots of copper, steatite, two gorgets, ground stone tool fragments, Jaketown perforators, a pumice hone, and a hematite plummet. Twelve projectile points were also recovered, and seven of these are very much like Delhi points, a popular type at the Poverty Point site. Seven of the points were produced on exotic chert, four on quartzite, and one on translucent quartz. Lazarus (1965) was only able to sample the site, but it is obvious from the collection he gathered that Alligator Lake exhibits some of the most dramatic evidence of Elliotts Point complex trade found to date.

Thomas and Campbell (1993) have hypothesized that Fourmile Peninsula, with its accretional mound and activity-specific sites, was a redistribution center for the Elliotts Point population, who gathered periodically to exchange local goods and obtain exotic items. In this scenario, Poverty Point–associated traders along the Gulf may have stopped at Alligator Lake; from there, they could move overland and continue northward up to the Choctawhatchee River and on into the interior or continue in either direction along the Gulf.

There is little doubt that Elliotts Point was a local manifestation of the Poverty Point trade network and it thrived on the exchange and distribution of goods. The chronology of Elliotts Point sites (Table 6.1) suggests the culture was flourishing without a ceramic industry at a time when fiber-tempered pottery was a well-established part of the assemblages along the Atlantic coast (Sassaman 1993a). For example, remains associated with a single-component, Elliotts Point site without any fiber-tempered pottery were found at the Eglin Federal Prison site (8OK898) in Okaloosa County. Feature 1 yielded a date on shell of 4200 ± 70 B.P. Meigs Pasture (8OK102), a horseshoe-shaped Elliotts Point midden mound with crude baked-clay objects, had dates on shell as early as 4100 ± 80 B.P. to as late as 3630 ± 50 (Thomas and Campbell 1993). The Stone Vessel site (8WL1005) is an Elliotts Point site with a cache of two nested steatite vessels; it yielded a date of

Table 6.1. Radiocarbon dates from selected sites in northwest Florida.

Site Name	Site #	Material	Component	Conventional B.P.	Calibrated 2 sigma B.C.	Lab #
Eglin Federal Prison	8OK898	Shell	Elliotts Point	4200 ± 70	2535–2140	Beta-129298
Meigs Pasture	8OK102	Shell	Elliotts Point	4100 ± 80	2425–1955	Beta-21253
Meigs Pasture	8OK102	Shell	Elliotts Point	3630 ± 50	1700–1455	DIC-3295
Stone Vessel	8WL1005	Organic Residue	Elliotts Point	3740 ± 50	2290–1975	Beta-81709
Unnamed	8SR44	Shell	Elliotts Point	3490 ± 70	1585–1245	Beta-39718
Alligator Lake	8WL29	Charcoal	Elliotts Point	3135 ± 125	1675–1025	AC-32
Alligator Lake	8WL29	Charcoal	Deptford	2575 ± 80	840–415	GX-155
Fish Fry	8OK126	Shell	Deptford	2580 ± 70	375–190	Beta-39712

3740 ± 50 B.P. on organic residue in the bowls (Hemphill et al. 1995). A few fiber-tempered sherds were found in other parts of the site, but none were in direct association with the steatite vessels. A later date was obtained on 8SR44 (no name), a prepottery shell mound that is one of a cluster of Elliotts Point sites on East Bay in Santa Rosa County, Florida. 8SR44 produced a date of 3490 ± 70 B.P. on shell but yielded only lithics—no baked-clay objects or other trappings of Elliotts Point culture were recovered from this component, which is relatively late in the complex (Thomas and Campbell 1993).

In contrast to the early appearance of pottery elsewhere, in some cases more than 4400 B.P. (Stoltman 1966, 1972a; uncorrected charcoal dates), fiber-tempered pottery occurs as a late addition to the Gulf Formational Elliotts Point inventory. A firm date on fiber-tempered pottery in the study area comes from Alligator Lake, which produced a date of 3135 ± 125 B.P. on charcoal (Table 6.1). This time frame is contemporaneous with the emergence of fiber-tempered pottery to the east in the Apalachicola region, where dates obtained by Phelps (1966) and White (1981, 2003) indicate an age as early as about 3970 B.P. to slightly later than 2962 B.P. (2900 to 806 2cal B.C.). These dates, along with the above-noted stratigraphic positioning of fiber-tempered wares underlying Deptford pottery, support the proposition that fiber-tempered pottery was an addition to an already well-established material culture in the prepottery Late Archaic.

In addition to the body of data confirming that fiber-tempered wares predated Deptford pottery, introduction of the latter seems well established at sometime after 2800 B.P. A recent calibration of Lazarus's (1965) date on Deptford materials from Alligator Lake establishes the presence of that culture by about 2575 ± 80 B.P. (Table 6.1), based on a date on charcoal. A Deptford date from 8OK126, the Fish Fry site, located on Eglin Air Force Base, was 2580 ± 70 B.P. It seems, therefore, safe to assume that the Deptford culture was firmly in place no later than around 2600 cal B.P.

The current database[2] for the study area lists 85 sites with fiber-tempered pottery, including 14 in Santa Rosa County, 46 in Okaloosa County, and 25 in Walton County. Although there are numerous sites with fiber-tempered pottery, the overall quantity of this pottery is unimpressive, with the exception of that at the Alligator Lake site, which seems aberrant overall and may actually have served some special purpose in the redistribution network.

Excluding Alligator Lake, the remaining 84 sites have yielded only slightly more than 200 fiber-tempered sherds in all, and most sites produced only one or two sherds. Only 12 sites have more than four fiber-tempered sherds. The next largest collection after Alligator Lake is that from the Pirate's Bay site on Santa Rosa Sound, where 25 sherds were recovered during large-scale excavations primarily focused on the Deptford occupation. Again, excepting Alligator Lake, there are no sites with a collection comparable to those on the Georgia and South Carolina coasts (Stoltman 1974) or even, for that matter, to that reported by Kimbrough (1990) to the east in the Apalachicola National Forest, where 171 Norwood Plain sherds were found at one site.

Despite the low pottery frequency, there is a widespread distribution of sites with fiber-tempered pottery (Figure 6.4). Their locations also suggest deliberate patterning in settlement choices. Sites are clustered around the shoreline, predominantly in areas where freshwater streams flow into the brackish-water bayous, and also around Santa Rosa Sound, East Bay, and Choctawhatchee Bay. Sites with fiber-tempered pottery also occur in more inland settings than was common for earlier Elliotts Point sites, being found along the major river valleys, such as along the Yellow and Shoal Rivers.

There are areas, however, that are completely devoid of sites with fiber-tempered pottery, and we do not believe that this is a result of sampling error. Live Oak and Turtle Creeks, two streams in the western part of Okaloosa County that flow from north to south into the East River, serve as excellent examples of this point. Both have been the subjects of intensive and extensive survey. Over 50 archaeological sites have been located along these creeks (Figure 6.5), but *not a single one* contains fiber-tempered pottery.

In contrast, Basin and Alaqua Creeks, in the eastern portion of the study area, have also been intensively surveyed, an effort that has identified an extremely high density of archaeological sites along both creeks (Figure 6.6). However, unlike Live Oak and Turtle Creeks, Basin and Alaqua, which flow into Choctawhatchee Bay, have a number of sites with fiber-tempered pottery, particularly along the southern reaches of Basin Creek (Figure 6.7).

With sites concentrated along the shore and the major rivers, interior fiber-tempered sites are sparse. An exception is another well-studied area, Turkey Creek, which has a high frequency of archaeological sites in general (Figure 6.8) and a noteworthy number of fiber-tempered sites (Figure 6.9); the linear distribution of fiber-tempered sites along Turkey Creek seems to mark a transportation or diffusion corridor from Choctawhatchee Bay north and northwest to the Yellow and Shoal Rivers.

The data indicate strong differential patterning to the location of sites with fiber-tempered pottery in the study area. The settlement patterns display (1) a coastal adaptation on the shores of brackish-water bays and bayous and (2) a preference for occupational loci following transportation arteries along major streams and, as far as we know, three minor streams, including Turkey, Basin, and Alaqua Creeks. It seems clear that preferential settle-

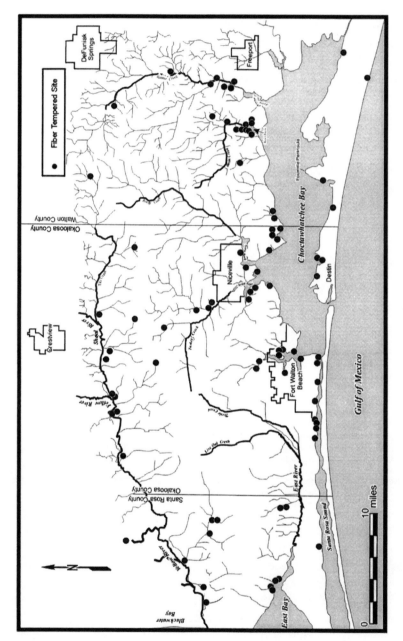

Figure 6.4. Clusters of Elliotts Point sites with fiber-tempered pottery in the study area.

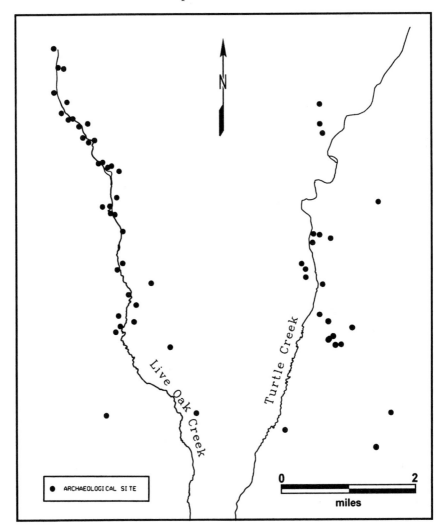

Figure 6.5. Prehistoric sites on Live Oak and Turtle Creeks. None have fiber-tempered pottery.

ment decisions were made on the part of the population producing the fiber-tempered pottery.

Perhaps even more noteworthy is the observation that the settlement patterning of sites with fiber-tempered pottery is divergent from that of sites with the main trappings of the Elliotts Point complex, the latter confidently identified at 57 sites. Consider, for example, Fourmile Peninsula. This nexus of activity, we suggest, was a redistribution center of Elliotts Point material

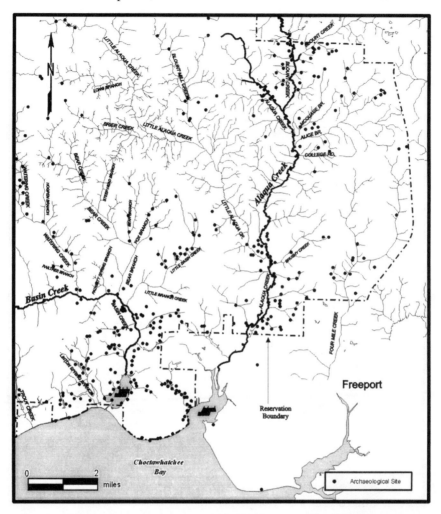

Figure 6.6. Prehistoric sites on Alaqua and Basin Creeks.

culture, but it has only two sites (8WL28 and 8WL36) with fiber-tempered pottery (Figure 6.10), and together they have produced only 10 sherds. In fact, of the 85 sites with fiber-tempered pottery in the study area, only 18 (21.2 percent) have evidence of classic Elliotts Point material culture. Most of the sites with fiber-tempered pottery have little in the way of other material culture besides debitage; only occasionally do the artifact assemblages contain a chipped or ground stone tool.

Looking at the data from a slightly different perspective, there are 57 sites with Elliotts Point components and, again, 18 have fiber-tempered pottery.

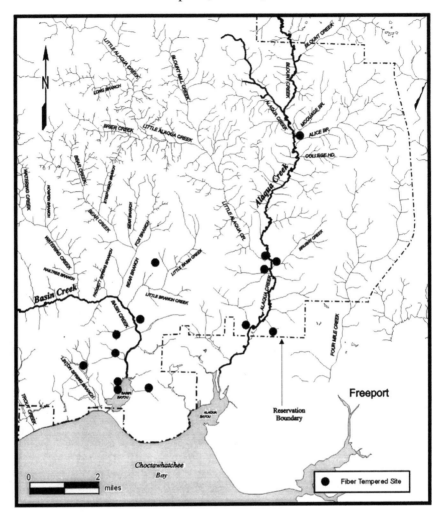

Figure 6.7. Elliotts Point sites with fiber-tempered pottery on Alaqua and Basin Creeks.

Thirty-nine sites, or 68 percent, have no evidence of fiber-tempered pottery whatsoever.

The combination of radiocarbon dates and distribution of fiber-tempered pottery vs. Elliotts Point components supports the position that pottery was a late arrival in Elliotts Point culture but clearly lingered longer than the distribution network that was the hallmark of early Elliotts Point assemblages. Evidence for this comes from the fact that 42.4 percent of the sites

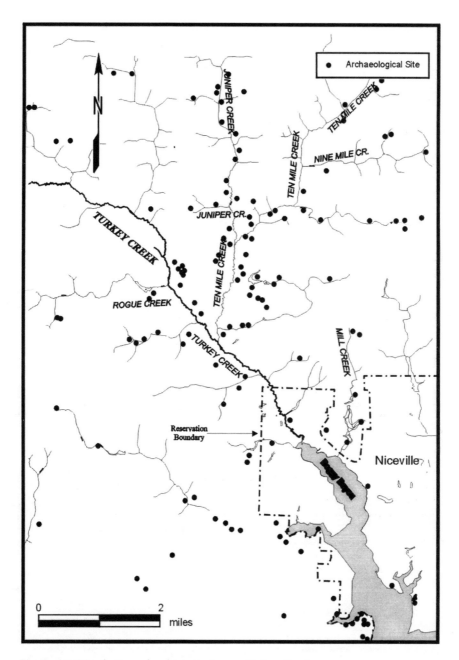

Figure 6.8. Distribution of prehistoric sites on Turkey Creek.

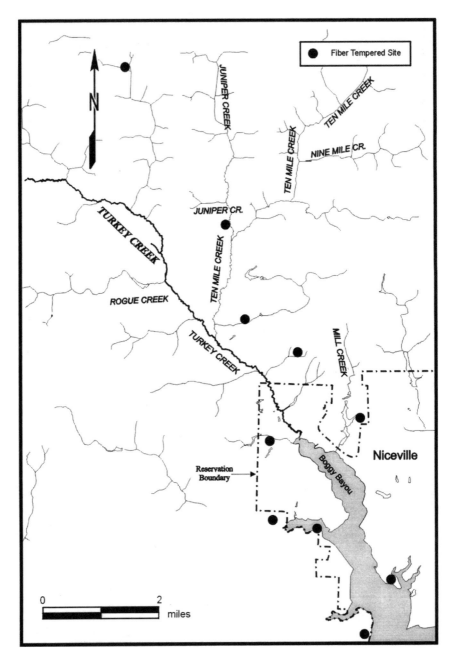

Figure 6.9. Elliotts Point sites with fiber-tempered pottery on Turkey Creek.

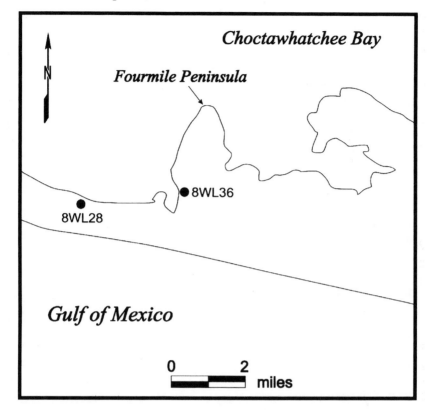

Figure 6.10. Distribution of sites with fiber-tempered pottery at Fourmile Peninsula.

with fiber-tempered pottery also had Deptford components, reflecting an-other wave of influence from eastern cultures.

The data seem to indicate that as fiber-tempered pottery dropped out, Deptford populations were on the increase and (though this topic is beyond the scope of this discussion) settled in different areas along the coast and bayous from the sites of Elliotts Point people. Also, Deptford populations established more substantial occupations with evidence of sizeable villages as well as hamlets and resource exploitation loci. Notably absent, however, were any mounds, accretional or otherwise. Clearly, the stimuli for redistri-bution and activities surrounding the mound and other special-function sites on Fourmile Peninsula played no role in Deptford cultural dynamics or interaction.

What we see in the study area, therefore, is a bustling population at the end of the Archaic with strong ties to the Poverty Point network and unambiguous evidence of participation in long-distance trade. Sometime near the end of the Elliotts Point heyday, fiber-tempered pottery made its appearance, but it does not seem to have been widely accepted, as the incidence of pottery is so low. There is no clear evidence that the population was eager to trade their steatite vessels for pottery ones. In contrast, it appears that after the diffusion of either Deptford pottery or the concept of Deptford pottery, both fiber-tempered and steatite containers were rapidly replaced.

Looking at the picture of settlement patterning and material culture change, there is no evidence that the appearance of fiber-tempered pottery heightened cultural interaction at all in the study area. In fact, it seems to have entered the scene at a time when widespread interaction had been ongoing for hundreds of years and may have been on the wane. We believe that the northwest Florida Gulf coast is paradigmatic of Sassaman's (1993a) posture on the slow and erratic movement of pottery after its introduction on the Atlantic coast. He believes that part of the reason for the tardy appearance of pottery to the west lay in the control of trade networks. Essentially, the people who controlled the Late Archaic trade networks probably enjoyed prestige and power and were likely also influential in shaping the direction and pace of technological change in a given region. Extremely important in that network was the trade of steatite for use as containers. Pottery vessels presented a direct threat to the value of steatite. Thus, the powerful Poverty Point trade network, viewed by some as the perfect conduit for the diffusion of pottery, may have instead worked to stall its spread and acceptance across the Southeast.

These concepts could be applicable to the northwest Florida study area. Steatite vessels are an integral part of the Elliotts Point assemblage, and they were in use well before fiber-tempered pottery came on the scene. The peddlers who controlled the network locally may have been highly resistant to the pottery innovation. The value of steatite and perhaps other exotics would have certainly plummeted if they were replaced by items that could be made in the region with locally available raw materials.

The data are clear that the replacement of stone vessels by pottery vessels ultimately did take place in the study area. Moreover, Sassaman (1993a) suggests that the decline of trade, coupled with increased social demands on labor and even shifts in gender-related contributions to group subsistence, led to the acceptance of pottery. This change is manifested on the Atlantic coast by an increase in shellfish collection and subsequent adoption of pottery, including active innovation with vessel form and type.

Shellfish collection already formed a major component of the prehistoric diet during Elliotts Point times; however, there was a shift in the availability of shellfish species that took place at the end of Elliotts Point times and may have had an effect on the distribution of labor. By around 3000 B.P., the restriction of flow between Choctawhatchee Bay and the Gulf of Mexico caused a reduction in the availability of shellfish like bay scallop and qua-hog that were exploited heavily by Elliotts Point populations, leaving oyster as the major species available (Goldsmith 1966; Johnson et al. 1986; Thomas and Campbell 1993). Associated with these shifts in the natural environment is an increase in inland, riverine settlement.

In summary, the data strongly argue that the appearance of fiber-tempered pottery had no observable impact on interaction in Elliotts Point culture, which was already characterized by intense interaction. Although fiber-tempered pottery arrived in the study area from elsewhere, we maintain that the diffusion of pottery production did not trigger any consequential cultural changes because, for whatever reasons, the introduction of fiber-tempered pottery did not result in warm or widespread acceptance. Whether this was because the entrepreneurs who controlled trade managed to limit its acceptance or whether there were other factors at work is undetermined. Nevertheless, by the time the local population was ready to switch from steatite to pottery vessels, Elliotts Point culture must have already been on the way out and with it the powerful group that controlled not only the flow of goods but also possibly the rate of technological change as well. It seems likely that the decline of such trade, coupled with changes in the division of labor, perhaps brought on by shifts in the availability of shellfish or other stimuli, led to an atmosphere in which local populations were re-ceptive to new ideas. However, fiber-tempered pottery was the Edsel of its day. It was the Deptford tradition that took hold in the area, and that culture would remain a sedentary, conservative, and virtually unchanged population for hundreds of years.

7

Early Pottery at Poverty Point

Origins and Functions

Christopher T. Hays and Richard A. Weinstein

The Poverty Point site (16WC5), located on the eastern edge of Maçon Ridge in northeast Louisiana (Figure 7.1), has fascinated archaeologists with its unique artifacts and earthworks ever since it was reported by S. H. Lockett (1873) and C. B. Moore (1913) in the late nineteenth and early twentieth centuries. These aspects of the site continue to attract archaeological research, and many have been the subjects of intensive investigations over the years. For example, recent studies have pondered the number and types of lithic materials brought in by an apparently elaborate exchange system (e.g., Johnson 1993), the structure of the monumental earthworks (e.g., Kidder 2002), and the function and stylistic characteristics of the ubiquitous baked-clay balls or Poverty Point Objects (e.g., Lear 1998). The pottery at Poverty Point, however, is one category of artifacts that has received very little systematic investigation.

We undertook our study of Poverty Point pottery as a follow-up to our examination of the pottery from the Bayou Jasmine site (16SJB2) in southeast Louisiana (see Figure 7.1), a site that contains both an extensive Tchefuncte component and a Poverty Point component (Hays and Weinstein 2000). One of the major research issues we wanted to address in that study was the technological development of the earliest pottery in the Lower Mississippi Valley (LMV). Since, however, the excavations at Bayou Jasmine did not reach the Poverty Point component of the site, we were unable to examine the transition in pottery technology from Poverty Point to Tchefuncte. We then turned our attention to the Poverty Point site itself.

Traditionally, most archaeologists have believed that fiber-tempered pottery represented one of the earliest pottery series in the Western Gulf coastal plain and the LMV, having been brought in from the east by the far-flung Poverty Point exchange system (e.g., Jenkins et al. 1986:548). Specifically, Jenkins et al. (1986:550; see also Sassaman 1993a:26) argue that steatite and fiber-tempered pottery were probably transferred together from the Alabama-Georgia piedmont to the Gulf Coast and eventually to redistribution

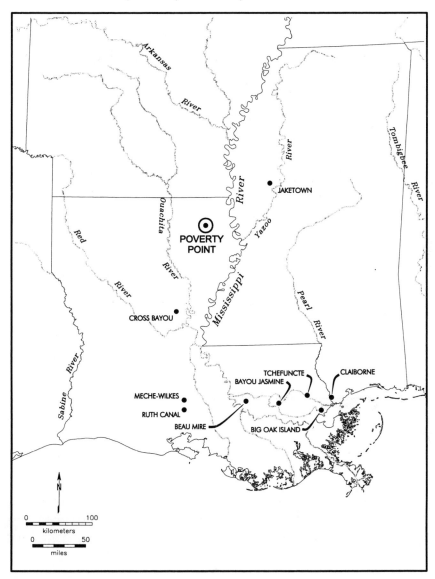

Figure 7.1. Location of the Poverty Point site in northeast Louisiana. Other sites mentioned in the text also are shown.

sites such as the Poverty Point–era Claiborne site (22HA501) (see Figure 7.1). However, in Gibson's excavations at Poverty Point, he found that the mean vertical position (the average excavation level) of Tchefuncte sherds was below that of fiber-tempered wares, and therefore he concluded that Tchefuncte pottery preceded fiber-tempered pottery at the site. He conjec-

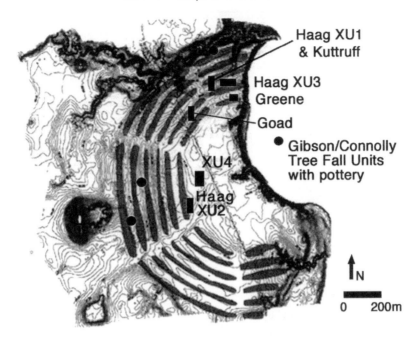

Figure 7.2. Contour map of the Poverty Point site, showing locations of excavation units from which pottery was analyzed. The six concentric ridges have been shaded for clarity (adapted from Connolly 1999).

tured that Poverty Point was a largely independent center of early Southeastern pottery manufacture, producing a pottery series that he labeled "Old Floyd" Tchefuncte. Specifically, he suggested that "the early age of 'Old Floyd' Tchefuncte at Poverty Point means that the Tchefuncte decoration complex arose in the Lower Mississippi Valley, possibly at or around the Poverty Point site" (Gibson 1995:70).[1] This hypothesis has important implications for the development and spread of pottery technology in the LMV, and one of the goals of our study is to evaluate and test it.

POTTERY SAMPLES AND METHODS

In the course of our study we examined 641 sherds. This pottery was collected during five major excavations at the site (Figure 7.2), including excavations by William Haag (1990) in the mid-1970s, Carl Kuttruff (1975) in 1973, Sharon Goad (Connolly 1999, 2001) in the early 1980s, Glen Greene (1990) in 1983, and Jon Gibson and Robert Connolly in the late 1990s (Connolly 1999). Goad's investigations consisted of six 5-×-5-m units excavated in the north sector of the site, and Gibson and Connolly's investigations consisted of 14 1-X-1-m units excavated in various areas where tree falls had disturbed the ground (Connolly 1999). Haag's investigations included a series of five "excavation units" (XU1 to XU5), most consisting of several contiguous 5-X-5-foot (1.5-X-1.5-m) squares, excavated in the north sector, the plaza, and Mound A. However, only XU2, XU3, and XU4 yielded pottery. Weinstein participated in the excavation of several of these units. Kuttruff's investigations consisted of three approximately 2-X-2-m test units placed adjacent to Haag's XU1 profile in the north sector, while Greene's investigations consisted of a 6-X-6-m unit excavated along the eroding bluff of Ridge 1 in the north sector.

In addition, we also examined a portion of the Carl Alexander surface collection (n = 229). These particular sherds, which until recently were housed at the University of Florida, are curated at the Poverty Point site and were loaned to us by Robert Connolly. They almost certainly were part of the Carl Alexander surface collection that Webb (1982:40–42) analyzed and reported on in his comprehensive study of the site. Since our examination of this pottery, an additional 962 sherds have been located and catalogued, and in the future we plan to examine them. The only recorded pottery collections from the site that we did not examine were those reported by Ford and Webb (1956) and those recovered by Gibson (1984, 1987, 1989, 1990b, 1993, 1994b, 1997). Ford and Webb (1956:105–106) recorded 53 sherds and classified 21 of them as clay tempered and 32 of them as fiber tempered. Gibson collected 1,273 sherds from 115 1-X-1-m test units that he excavated at various locations throughout the site.[2]

POTTERY CLASSIFICATION AND DESCRIPTION

We classified each sherd, where possible, according to the type-variety system developed for the LMV by Phillips (1970). A small sample of sherds (n = 6) was unclassifiable. We examined each sherd microscopically to a power of 60–70X and recorded the presence of large aplastic inclusions (e.g., sponge spicules, fiber, grog) and other information on paste composition. For each sherd in the Goad and Gibson/Connolly collections, we recorded Munsell colors (for the interior, exterior, and core), the vessel part (rim, body, base), thickness (rim and body), maximum diameter, and weight.

About half the pottery examined (49 percent) consists of grog-tempered sherds that postdate the main Late/Terminal Archaic period (ca. 3650–3050 rcybp) occupation of the site (Connolly 2002). Most of these are classified as sherds of Baytown Plain, *var. unspecified,* but there are a number of decorated grog-tempered specimens. Some of these decorated sherds clearly indicate the presence of a Late Woodland period, Coles Creek culture occupation. Others indicate the presence of a previously undocumented Marksville culture component (Hays and Weinstein 2000). The number and characteristics of the Coles Creek and Marksville pottery at Poverty Point will be discussed in some detail in a later paper.

The other three common types of pottery in the collections are among the earliest in the Southeast, and they are the main subjects of this chapter (Figure 7.3). They include chalky-paste pottery, pottery of the Tchefuncte series, and fiber-tempered pottery. The chalky-paste pottery, so named because it has a chalky or silty feel to it (cf. Borremans and Shaak 1986; Goggin 1952), could be divided into two distinct groups.

The vast majority of the chalky pottery has abundant siliceous sponge spicules in the paste. Siliceous spicules are the skeletal structure of freshwater sponges, which remain after the creatures die and the soft tissue decomposes. The chalky texture of the pottery is a result of the sponge spicules being sloughed off the surface when the sherds are touched (Borremans and Shaak 1986:127–128). The spicules appear as abundant, unarticulated whitish rods (see Figure 7.3). We classified this pottery as part of the St. Johns series, originally described from eastern Florida, since it is the only known series in the Southeast to contain abundant sponge spicules.[3,4] Stoltman's (this volume) petrographic analysis of three of our St. Johns sherds from Haag's excavations strongly supports the argument that the St. Johns pottery was imported to Poverty Point from Florida. Ortmann and Kidder's (this volume) petrographic analysis of three St. Johns sherds from Poverty Point also indicates that they were almost certainly imported from Florida. Recently, Rolland and Bond (2003) have determined that sponge spicules in St. Johns pottery are most likely an intentional temper added during the manufacturing process, but sponge spicules have been found naturally occurring in at least one clay source in Florida (Cordell and Koski 2003).

The second group of chalky-paste pottery has the characteristic chalky feel of the St. Johns series, but it does not have any spicules in the paste and indeed has no temper at all. This pottery is very similar to Tchefuncte Plain, *var. Tchefuncte,* but it does not have the contorted and laminated paste typical of that latter variety. Since we have observed similar pottery in Tchefuncte collections at the Bayou Jasmine and Beau Mire (16AN17) sites in southern Louisiana (see Figure 7.1), we tentatively classified this chalky, temperless, nonlaminated pottery as Tchefuncte Plain, *var. unspecified.*[5]

ASSEMBLAGE COMPOSITION AND DESCRIPTION

The analyzed assemblage of early pottery includes 324 sherds, but only 175 are from excavated contexts with provenience (Table 7.1). The total number of vessels represented by these sherds has not been determined, but it must

Figure 7.3. Examples of some of the early pottery wares from Poverty Point, along with enlargements of their respective pastes: a–d, plain and incised sherds with St. Johns paste (a–c, St. Johns Plain, *var. St. Johns;* d, St. Johns Incised, *var. St. Johns*); e–h, punctated and scored sherds with fiber-tempered paste (e–g, Wheeler Punctated, *var. unspecified;* h, Norwood Simple Stamped, *var. unspecified*); i–n, plain, stamped, and incised sherds with Tchefuncte paste (i–k, Tchefuncte Plain, *var. Sky Lake;* l, Tchefuncte Stamped, *var. Shell Brake;* m, Tchefuncte Incised, *var. Sanders;* n, Tchefuncte Incised, *var. Tchefuncte*). a, c, e, g–i, k, and m–n from Goad excavations; b, j, and l from Gibson/Connolly excavations; d and f from Haag excavations.

Table 7.1. Early pottery types believed associated with the Poverty Point component at the Poverty Point site.

	Collections Analyzed						Total
	Gibson/Connolly	Goad	Haag	Kuttruff	Greene	Alexander	
St. Johns paste							
St. Johns Plain	8	15	8[a]	3	2	19	55
St. Johns Incised	1		2			4	7
St. Johns Punctated					2		2
Fiber tempered							
Wheeler Plain	7	36	9	9	2	27	90
Wheeler Punctated		2	3		1	6	12
Wheeler Simple Stamped						1	1
Norwood Simple Stamped		1					1
Tchefuncte paste							
Tchefuncte Plain	28	17	9	4		63	121
Tchefuncte Incised		3				2	5
Tchefuncte Stamped	1					18	19
Tammany Punctated			2			6	8
Jaketown Simple Stamped						2	2
Alexander paste							
Alexander Pinched						1	1
Total	45	74	33	16	7	149	324

Note: No pottery types with Baytown or later pastes have been included, although such items are present in relatively large numbers at the site.
[a]Includes one sherd with fiber.

be a relatively small number. The total weight of the 175 excavated sherds, for example, is ca. 1,000 g, which is less than the weight of two typical Tchefuncte bowls (bowls weighed at Louisiana State University, Museum of Natural Science Laboratory of Anthropology). Of the total 324 sherds, 20 percent are St. Johns, 48 percent are Tchefuncte, and 32 percent are fiber tempered. Notable for its near absence from the collection is the sandy/gritty Alexander series pottery. Webb (1982:40) reported finding 51 O'Neal Plain and nine Alexander Pinched sherds in surface collections, but the only Alexander sherd that we found was a single example of Alexander Pinched in the Carl Alexander collection. Also notable, principally because of its sparse numbers, is Jaketown Simple Stamped, which was abundant in the Tchefuncte levels at the Jaketown site (22HU505) (see Figure 7.1). Webb (1982:40) reported finding 15 Jaketown Simple Stamped sherds in surface collections, but we only found two specimens in our examination of the Carl Alexander surface collection.

Fiber-Tempered Pottery

All but one of the fiber-tempered sherds appear typical of the Wheeler series (Phillips 1970) (see Figure 7.3). This series is centered in the western Tennessee River valley of northern Alabama and west Tennessee, but it is also found in eastern Mississippi, western Alabama, and, in small numbers, in eastern Louisiana (Jenkins and Krause 1986:33; Weinstein 1995). Wheeler vessels are flat-bottomed, wide-mouthed beakers and simple bowls that are typically plain, but when decorated the styles include punctations, dentate stamping, and simple stamping.

Most of our Wheeler sherds are plain (n = 90), but there are also 12 punctated sherds and one simple-stamped sherd (see Table 7.1). The only apparent non-Wheeler fiber-tempered sherd in the collection is classified as an example of Norwood Simple Stamped. It has the wide interior stamping typical of that type, which is associated with the northwest region of Florida (Phelps 1965). To the best of our knowledge, this type has not been found previously in the LMV, and it most likely represents a trade ware from western Florida. One particularly interesting fiber-tempered sherd in the collection is a podal support from the base of a Wheeler pot. Again, to the best of our knowledge, podal supports are previously unknown for Wheeler pottery or indeed for any fiber-tempered pottery.

The number of fiber holes evident in a sherd ranges from few to abundant, and the paste often includes a variety of other materials, such as quartz or abundant sand, that appear to be unintentional inclusions. Some of the pastes are very sandy, whereas others contain little sand. The Munsell colors of the exterior surfaces of the sherds range quite widely between yellowish red (5YR 5/6) and light yellowish brown (10YR 6/4). Even on a single sherd, the exterior color can range widely, suggesting that the pot was fired unevenly. The core colors of the sherds are commonly dark gray (10YR 4/1) but range to 10YR 6/4. The interior colors also range from yellowish red to light yellowish brown, but the majority are dark gray (10YR 4/1). As is typical of fiber-tempered pottery, the sherds are relatively thick, ranging from approximately 7 to 11 mm. There are three discernable rim profiles: two flat and one pointed.

St. Johns Pottery

The St. Johns series also consists mostly of plain wares (n = 55), with a few incised pieces (n = 7) and two punctated sherds (see Table 7.1, Figure 7.3). One plain sherd from Haag's excavations contains both sponge spicules and fiber in the paste. The exterior Munsell colors of the St. Johns pottery range from reddish yellow (7.5YR 6/6), which is relatively common, to yellowish brown (10YR 6/4). Like the Wheeler pottery, the exterior colors often range widely on a single sherd, suggesting that the pot was fired unevenly. The core colors are mostly very dark, ranging from very dark gray (10YR 3/1) to gray (10YR 5/1). The interior colors range from dark gray (10YR 4/1) to very pale brown (10YR 7/4). The vast majority of this pottery has a very soft paste and appears to be poorly fired. Indeed, when two St. Johns sherds from the Kuttruff excavations were submitted for chronometric dating to the Luminescence Dating Laboratory at the University of Washington, they were found to be "too poorly fired to yield luminescence dates valid for the time of manufacture" (Feathers 2000:2). Sherd thickness ranges from about 5 to 10 mm. The three discernable rim profiles include two flat rims and one pointed rim.

Tchefuncte Pottery

Most of the Tchefuncte pottery is also plain (n = 121) (see Table 7.1). In addition, there are five Tchefuncte Incised, 19 Tchefuncte Stamped, and eight Tammany Punctated sherds (see Figure 7.3). It is worth noting that this is a relatively bland and nondiverse assemblage compared with the manifold suite of types and varieties that one sees at classic Tchefuncte sites such as the Tchefuncte type site (16ST1), Bayou Jasmine, and Big Oak Island (16OR6) (see Figure 7.1). For example, the Poverty Point assemblage lacks any clear examples of the common types Orleans Punctated and Lake Borgne Incised, and the range of varieties is also very limited. The Munsell colors of the Tchefuncte pottery show less variability than those of the other two series. The exterior colors range from reddish yellow (7.5YR 6/6) to yellowish brown (10YR 6/4), and both the core and interior colors range from dark gray (10YR 4/1) to yellowish brown (10YR 6/4). The two discernable rim profiles are both rounded. Sherd thickness ranges from about 6 to 9 mm.

VERTICAL AND HORIZONTAL DISTRIBUTION OF THE POTTERY

Our analysis of the vertical distribution of the pottery is based on the stratigraphic position of the sherds. Robert Connolly (2001), former station archaeologist at Poverty Point, has worked out a general stratigraphic sequence for the units excavated on the ridges. The youngest stratum, Stratum 1, is the plow zone and it contains artifacts from potentially mixed strata and levels. The next stratum, Stratum 2, consists of the lower plow zone and upper midden, and its contents are also potentially mixed. Stratum 3 consists solely of upper-midden materials and is the first completely in situ stratum. Stratum 4 consists of the interface of the ridge construction levels and upper midden. Stratum 5 consists of ridge construction contexts and predates all upper midden. Finally, Stratum 6 consists of a buried A horizon/ midden that was deposited prior to all ridge construction. Where possible, Connolly assigned each sherd in the Goad collection and in his tree-fall collections to a particular stratum. The stratigraphic contexts for the sherds from the Haag, Greene, and Kuttruff collections have yet to be determined; consequently, this portion of our analysis focuses exclusively on the pottery from the Gibson/Connolly and Goad collections.

Each of the three pottery series has a distinct stratigraphic signature (Figure 7.4). The St. Johns pottery is found exclusively in the lower four strata (3 to 6), and 55 percent is found in the buried A horizon prior to ridge construction. This distribution strongly suggests that St. Johns pottery was brought into the site during the earliest occupations and during the ridge construction phase. Radiocarbon samples taken directly above and below a St. Johns Incised sherd in the construction horizon (Strata 4/5) yielded dates of 3040 B.P. and 3160 B.P., respectively (Connolly 2001:64–65).[6] It is important to note that these dates are surprisingly early since St. Johns series pottery has traditionally been thought to begin about 1950 rcybp in eastern Florida (e.g., Milanich 1994). However, sherds with abundant sponge spicules—indistinguishable from St. Johns—have been found in proveniences dated to 3425 B.P. at the Joseph Reed Shell Ring (Russo and Heide, this volume; see also Sassaman 2003a).

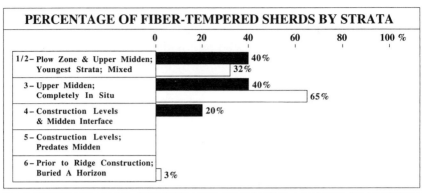

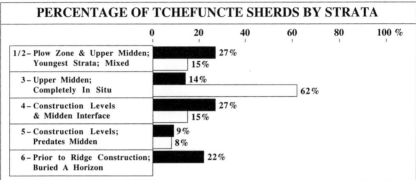

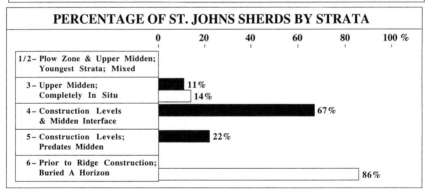

	Fiber Tempered	Tchefuncte	St. Johns		
Gibson/Connolly	n=5	n=22	n=9	■	Gibson/Connolly
Goad	n=31	n=13	n=14	□	Goad

Figure 7.4. Stratigraphic position of fiber-tempered, Tchefuncte, and St. Johns pottery recovered during Gibson/Connolly tree-fall excavations and Goad's large block excavation.

The fiber-tempered pottery (almost all Wheeler), in contrast to the St. Johns series, is found almost exclusively (ca. 94 percent) in the upper three strata at the site. Indeed, there are only two fiber-tempered sherds below Stratum 3: one in Stratum 4 and one in Stratum 6. This distribution strongly suggests that fiber-tempered pottery was brought into, or manufactured on, the site during the latter phases of ridge construction and occupation.

Finally, the Tchefuncte pottery is distributed more evenly in the strata, with more of the sherds occurring in the upper three strata, although there are also a small number of sherds in the lowest strata. This distribution suggests that Tchefuncte pottery may have been present during the earliest stages of occupation and construction at the site, and on through the site's latest Late/Terminal Archaic occupation. It is worth noting, however, that the Goad excavations produced only one sherd below Stratum 4, whereas the Gibson/Connolly excavations produced seven Tchefuncte sherds below Stratum 4.[7]

The horizontal distribution of the fiber-tempered, St. Johns, and Tchefuncte sherds indicates that they were used widely across the site. They are present in the west sector in the Gibson/Connolly tree-fall units, in the north sector in Goad's, Gibson/Connolly's, Kuttruff's, and Haag's units, and in Greene's unit along the eroding bluff edge of the north sector (see Figure 7.2). Finally, they are present in the plaza area in Haag's XU2 units. Within these areas, however, there is no apparent clustering of pottery. Several sherds occur together in some unit levels but none have been found in any feature, such as a pit or a hearth.

ORIGINS

We turn now to the issue of the origin of these three types at Poverty Point. As we noted above, the St. Johns pottery almost certainly represents a trade ware from eastern Florida (Figure 7.5). The strength of the Florida-Louisiana connection at this time is further demonstrated by the presence of the Norwood Simple Stamped sherd. Interestingly, the Tick Island site (8VO24), in the heart of the St. Johns region, has some Poverty Point Objects and plummets that are considered to be either derived from, or heavily influenced by, Poverty Point (Milanich 1994).

Several researchers (Blitz and Mann 2000:20; Jenkins et al. 1986:550; Webb 1982) have suggested that the Poverty Point–age Claiborne site near the mouth of the Pearl River may have served as a conduit for dispersing valued goods from the Mississippi Sound to the LMV. This seems to be a

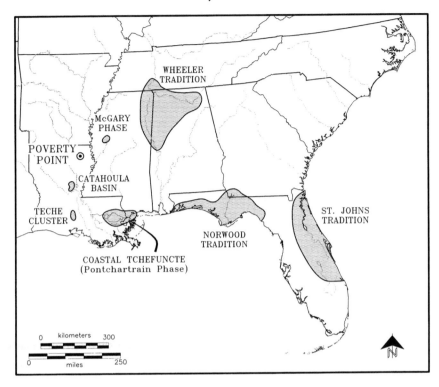

Figure 7.5. The southeastern United States, showing regions with probable and/or potential pottery connections to the Poverty Point site (based on Sassaman 1993a:fig. 3; Shannon 1987:fig. 1; Weinstein 1995:fig. 3; Williams and Brain 1983:fig. 11.6).

reasonable route for the St. Johns pottery to have traveled, given that Claiborne is the only other known Poverty Point–age site with true St. Johns pottery (Gagliano and Webb 1970).[8] We have examined some of the St. Johns sherds from the Claiborne site that are curated at Coastal Environments, Inc., in Baton Rouge, and they appear macroscopically and microscopically identical to the St. Johns sherds found at the Poverty Point site.

The stratigraphic position of the St. Johns sherds indicates that they represent, possibly along with some Tchefuncte sherds, the earliest pottery at the site. Apparently, however, little or none was imported during the latter stages of occupation and construction of the site. The horizontal distribution of St. Johns sherds at Poverty Point suggests that there were at least several vessels imported to the site and that they were used in several locations across the ridges and plaza.

It seems likely that the majority of Wheeler pottery was brought to Poverty Point from the east (e.g., the Yazoo Basin), where it has been found in modest quantities at sites of the McGary phase (Williams and Brain 1983:355) (see Figure 7.5). The vertical and horizontal distribution of the Wheeler pottery at Poverty Point indicates that it was in widespread use across the site but that it was present almost exclusively during the latter phases of ridge construction and site occupation. Stoltman's (this volume) petrographic analysis of our four Wheeler series fiber-tempered sherds from Haag's excavations suggests that two of them probably were imported while the other two may have been manufactured at Poverty Point.

The origin of Tchefuncte is the most problematic of the three series. We found some sherds in the Gibson/Connolly excavations in the pre-ridge stratum, which tentatively supports Gibson's (1995) finding that Tchefuncte appears at the earliest stages of the site and then continues to be used up to the end of the main Poverty Point occupation. We are, however, not as certain about the question of where these vessels originated, mainly because few early Tchefuncte sites have been confirmed. As reviewed earlier, Gibson believes that Tchefuncte pottery was manufactured at the Poverty Point site. In contrast, we argue that most, if not all, of the Tchefuncte pottery was manufactured off the site. It is worth noting also that Stoltman's (this volume) petrographic analysis of three of our Tchefuncte sherds from Haag's excavations indicates that they were *not* constructed of the loessic sediments present at the Poverty Point site.

We make this argument because the number and composition of the Tchefuncte pottery at Poverty Point are unlike those of any other early Tchefuncte assemblage with which we are familiar. For example, the Tchefuncte sherds found in the lowest excavated levels at the Bayou Jasmine site are associated with a radiocarbon date of around 2870 B.P. and thus represent the earliest Tchefuncte pottery found to date. However, in a context that is presumably very early in Tchefuncte, and probably just after the Poverty Point occupation, the number of Tchefuncte sherds at Bayou Jasmine is abundant and essentially the entire range of Tchefuncte types is well represented (e.g., Tchefuncte Plain, Tchefuncte Stamped, Tchefuncte Incised, Lake Borgne Incised, Orleans Punctated, and Tammany Punctated). In other words, the full suite of Tchefuncte pottery is present in the earliest levels at Bayou Jasmine. This same pattern is found in the earliest levels at the classic Tchefuncte site, at Big Oak Island (Shenkel 1980), and, most interestingly, also at Jaketown, which contains both well-stratified Tchefuncte and Poverty Point occupations. Based on their work at Jaketown, Ford et al. (1955:62) reported that "at this point, we can make one of the few unqualified statements in this report, to wit, that pottery was not used at Jaketown in the Poverty Point period . . . there is every indication that pottery appeared at

Jaketown abruptly as a fully developed complex." In other words, the earliest Tchefuncte levels at the Jaketown site contain, again, numerous sherds and essentially the full suite of Tchefuncte types.

In summary, we suggest that most, if not all, of the Tchefuncte pottery was not manufactured at Poverty Point and, consequently, like many of the other artifacts, it may have been brought into the site as part of the exchange network. This, of course, raises questions about the site or region from which the Tchefuncte pottery at Poverty Point derived and, ultimately, the place(s) of origin of the series. This brings us full circle back to our initial research questions on the technological and stylistic development of the earliest pottery in the LMV—unfortunately without any clear answers. Future research on this question could focus on the only known locations to have produced the earliest radiocarbon-dated Tchefuncte assemblages: the Catahoula Basin and coastal Louisiana. The Catahoula Basin, located about 135 km south-southwest of Poverty Point (see Figure 7.5), contains the Cross Bayou site (16CT354) (see Figure 7.1), a locale with a Tchefuncte occupation dated initially to 2680 B.P. (Gibson 1991; McGimsey and van der Koogh 2001). Sites of the Pontchartrain phase in coastal Louisiana, such as Bayou Jasmine with its deep, thick, and relatively early Tchefuncte deposits that have produced calibrated radiocarbon dates between 3370 and 2730 B.P. (Hays 1995, 1997; Hays and Weinstein 2000; Kuttruff et al. 1993), also may be good candidates for discovering the origins of Tchefuncte. Finally, sites of the McGary phase in the Yazoo Basin (Williams and Brain 1983:355) and/or the so-called Teche cluster (Weinstein 1995) in south-central Louisiana (see Figure 7.5) may provide keys to understanding the development of Tchefuncte pottery. These sites, including such locales as Meche-Wilkes (16SL18) and Ruth Canal (16SM20) (Gibson 1976, 1990a) (see Figure 7.1), contain some of the largest assemblages of fiber-tempered pottery from the LMV, plus significant quantities of Tchefuncte ware. Although the exact relationship between the fiber-tempered and the Tchefuncte pottery is not yet known, these locations may contain clues to the origins of early, locally produced pottery within the LMV.

FUNCTION

We initially attempted to evaluate the function and usage of the pottery by determining vessel shape and looking for the presence of sooting on the sherds (see Gibson and Melancon, this volume, for another discussion of early Poverty Point–era pottery vessel function). These efforts, however, produced little useful information. Since most of the sherds are relatively small and fragmentary, we were able to refit only a few of them, and there are only 11 rim sherds in the sample. Consequently, we were only able to determine vessel shape for 11 sherds: 10 bowls and one jar. None of the sherds in the sample has clear evidence of sooting on the exterior or interior. This suggests that, if the vessels were used for cooking, the source of heat was indirect, probably from some type of hot-rock heating. Alternatively, the vessels may have been used primarily for serving or storage.

Since we have relatively little direct information on vessel function, we address the issue obliquely from two angles. First, the small amount of early pottery found at Poverty Point strongly suggests that it played either a very minimal or very specialized role in the society. Specifically, it seems clear that pottery played, at best, a very minor role in the culinary tool kit of the Poverty Point people. This is particularly apparent when the amount of pottery at the site is contrasted with the ubiquitous Poverty Point Objects, whose primary function is attributed to earth-oven cooking (Ford and Webb 1956). For example, the Goad excavations recovered ca. 9,925 g of Poverty Point Objects in features alone (Connolly 2001:113), whereas the total weight of the early pottery from all locations in the Goad excavations was ca. 520 g.

This observation, however, raises the question, If the Poverty Point people knew of pottery and how to make it, why did they not produce it in large quantities for use in cooking and other utilitarian tasks? One possibility is that steatite may have served as the primary container for the Poverty Point people and, thus, it may have obviated the need for pottery. However, as Gibson and Melancon (this volume) note, given the undoubtedly high cost of importing steatite vessels from the Appalachian Mountains, it seems extremely likely that most Poverty Pointers would have opted instead to use local clays to make their cooking vessels—that is, if they were given a choice. Sassaman (1993a) has proposed that, in fact, Late Archaic communities throughout the lower Southeast were slow to adopt pottery manufacture precisely because the leaders of the Poverty Point exchange network viewed it as a threat to the prestige and power they gained through their control of the steatite trade. In other words, he suggests, the Poverty Point leaders in control of the steatite trade may have actively suppressed the manufacturing of pottery in their communities. If Sassaman is correct, then it is likely that the suppression of pottery manufacture at the Poverty Point site itself would have been extraordinarily powerful.

Still, the question remains, for what was the pottery at the site being used? Hayden's (1998) hypothesis that pottery initially was used on special occasions by the elite for ritualized drinking and feasting seems to fit the

Poverty Point data well (see also Saunders, Gibson and Melancon, and Russo and Heide [all this volume] for other uses and evaluations of Hayden's hypothesis). This highly specialized function would explain the lack of sooting on the vessels, the small amount of pottery at the site, and the fact that most, if not all of it, was imported. Helms (1988) and others have eloquently made the case that exotic items and exotic knowledge are frequently used by elites in a society to enhance and establish their prestige. Beyond this suggestion, we are reluctant to speculate about the function of the pottery, given the small sample sizes. Future studies on the function of Poverty Point pottery should undoubtedly incorporate use-wear studies (e.g., Hally 1986; Skibo 1992).

DISCUSSION AND CONCLUSION

As noted at the beginning of this chapter, the major research issue we wanted to address in our studies of both Bayou Jasmine and Poverty Point pottery was the technological development of the earliest pottery in the LMV. The view of this issue from Bayou Jasmine was limited by the fact that the excavations did not reach the Poverty Point level. However, our study did show that in the very earliest levels associated with Tchefuncte culture, sherds were abundant and essentially the entire range of Tchefuncte types was well represented.

The view from Poverty Point is both more enlightening and more complex. Our study demonstrates that the vast majority of early pottery at the site can be classified into three groups: St. Johns series pottery, fiber-tempered pottery, and Tchefuncte series pottery. As noted previously, most archaeologists have believed that fiber-tempered pottery represents, perhaps, the earliest series in the LMV, having been brought in from the east together with steatite by the far-flung Poverty Point exchange system (e.g., Jenkins et al. 1986:548). Based on our stratigraphic view of the three pottery types, we have demonstrated that, in fact, fiber-tempered pottery is the latest of the three series to arrive at Poverty Point. When this result is coupled with Connolly's (2001:162–167) recent stratigraphic analysis of steatite at Poverty Point, another interesting result emerges. Connolly demonstrated that steatite is present from the earliest to the latest Poverty Point culture occupations of the site. Therefore it is clear that, once again contrary to the traditional view, steatite and fiber-tempered pottery have no necessary relationship to each other.

Our study has also provided data to evaluate Gibson's hypothesis that Tchefuncte is the earliest pottery at Poverty Point. Our stratigraphic view of the pottery offers some very limited, but also equivocal, support for his position. The Gibson/Connolly excavations contained a small number of Tchefuncte sherds in the lowest strata, but Goad's excavations did not. Furthermore, our analysis demonstrates that most of the Tchefuncte sherds were present in both sets of excavations in the upper strata. It would appear, therefore, that Tchefuncte is more closely associated with the later occupations of the site.

Finally, our study has demonstrated that the pottery that is most clearly associated with the earliest occupations of the site is that of the St. Johns series. Radiocarbon dates associated with St. Johns pottery at Poverty Point indicate that it arrived by at least 3250 B.P. and therefore is unquestionably the earliest pottery known in the LMV. The fact that the initial occupation of Poverty Point included spiculate-tempered pottery brought from eastern Florida over 800 km (500 miles) away is both fascinating and perplexing. We have suggested that St. Johns pottery and indeed almost all the early pottery at the site may have been imported into Poverty Point by the site's elite population for use in feasting rituals. This compelling interpretation raises more questions than it really answers, which leaves us, and others, plenty of room for future research.

ACKNOWLEDGMENTS

We wish to thank the following individuals for their help during the research and production of this essay. Robert Connolly, former station archaeologist at the Poverty Point State Commemorative Area, made available for study those relevant collections housed at the Poverty Point Museum. Rebecca Saunders, associate curator of anthropology with the Museum of Natural Science at Louisiana State University, Baton Rouge, allowed us access to the Haag collection while that collection was stored at LSU. Carl Kuttruff allowed us to study his collection of pottery from his 1975 excavations at Poverty Point. Joe Saunders, regional archaeologist at the University of Louisiana at Monroe, allowed us to study the sherds from Glen Greene's 1983 excavations at Poverty Point. Jon Gibson, retired professor with the Department of Anthropology and Sociology at the University of Louisiana at Lafayette, allowed the junior author access to the Meche-Wilkes collection housed at that university. Ann Cordell, senior biological scientist with the Florida Museum of Natural History, Gainesville, examined several of our St. Johns sherds for comparative purposes. Cherie Schwab of Desktop Publishing, Baton Rouge, helped to organize and format Figure 7.3, while Curtis Latiolais, draftsman at Coastal Environments, Inc., Baton

Rouge, created Figures 7.1 and 7.5. Some of the research conducted by the senior author for this article was conducted through the State of Louisiana's Regional Archaeology Program at Louisiana State University, which is financed with state funds and with federal funds from the National Park Service, U.S. Department of the Interior. The senior author also acknowledges the support of the University of Wisconsin Colleges.

8

In the Beginning

Social Contexts of First Pottery in the Lower Mississippi Valley

Jon L. Gibson and Mark A. Melancon

For three-quarters of a century, archaeologists have been told that the earliest pottery in southeastern North America was fiber tempered and was followed by sand- and clay-tempered wares. We instead propose that the fabric of early pottery was contingent on where, when, and why ceramics first appeared and was not dictated by some inviolate, step-by-step progression or historical tradition. Since the earliest pottery created at any given spot appeared at a different time from that appearing elsewhere and under differing local conditions, it follows that ceramic progression is not the same everywhere. In the Lower Mississippi Valley, at sites such as Poverty Point (16WC5), Jaketown (22HU505), Meche-Wilkes (16SL18), Ruth Canal (16SM20), and a few others, clay-tempered wares bearing Tchefuncte designs appear in preceding or coeval contexts with earlier fiber-tempered materials.

LAST CHANCE FOR OLD-FASHIONED GUESSING

If abundance means importance, then the appearance of first pottery in the Lower Mississippi Valley is an extraordinarily insignificant moment, a nonevent in the history of the arts and famous chefs (cf. Smith 1986). A handful of early potsherds from several places—Poverty Point, Teoc Creek (16CR504), Jaketown, Claiborne (22HA501), Meche-Wilkes, Ruth Canal, and a few others—is all we have to mark the occasion (Gibson 2000; Webb 1977; Figure 8.1). We don't know whether pottery appears everywhere at once, sweeps across the region like a row of toppling dominoes, or pops up like targets on a shooting range. Being scarce and isolated has not helped archaeologists figure out its chronological history either. We have managed to put radiocarbon brackets around a sherd buried deep in Poverty Point's earthen rings—a sherd that we suspect may be from the mother pot—but in archaeology, there's always a chance that an older one will turn up, some-

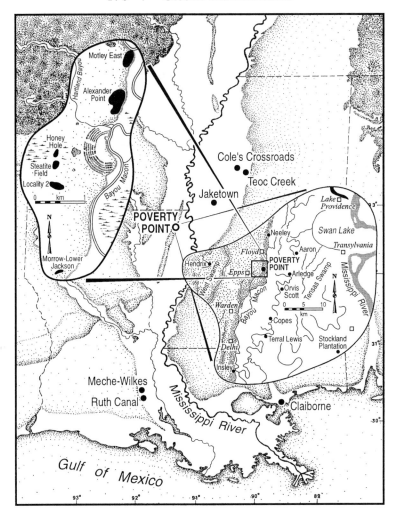

Figure 8.1. The Lower Mississippi Valley. Poverty Point sits on the Maçon Ridge in northeastern Louisiana, and other contemporary sites are scattered up and down the valley. Insert on right shows Poverty Point components in the Poverty Point vicinity. Insert on left shows residential core components surrounding Poverty Point's rings.

where. Once we looked to Alabama's Tombigbee Valley, the south Georgia–north Florida coast, or the Mesoamerican Gulf coast for the source of inspiration for Lower Mississippi pottery (Ford 1969; Haag 1978, 1990; Jenkins et al. 1986; Walthall and Jenkins 1976). Some investigators still do (Hays and Weinstein, this volume), but others have started looking no farther than beneath their own feet (Gibson 1995).

Using abundance to gauge pottery's importance makes sense when you're talking about everyday cooking. But if first pottery was used only for special occasions, such as serving sacramental drink or food during rituals (see Clark and Blake 1994; Clark and Gosser 1995; Hayden 1995a; Hoopes 1995), then importance would not be measured by abundance but by scarcity. By the same measure, if pottery was used to prepare fast food or deliver drinking water to work gangs busy building mounds (Gibson 2000), then we ought not expect it to be as plentiful as cooking wares routinely used when building was suspended. Again, scarcity, not abundance, would mark pottery's value.

It is precisely because we know so little about all of this, especially the circumstances and motives behind its debut, that we seize the moment to think out loud about first pottery in the Lower Mississippi Valley. We aren't constrained by data or opinion—there are too few of the former and there's too much of the latter to show the straight and narrow path. Ambiguity reigns. A half century ago, the advent of radiocarbon dating brought Philip Phillips, James Ford, and James Griffin to a similar crossroads: "We stand before the threat of the atom in the form of ^{14}C dating. This may be our last opportunity for old-fashioned uncontrolled guessing" (Phillips et al. 1951:455). This essay may be our last chance for old-fashioned uncontrolled guessing before hard data get in the way.

SOUTHEASTERN ARCHAEOLOGISTS LOVE THEIR POTTERY

Southeastern archaeologists love their pottery. They spent the larger part of a century naming it and figuring out how old its many types were. There's not a major culture-historical sequence that's not made out of it (Gibson 1994b). Origins have been a favorite topic, especially trying to figure out when pottery was "introduced" and from whence it came—and, in the Lower Mississippi Valley, the Poverty Point site and culture figure prominently on both accounts.

At first, Poverty Point was considered prepottery. After their excavations at Jaketown, James Ford and associates Philip Phillips and William Haag averred: "we can make one of the few unqualified statements in this report, to wit, that pottery was not used at Jaketown in the Poverty Point Period" (Ford et al. 1955:62). Yet, less than a year later, Ford and Clarence Webb did qualify that statement: "The principal surprise of the 1955 field season was the discovery that pottery is undoubtedly an element of the Poverty Point cultural complex [at the Poverty Point site]" (Ford and Webb 1956:105). Later, Ford pointed to Gulf coastal Mexico and ultimately South America as the source of inspiration for pottery (Ford 1969), but Phillips wasn't convinced. He stated: "We are now bracing ourselves against the shock of discovering that [pottery and Poverty Point culture were] introduced into the Lower Mississippi Valley by a series of relayed diffusions originating in Valdivia on the Ecuadorian coast. . . . Both [Stephen] Williams and the present writer stubbornly persist in the disbelief that [Carl] Alexander's pottery is associated with the Poverty Point component in the Poverty Point site" (Phillips 1970:876). Phillips believed that pottery "came in" during a brief fiber-tempered horizon after Poverty Point (see Williams and Brain 1983:354–356).

Stubbornness persists, but by and large, associational and stratigraphic data amassed over the past half century cannot all be blamed on careless excavators or aboriginal posthole diggers (Connolly 2001; Gibson 1973, 1984, 1987, 1989, 1990b, 1993, 1994a, 1997, 2000; Greene 1990; Haag 1990; Hillman 1987; Kuttruff 1975; Webb et al. 1970). Modest in number but heavy with evidentiary weight, these data enable us to make one of the few unqualified statements in this chapter—to wit, that pottery was made during Poverty Point times *by Poverty Point potters* (Gibson 1996b). Poverty Point pottery stratigraphy even holds a few surprises, especially for the relative positions of fiber-, clay-grit-, and sand-tempered wares, untempered wares, and soapstone vessel fragments (Gibson 1995, 2001, 2002). When relative stratigraphic patterns are compared sitewide (rather than looking at successions in individual test pits or small isolated sections of individual rings), we find that clay-grit ware peaks below fiber-tempered ware and soapstone. But as previously argued (Gibson 2001, 2002), we regard this as a nuance of building succession rather than a wrinkle in time or evidence of avant-garde designers. While this discovery has profound local implications— especially for the appearance of clay-grit pottery—it in no way contravenes the well-known southeastern historical sequence with its fiber-tempered roots (Bullen and Stoltman 1972; Ford 1966, 1969; Jenkins et al. 1986; Sassaman 1993a; Walthall and Jenkins 1976).

We choose not to call these wares by their historical type names, because those names convey the appearance of cultural relationships where none may exist. Even if they do, naming leaves us with no earthly idea as to how relationships were established. All too often, type names substitute as proof of those relationships—proof by typology instead of empirical demonstration. Just because we call a potsherd Wheeler Punctated and automatically assume that the pot, the potter, or the decorative idea came from the Tombigbee Valley doesn't make it so. Too bad, too. Type names ease archaeological conversation—if only archaeologists didn't let type names substitute for the search after historical and cultural relatedness. But then, if analysts didn't, historical types wouldn't be historical types (e.g., Ford 1954; Krieger 1944; Rouse 1939). Philip Phillips (1970:23) said it best in his Yazoo Basin opus: "They [types and varieties] have been selected from an endless number of possible variations solely because we think they are likely to reveal significant relationships. . . . To demand that typological classification be uncontaminated by implications of culture-history . . . is not realistic." Phillips is right, of course, unfortunately. So, we choose not to use their given names to avoid contamination.

Fortunately, there are analysts around who seek to verify presumed historical relationships by rigorous, empirical means, such as petrographic thin-section analysis, microscopic and materials analysis, and even trace-element analysis (Stoltman 1989, 1991, this volume; see also Cordell, Hays and Weinstein, and Ortmann and Kidder, this volume). Sometimes, such analyses are done in the name of eliminating the possibility of external origins and, sometimes, of supporting them, but rarely are they done when local origins are suspected. The logical follow-up when nonlocal interactions are suspected or demonstrated is attempting to figure out the historical circumstances and social means responsible for them. And we don't mean blaming direct contact, stimulus diffusion, independent invention, or old, common technology or ideology (e.g., Herbert Spinden's "archaic" culture foundation [Spinden 1917]; James Ford's "psychic unity of mankind" [Ford 1969]; and Malcolm Webb's "old and widely shared ideological orientation" [Webb 1989]).

Traditional "catch-all, explain-all" explanations like these only beg the question. At best, they only identify the context toward which the search for real answers ought to be focused. A serendipitous transpacific voyage doesn't explain why first Ecuadorian Valdivian pottery and Japanese Jomon pottery look alike. Neither does long-distance trade account for fiber-tempered wares at Poverty Point. The real accounting lies in the motives, politics, and social relations behind trade. And what, pray tell, would compel fisher-hunter-gatherers from eastern Florida to pass along or carry soft, breakable St. Johns spiculate ware 2,560 km (1,600 miles) to Poverty Point? The real burden of explanation lies in telling how such "events" came to be and how they were carried out (e.g., Clark and Blake 1994; Clark and Gosser 1995; Sassaman 1993a, 1995b, 2000).

The calendar age of first Lower Mississippi pottery is not crucial to our search. First pottery is first pottery, no matter when it appeared. But for the sake of the record and until someone finds something older, the oldest piece of pottery found so far in the Lower Mississippi Valley is an untempered incised sherd excavated from the first building level in the third ring in the lower western compartment of Poverty Point's enclosure. Radiocarbon samples taken by the senior author a few centimeters above and below the sherd date to sometime between 3691–2971 2cal B.P. (1735–1020 B.C.), most likely between 3378 cal B.P. (the intercept of the stratigraphically higher date, Beta-122916; 1420 B.C.) and 3312 cal B.P. (the intercept of the lower date, Beta-122917; 1285 B.C.), or squarely during Poverty Point's peak (Gibson 2000; see Connolly 2001 for an alternative stratigraphic interpretation). Other radiocarbon-dated early pottery sites—Teoc Creek (Connaway et al. 1977) and Claiborne (Bruseth 1991)—are of similar age, statistically speaking.[1] Jaketown's dates run later (Ford et al. 1955), but they were assayed during the early days of radiocarbon dating and are not representative of the age of the Poverty Point component.[2] Jaketown's dating dilemma is confounded because James Ford and colleagues concluded that the Poverty Point occupation was prepottery and that first pottery came in during the ensuing Tchula period or possibly slightly before, during a postulated fiber-tempered horizon (Ford et al. 1955). The chances of finding a fiber-tempered horizon that fits that interval are about as remote as spotting a 6-foot-4 hobbit with piercing, deep-set eyes (Gibson 1995).[3] Ruth Canal and Meche-Wilkes have not been radiocarbon dated, but we fully expect that their campfires burned before Poverty Point's last fire flickered out.

FIRST POTTERY

Clarence Webb's (1977:fig. 16; Webb et al. 1970) characterization remains the best general description of Poverty Point pottery to date (also see Ford et al. 1955 and Phillips et al. 1951 for typological descriptions). Webb identifies four ware classes: fiber tempered (often called Wheeler after the early Alabama series [Sears and Griffin 1950]); sand tempered (often called Alexander after the Alabama series [Haag 1939]); untempered (often referred to as St. Johns after the Florida series [Goggin 1952; Griffin 1945b]); and clay and clay-grit tempered (often called Tchefuncte or "Old Floyd" Tchefuncte after the resident Lower Mississippi series [Ford and Quimby 1945; Gibson 1995]). By adhering to Webb's characterization, we are only following long-standing convention. Not all sites with Poverty Point components have all four pastes; some do, but others have fewer. Teoc Creek, for instance, has only fiber-tempered ware; Claiborne, fiber tempered and untempered; and Meche-Wilkes, fiber tempered and clay-grit tempered.

First pottery includes both plain and decorated surfaces—sometimes decorations are rare, sometimes common (Figures 8.2 and 8.3). Gibson's detailed breakdown of Poverty Point pottery reveals that the assemblage contains decorative techniques and motifs found on early ceramics across the Gulf Coast (Gibson 1973, 2000; see also Webb 1977; Webb et al. 1970). Free

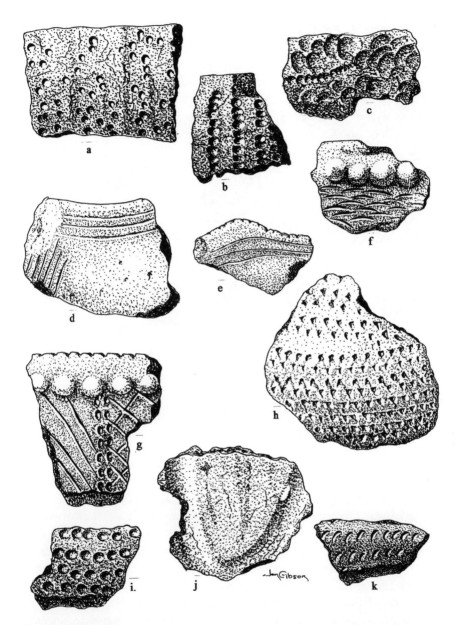

Figure 8.2. First pottery from the Poverty Point site: a, free fingernail punctating, fiber tempered; b, vertically aligned tool punctating, fiber tempered; c, free fingertip dimpling, fiber tempered; d–e, multiple-line incising, chalky untempered; f, nondentate rocker stamping, clay-grit; g, paneled incising and cross-hatching, clay-grit; h, two-pronged tool rocker stamping, clay-grit; i, horizontally aligned tool punctating, clay-grit; j, fingertip grooving, clay-grit; k, horizontally aligned fingernail punctating, clay-grit. Carl Alexander and Clarence Webb collections. Drawn from illustrations in Webb et al. 1970 by Jon Gibson.

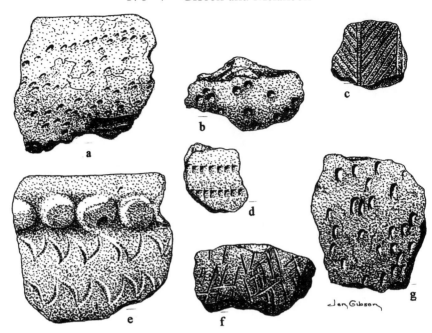

Figure 8.3. First pottery from the Jaketown site: a, free tool punctating, fiber tempered; b, free tool punctating, clay-grit; c, simple narrow incising, clay-grit; d, drag and jab incising, clay-grit; e, nondentate rocker stamping, clay-grit; f, simple stamping, clay-grit; g, free fingernail punctating, clay-grit. Drawn from illustrations in Ford et al. 1955 by Jon Gibson.

and vertically aligned fingernail and tool punctation (Figure 8.2a–b, Figure 8.3a), vertical fingertip grooving, free fingertip dimpling (Figure 8.2c), and simple stamping adorn fiber-tempered wares. Clay- and clay-grit-tempered wares display fingernail and fingertip punctating-pinching (horizontal rows of vertically oriented nail impressions; closely spaced horizontal rows of shallow nail impressions [Figure 8.2k]; all-over vertically aligned back-to-back fingernail impressions resembling gar fish skin; vertical or horizontally oriented fingernail gouging; free or nonaligned fingernail impressions [Figure 8.3g]; shallow fingertip grooving [Figure 8.2j]; and two-finger ridge pinching). Also found on clay- and clay-grit-tempered wares are unzoned tool punctating (horizontally oriented [Figure 8.2i] and free [Figure 8.3b]); zoned tool punctating (bordered by drag and jab lines); simple incising (wide-line incising and panels filled with narrow-line diagonal or hatched incising separated by lines of fingernail punctating or drag and jab incising [Figure 8.2g, Figure 8.3c]); drag and jab incising (horizontally or diagonally oriented [Figure 8.3d]); simple stamping (Figure 8.3f); and rocker stamping (plain [nondentate; Figure 8.2f, Figure 8.3e], wide rows of stamping with accentuated indentations at ends of rocker impressions, and two-pronged tool stamping [Figure 8.2h]). Free and linear fingernail-impressed and tool-punctated designs rarely appear on sand-tempered ware.

Clarence Webb and Gibson call the fourth ware untempered (Figure 8.2d, e). This is a chalky white to crème-colored, smooth-textured pottery that when rubbed leaves a residue on the fingers. The reference "untempered" is ill-chosen, for the possibility looms large that much of the other early pottery is untempered too, although it contains natural pedogenic or anthropogenic inclusions (see Gertjejansen et al. 1983; Gibson 1993:80).[4] In the days before trace-element analysis became routine, Webb and Gibson presumed this crème-colored pottery was made of kaolin clay (see Gagliano and Webb 1970). Small to minute lumps of white clay (kaolin or kaolinite?) are shot through Poverty Point's building fill, and occasionally this clay is used to form pavements atop lenses of fill (Gibson 1993:16–17). And white to olive-colored clay, which is or looks kaolinitic, occurs naturally in the Crowley soil stratigraphic unit, which lies 2 to 3 m below the loess mantle on the landform on which Poverty Point sits (Allen 1990; Allen and Touchet 1990). These white clays are exposed in the walls of deep ravines and along the eroding bayou bank.

Webb (1977:fig. 20 [10–12]) points out that designs on this soft, chalky, nonfiber-tempered pottery resemble those of Orange Incised (Figure 8.2d–e)—rectangular bands or zones of narrow multiple-line incising separated by plain lands (cf. Ford 1969:181–182). It is this pottery that Haag (1990) and Hays and Weinstein (this volume) identify as St. Johns spiculate ware from Florida—a pronouncement neither proven nor disproven by petrographic analyses. James Stoltman (this volume) finds that the chalky pottery is not made from Poverty Point's native loess (at least not from the deep, unweathered loessial sediment), which leaves open the possibility of a Florida origin. But just because the untempered chalky ware resembles St. Johns pottery and contains sponge spicules like St. Johns does not mean, ipso facto, that it is St. Johns pottery from Florida. Decorations, when present, look like Orange 3 styles. And Laura Tanley (1999) has found sponge spicules in Tchefuncte pottery pastes at a site located west of Lake Pontchartrain in southeastern Louisiana. Analysts simply are going to have to do a lot more systematic petrographic testing of local clay sources before some of us replace Occam's Razor with St. Johns oyster knives.

Stoltman's studies also reveal that Poverty Point's clay-grit and most fiber-tempered wares are not made from loess either. Yet as sandy, silty, and clayey alluvium all occur along the bayou and swamp immediately adjacent to the earthen rings, and as this has not been analyzed, Stoltman's discovery that loess was not used does not necessarily implicate exotic origins. On the other hand, Anthony Ortmann and Tristram Kidder's petrographic analysis is unable to distinguish "clay" used for Poverty Point pottery from Poverty Point's native soils (Ortmann and Kidder, this volume), which leaves open the possibility of local origin.

PRESUMPTIONS ABOUT FUNCTIONS

A simple matter worries us: If first pottery is used for cooking, then why is it so uncommon? If it is revolutionary and lifestyle altering (Smith 1986), how do imported soapstone vessels manage to gain and keep a corner on the container market after pottery appears? Why does cooking with loess briquettes continue to be the number-one means of preparing food? Could it be that first pottery isn't technologically suitable for use over open fires? Could it be that it isn't used for daily cooking at all (see Clark and Blake 1994; Clark and Gosser 1995; Hayden 1995a, 2001; Hoopes 1995)?

We look into the function issue from two angles, archaeological and physical. Archaeological context bears directly and indirectly on pottery function, and physical utility or performance shows us just how efficacious first pottery may have been as cookware. Although association and fitness do not in and of themselves answer the question of function, they do inform possibilities.

Our study builds on presumptions about functions. We presume that baked-earth briquettes were heating elements for earth ovens and hearths (Ford and Webb 1956; Webb et al. 1970). If the results of modern experiments are adequate measures, and we have every reason to believe they are, they uphold the solid performance of the earth oven–clay briquette cooking appliance (Gibson 2000; Hunter 1975; Mitchell Hillman and Dennis La-Batt, personal communications, 1978). Loess briquettes scattered in the coals of fire pits should prolong cooking temperatures without the need to add more wood. We presume that hot rocks were also used as heating elements (Jones 1997; Oyuela-Caycedo 1995), only not in ovens and open fire pits. Why? Fire-cracked rock (FCR) is not concentrated in or around hearths but is widely scattered throughout Poverty Point–age middens. Comparing data from Gibson's (1987, 1989, 1990b, 1993, 1997) excavations, Joe Saunders (2002:12–13) reports a strong statistical correlation between the distributions of loess briquette fragments and FCR, which could very well stem from both being used for some common household task like cooking. In our experience FCR appears before loess cooking briquettes in the Lower Mississippi Valley, but it is important to remember that at Poverty Point both means of cooking are employed at the same time. We think it likely that hot rocks are plopped directly into stews and court bouillons heating in stone and clay vessels (what Sassaman [1995b] calls moist indirect cooking), leaving the resulting shrapnel to be thrown out with the garbage. Shrapnel would have settled on vessel bottoms, so food or drink could have been consumed without diners being overly paranoid about cracked teeth or perforated intestines. However, kids would have had to be warned early on not to scrape the bottom of the pot. We don't believe that exploding rocks would have packed enough wallop to break pots, except possibly a big, poorly made, thin-walled clay-grit container, but then we imagine cooks knew which pots they could use and which ones they couldn't. We also envision stone and clay pots simmering away over glowing coals.

PERFORMANCE AND UTILITY OF PORTABLE CONTAINERS

We like to think that most of the time it is the intrinsic qualities of equipment that make it better suited for certain jobs than others. With this caveat in mind, we consider how well pots performed and how easy they were to use. Although our arguments are based on efficiency and reliability in cooking as the comparative standard, we are not prejudging portable containers to be cooking pots—we are only assessing how well they would have functioned in that capacity.

Fiber-tempered pots would have been better suited for indirect cooking (or heating from within) than for cooking over flames or in beds of coals (Sassaman 1993a, 1995b). Thick vessel walls and fiber tempering would have acted as insulation against heat loss. Wide mouths would have facilitated the introduction of hot rocks and removal of shrapnel—easy in, easy out.

Although our claims have not been experimentally confirmed, what we remember from high school physics leads us to believe that thinner-walled clay-grit pots would have heated up more quickly over open fires. Also, we think that deep bowl and jar shapes would have held heat, which otherwise would have been lost if vessels had been shallower or orifices wider (relative to height). Four-lobed basal architecture is more suitable for building taller vessels (see Gertjejansen et al. 1983). Pot legs and ring bases (kickups) would have distributed heat evenly during firing and cooking, lessening chances of vessel failure from differential heat absorption. They additionally would have promoted thermal efficiency by raising the pot above cooler ashes and permitting flames to circulate underneath, and efficient pots would have conserved firewood over the long run—good news for kids delivering firewood. We also think that low-fired, untempered (loessial or kaolinitic clay) pots would have made poor boilers because fabrics would rehydrate during cooking, adding mud flavor to contents, but floated surfaces on clay-grit pots would have combated the mud-seasoning problem.

Soapstone vessels would have been tough and durable, resistant to thermal shock, rough handling, and klutzes (Sassaman 1993a, 1995b). But they would have been hard to replace, as they were long-distance imports from the Appalachian foothills, and they were heavy, weighing when full anywhere from a few to upwards of 12 to 15 pounds (which is why they often bore lugs or handles). They also would have lacked flexibility, not because they are made of stone, but because Georgian or Alabaman stone carvers shaped and sized them, not their Poverty Point owners.

SPECULATIONS BASED ON PERFORMANCE CAPABILITIES, WHIMS, AND GUT FEELINGS

Given these arguments, we suggest that more thermally efficient clay-grit vessels and soapstone containers would have been better suited for open-fire cooking, whereas fiber-tempered and untempered pots would have been better for indirect hot-rock cooking. If so, then it follows that different kinds of pottery vessels and soapstone pots helped resolve conflicting work and meal-preparation schedules, including giving feasts. Reusable, easy-to-carry, clay-grit pots would have solved the problem of cooks having to dig new earth ovens every time old ones got covered with a new layer of construction dirt. Portability would have been crucial. Easy-to-carry clay-grit- and fiber-tempered pots taken to active construction sites enabled construction workers to fix meals and render oil and lard while they hauled dirt. Clay-grit- and fiber-tempered pots were lighter than soapstone hernia-makers, evoking a Pyrex dish vs. cast-iron Dutch oven comparison. If clay-grit pots got broken in the hustle and bustle around construction areas, all would not have been lost. All a cook had to do was fetch another from home or make a replacement. But breaking soapstone cookware would have been a calamity. A new soapstone container might have cost your favorite daughter in exchange or a long, arduous journey into the Georgia outback. The bottom line in this cascading speculation is that pottery vessels of all kinds caught on as labor-saving devices during busy construction periods and continued afterwards because they simplified meal preparation—they were Poverty Point's equivalent of cheap or disposable, all-purpose cookware. They turned out some tasty mulligans and court bouillons, too, providing relief from the usual fare of roasted venison, baked fish, and kunti bread. Besides, pots used in open-fire cooking did not leave all that crunchy FCR in the gumbo.

May, might, can, would, could—we could go on marshaling physical performance and utility arguments, pro and con, about clay and stone vessels' cooking capabilities, but one overriding truth renders all performance arguments inconsequential. If ceramic and stone vessels had been the primary means of fixing food, then residents of Poverty Point and Jaketown would have starved to death within a short time and would have been gaunt and hollow-eyed at Meche-Wilkes. Most, if not all, everyday cooking was in the hands of bakers, grillers, and hot-rock cooks using built-in appliances and perishable containers. The sheer abundance of earthen briquette residue and FCR makes cooking in pottery and stone vessels of small importance, no matter how good and thermally efficient the pots were. First pottery simply is too scarce everywhere in the Lower Mississippi Valley to have bolstered or eased food preparation, except during busy construction moments or other extraordinary events. And I emphasize that first pottery's scarcity does not seem to be a case of a brand-new technology struggling to grab a foothold. Pottery was known from the outset of monumental construction.

But do we have empirical support for pottery's link to such special moments? And if not spicy court bouillon or mulligan-on-the-stick, what engendered first pottery?

COMPARING COOKING RESIDUES OR "APPLES AND ORANGES"

We begin our inquiry by comparing first pottery with other presumed cooking residues at Poverty Point, Jaketown, and Meche-Wilkes, three sites with substantial excavated data. This comparison is designed to show how pottery meshed with other food- and drink-preparation technologies. Enmeshed thus, pottery's place in Poverty Point's domestic and political economies, as well as its social interactions, both local and far-reaching, ought to be illuminated. Pottery is compared with residues from earth oven–baked loess briquette, hot-rock, and stone-pot cooking technologies. All are historically coextensive, but whether they are complementary, optional, or alternative cooking methods or something completely different is at issue.

At all three sites, early pottery is limited in comparison with other cooking residues. Earthen cooking briquette fragments make up over 90 percent of the materials everywhere. Although inconsistently collected and reported, FCR seems to be less abundant—one piece for between 30 and 80 briquette fragments at Poverty Point and Meche-Wilkes (Gibson 1990a:tables 26–27, 2000). And this difference is not because hot loess breaks more readily than hot rocks. Our cooking experiments have shown just the opposite; apparently rock is more susceptible to thermal shock than loess. FCR has not been reported from Jaketown. Soapstone vessel fragments are less common than fire-cracked shrapnel, but soapstone representation is highly variable. Soapstone is more plentiful than pottery at Poverty Point—one large collection contains about nine soapstone vessel fragments for every piece of pottery—and less plentiful at Jaketown (Ford et al. 1955; Lehmann 1982). Soapstone is not reported at Meche-Wilkes. Among pottery classes, sherds of clay- or clay-grit-tempered ware are more common than pieces of fiber-tempered ware by about three to one (Gibson 1973; Webb 1977); untempered ware is rare at Poverty Point and Jaketown and missing at Meche-Wilkes. The important thing to remember is that pottery of all kinds is the least common material of all.

Stratigraphic comparisons reveal interesting statistical associations, which we consider important for modeling practical and social dimensions of first pottery. Those comparisons are enabled by a simple, time-honored descriptive statistic, mean vertical position (MVP; Ford et al. 1955). MVPs are critical to our analyses. They allow us to plot building succession in the rings, thereby revealing the relative "popularity" of cooking and containing utensils during construction. MVPs are precomputer statistics. All you need to do the math is, as William Haag used to say, "One eye and half a brain." Plus a pencil. What you do is multiply the number of artifacts—say, for instance, fiber-tempered sherds—recovered from each excavation level by the number of the level (e.g., Level 1, Level 2, and so on). Then you add up those products and divide the sum by the total number of artifacts. Voilà, you have the MVP, or average excavation level, of fiber-tempered pottery.

Poverty Point and Jaketown MVPs are taken from Gibson (1995) and Ford et al. (1955), respectively (see Table 8.1). MVPs are only good for intrasite comparisons, and even then caution is needed when comparing excavations from constructed areas with those from nonconstructed areas, especially when separate earthworks or widely separated parts of the same large earthwork are involved. For example, Gibson finds that clay-grit-tempered ware has the lowest overall stratigraphic position (largest MVP) of all Poverty Point's pottery. But as he maintains (Gibson 2001, 2002), having the lowest average position in Poverty Point's massive earthen rings does not necessarily make clay-grit pottery earlier than untempered, sand-tempered, or fiber-tempered ceramics. All four ceramics seem to have been made from the start of ring construction to the finish (although sand-tempered ware is too scarce to verify the claim). What is actually revealed by comparing MVPs from different sections of the Poverty Point site is a ceramic record of building progression—which section of the rings was put up first, second, third, and so on (Gibson 2001, 2002). Gibson contends that the ring-building span was too short to incorporate long-term historical or evolutionary trends.

At Poverty Point, relative stratigraphy as shown by MVPs discloses that

Table 8.1. Relative stratigraphy based on MVPs, Poverty Point and Jaketown.

	Poverty Point	Jaketown
Poverty Point Objects		
Biconical	4.9	15.2
Cross grooved	4.6	17.0
Cylindrical grooved	6.5	10.9
Melon grooved	4.8	—
Pottery		
Sand tempered	3.5	4.7
Clay-grit tempered	4.7	5.0
Fiber tempered	2.6	5.5
Unspecified temper	6.0	—
Untempered	3.3	—
Soapstone	3.5	Present
FCR	3.3	—

Note: These statistics are not available for Meche-Wilkes excavations. Poverty Point data are based on 95 test units excavated by Gibson in all sections of the earthen rings, as well as in some off-ring locations. Jaketown data are based on Trench 5 excavated by Ford and associates (Ford et al. 1955:table 7).

cylindrical grooved briquettes peak first (have the lowest average stratigraphic position, MVP = 6.5), followed by biconical (4.9) and melon-shaped (4.8) briquettes, clay-grit-tempered pottery (4.7), and cross-grooved briquettes (4.6). Higher in the stratigraphic succession are untempered pottery (3.3), soapstone vessel fragments (3.5), FCR (3.3), and finally fiber-tempered pottery (2.6). We won't go into details of building progression. For our purposes here, these sitewide MVPs suffice to compare kitchen-gear popularity, or rather utilization, through time and thus provide us with evidence of short-term historical shifts in use during construction of Poverty Point's central rings.

Our preliminary observations are that clay-grit- and fiber-tempered fabrics occur from top to bottom in the mound at Meche-Wilkes with fiber-tempered pottery spiking below clay-grit tempered. FCR is too scarce to matter, as is stonework of all kinds (Gibson 1990a:table 27). Despite being plentiful, briquette fragments defy stratigraphic ordering, because they are generally too small to identify, and the few bigger pieces are broken from unique forms lacking counterparts at Poverty Point and Jaketown. The intriguing thing about Meche-Wilkes is that briquettes and fiber-tempered pottery are confined to the mound and are essentially missing in the adjoining midden (Gibson 1990a:110–111). At Jaketown, cross-grooved briquettes peak first (MVPs = 14.6 and 17.0 in Trench 1 and Trench 5, respectively; Ford et al. 1955), followed by biconical (14.0, 15.2) and cylindrical grooved (8.7, 10.9) briquettes. Early pottery is much higher—fiber tempered (MVP = 5.5, Trench 5 only) and then clay-grit tempered (4.2, Trench 1; 5.0, Trench 5). These MVPs are for decorated fractions of these wares only (identified as early pottery from their type names; Ford et al. 1955:table 7). MVPs for plain wares are not calculated and cannot be, because data are presented graphically and not as frequencies. Although decorated fiber-tempered ware in general is lower stratigraphically than decorated clay-grit materials, a clay-grit-tempered type, Tchefuncte Incised, actually has the distinction of peaking below all other types of pottery (MVP = 6.5, Trench 5), and another clay-grit-tempered type, Jaketown Simple Stamped, is lower too (MVP = 5.7, Trench 1).[5] So, at Jaketown as at Poverty Point, we have indications that clay-grit-tempered pottery peaked stratigraphically below fiber-tempered pottery. What makes this all the more interesting is that these indications come from Ford and associates' own hands (Ford et al. 1955), a clear case of normative reasoning (viewing data as averages) and of a favorite theory (fiber-tempered horizon) absorbing data that don't fit.[6]

ASSOCIATION BETWEEN POTTERY AND PLACES OF MOUNDS AND RESIDENCES

One of archaeology's basic premises is that association and context hold functional meaning. An obvious area to look for a potential association is between mound building and food containers. Our argument about pottery being a labor-saving utensil presumes just such a relationship, but do empirical associations warrant that interpretation?

First pottery is found on Poverty Point components with and without mounds. Poverty Point–age earthworks are confirmed at greater Poverty Point, Jaketown, and Meche-Wilkes. Claiborne once had a mound, but Teoc Creek didn't. More than two decades ago, Webb (1977:table 18) reported early pottery from 18 Poverty Point or related components located east of the lower Mississippi River, but he records only four, including greater Poverty Point, west of the river. Despite recognizing that other paste classes are early too, Webb includes only sites with fiber-tempered pottery on his checklist. Why? Because he knows archaeologists will have no qualms accepting fiber-tempered pottery as early, but to suggest that other pastes are as early would be heretical and scandalous beyond redemption (see endnote 6). As nearly as we can tell, of all the east-bank sites with fiber-tempered pottery, only Jaketown and Claiborne have mounds (Webb 1977:table 18).

Coles Crossroads has mounds—although not certainly of Poverty Point age —but no pottery (Webb 1977:table 18). Only two of the four west-bank sites recorded by Webb (1977:table 18) have mounds: Insley is one (Griffing 1990) and Poverty Point itself, the other. Webb was unaware of the Meche-Wilkes mound.

Ongoing research within Poverty Point's immediate vicinity has updated Webb's checklist (Gibson 1996a, 1998b; Griffing 1990). Four additional pottery-bearing Poverty Point components are among the 55 components now known. Yet, except for greater Poverty Point, Insley is the only one with mounds (Beyer 1900; Griffing 1990). The other three early pottery–bearing sites—Orvis Scott, Terral Lewis, and Stockland Plantation—are moundless (Gibson 1996a, 1998b; Gregory 1991).

About one in three (16 of 55) components produce soapstone-vessel fragments (Gibson 1998b), and fewer than half of them—greater Poverty Point, Alexander Point, Motley East, Steatite Field, Honey Hole, Locality 2 (16WF54), and Morrow–Lower Jackson (16WC10)—support nearby mounds. Yet, all but Insley (16FR3) and Neely Place (16WC4) are core components lying in the shadow of greater Poverty Point's mounds. Their mounds are its mounds. Soapstone-bearing components without mounds in Poverty Point's periphery include Hendrix, Aaron (16EC39), Arledge (16EC119), Orvis Scott, J. W. Copes (16MA47), Terral Lewis (16MA16), and Stockland Plantation.[7]

A fifty-fifty correlation is not a ringing endorsement for a functional link between soapstone-vessel use and mound building, especially when nearly half of the half that do have soapstone are neighborhoods of greater Poverty Point. But mound building and early pottery are associated. Although early pottery is not limited to mound components, nearly all mound-bearing Poverty Point components have pottery, generally bearing the combination of pastes crucial to the multiple-use hypothesis (Gibson 2000). Out in Poverty Point's periphery, only Insley and Neely (no early pottery recorded) have mounds, but whether they are Poverty Point–age constructions has yet to be confirmed. As a matter of fact, the only sure Poverty Point–age earthworks occur at greater Poverty Point. Outside Poverty Point's homeland, Jaketown, Claiborne, and Meche-Wilkes have mounds and early pottery. Throughout the Lower Mississippi Valley, all components with proven Poverty Point–age earthworks also yield the combination suite of early pottery pastes.

So, mounds and early pottery go together. Mounds and soapstone don't. And these findings nicely fit our speculations about varied sorts of containers filling distinctive functional niches during ongoing construction.

Another means of seeing how container technologies are enmeshed is by comparing their dispersal at field camps and residences. Of the known Poverty Point components in Poverty Point's homeland, only a quarter yield sufficient information to be identified as field camp or residence (Gibson 1998b). Soapstone is found on five of the seven field camps but early pottery on only one. Among the eight residences, soapstone is found on seven and early pottery on only two. Thus, soapstone enjoys wide use in Poverty Point's homeland no matter whether the encampment is a field camp or residence. Pottery, on the other hand, simply is not an integral part of the gear at camps or residences. Out in Poverty Point's hinterland, the use of durable soapstone vessels smacks of practicality. To be sure, stone pots are heavy if carried on the pate or shoulder but not if stowed in the dugout. Even fishing or root-grubbing parties spending a night or two away from home have to eat, and durable soapstone cooking pots provide a perfect solution for the knocks and bumps of trail and boat road. Breakable pottery doesn't. Still, we suspect that fragility is only part of the reason pottery is not used more widely. The main reason, we contend, is that it is used only during special occasions—those busy times when fixing fast food and supplying drinking water for hot, thirsty construction workers or serving special food and drink to celebrants at feasts and other ceremonies is demanded. Pottery, in our view, has both practical and social uses, but we suggest the practical is limited to busy construction moments, the social, to festive occasions. Places where both building and celebrating occur are where first pottery is found.

TIES TO EARTHWORKS

First pottery is associated with earthwork-bearing components, but is it tied directly to the earthworks themselves? Do actions undertaken on mounds during or after construction entail use of pottery, or is pottery produced by other actions that prevail on mound components but that are carried out less frequently on sites without mounds? How can we tell? Well, for one thing, we can check intrasite pottery distribution to see whether it peaks in, on, or around earthworks. For another, we can come up with performance and utility arguments about pottery as drinking and serving vessels, just as we did about its performance as cooking pots. So, our case builds partly from empirical distribution but primarily from argument.

First, witness these contexts and associations. At Poverty Point, pottery occurs throughout the vertical extent of various ring segments, as well as off-earthwork areas. Excavations in one of Poverty Point's small mounds inside the plaza expose several successive platforms, arguably ritual stages, but produce no pottery (Gibson 1984). A small bit of pottery is recovered from Meche-Wilkes mound, but most derives from the adjoining midden (Gibson 1990a, 2000; Melancon 1999). Meche-Wilkes mound contains primarily fragments of cooking briquettes. We can't say for sure about Jaketown. A small Poverty Point–age mound apparently produces no pottery (Ford et al. 1955), but there is a possibility that some stratigraphic layers previously interpreted as natural fluvial deposits actually may be mound fill, in which case Jaketown's first pottery is associated with mound construction. By and large, too few excavations and first pottery's rarity combine to prevent a confident conclusion, one way or the other, about pottery's direct ties to mounds.

Second, witness vessel morphology. Size and shape can help us determine which pots are better for cooking and which for drinking and serving. We have previously rated vessels on cooking performance, but what about drinking and serving? You don't want a mug that's too heavy (soapstone pot) or that spills more in your lap than down your throat (wide mouths). Cup- or dipper-shaped bowls are better suited for serving hot beverages such as holly tea and soupy dishes such as mulligan and court bouillon, and cup and bowl forms occur in both pottery and soapstone (Webb 1977; Webb et al. 1970). The main difficulty is that we can't tell how common these forms are compared to shapes better suited for simmering or boiling liquids (e.g., big bowls, deep wide-mouth pots, and neckless jars). All we can say without a complete reanalysis is that vessels suitable for cooking and for serving occurred at Poverty Point (Webb et al. 1970). We have no idea about sizes and shapes at Jaketown. Meche-Wilkes provides the only empirical data at the moment, and wouldn't you know, they are just the opposite of our expectations. In general, mound vessels have mouths a third again wider than pots in the midden (23 cm as opposed to 17 cm).[8] Decorated vessels, ostensibly the most special of the special, have orifices a third again wider than plain ones (27 cm as opposed to 17 cm). In fact, decorated pots from the mound are almost twice as big as decorated pots from the midden, and we expected just the opposite.

Neckless, globular-bodied vessels, or tecomates, in either pottery or soapstone, make the best containers for fermentation, but Lower Mississippi Valley natives lack a beer-making tradition, or else conservative Archaic heliolaters are closet drinkers. They have neither corn nor palm fruit to brew, although native fruits and berries abound, which keeps the prospect of fruit cocktail wine from being dismissed out-of-hand.

Some soapstone and pottery forms have such small, rounded, even conical, bottoms that they cannot stand upright (Gagliano and Webb 1970:fig. 6). Although they can be stabilized by pushing them deep into ash beds or soft ground or putting them in racks or frames, lacking support, they make better dippers and serving dishes than cooking pots. Obviously, liquid- and food-holding vessels need to be free-standing or propped up somehow.

Size and shape details are a good source of information and ideas. Unfortunately, they are not as helpful as they could be, because they are inconsistently reported and, even when reported, usually are given as averages rather than as discrete measurements and attributes.

POTTERY'S PLACE IN THE SUN

What is the point of all this talk about first pottery's correlation with mound components and link to mounds? What is wrong with pottery being used for everyday cooking? Absolutely nothing from a physical viewpoint; absolutely everything judging by its scarcity. If pottery is daily cookware, it ought to be one of the most abundant materials remaining at residences. It is not. So, we are left grasping at functional will-o'-the-wisps that can make sense of its rarity and its association with mounds and mound sites. We are searching for first pottery's place in the sun.

Discovering how first pottery is used is not the Holy Grail. Yet, how it functions and the contexts in which it functions lie close to the heart of the matter—why pottery is adopted in the first place. Poverty Point and the Lower Mississippi Valley are not cradles of the "container revolution" (Smith 1986). First potteries "came into" the Lower Mississippi Valley via stimulus diffusion from the eastern Gulf area, where they date as much as a thousand years earlier (Walthall and Jenkins 1976). Even homegrown clay-grit-tempered pottery (Tchefuncte) derives artistically, though not technologically, from eastern Gulf prototypes (Ned Jenkins, personal communication, 2003; cf. Hays and Weinstein, this volume). Are you proud of us yet, Ned Jenkins? The sort of stimulus diffusion we think responsible has been described as dependent invention—a case of one group assimilating ideas and technical know-how from another while adapting the technology to suit its own ends, often in ways that differ from how the technology was used in the donor group (Clark and Gosser 1995:209–210). It reminds us of the eighteenth-century Tunica-Biloxi group living on the Red River who acquired Spanish and French silver coins, not to spend, but to convert into ornaments (Gregory and Webb 1971) or the eighteenth-century Attakapa of upper Bayou Teche who chipped scrapers from French wine bottles (although we're confident the Attakapa and the French Acadians used the contents the same way). Pottery may have been practical cookware in the eastern Gulf area, but it doesn't seem to have caught on that way in the Lower Mississippi Valley, at least at first.

Too rare to be used for daily cooking, pottery, we contend, served ritual and/or labor-management purposes—specialized contexts that mark pottery's place in the sun. From coastal Panama to coastal Georgia, first pottery is envisioned as ritual drink- and food-serving containers (Clark and Blake 1994; Clark and Gosser 1995; Hoopes 1995; Russo 2004; Russo and Heide, this volume; Saunders, this volume). Employed thus, pottery becomes a prestige technology for individuals and families striving to gain esteem and influence via competitive or reciprocal feasting (Hayden 1995a, 1995b, 2001). Yet, there is nothing inherently contradictory about a prestige technology having a practical side too, such as turning out labor-saving, expedient cookware for use during peak construction periods.

Public-event and construction service may explain why Poverty Point pottery is linked with earthworks and earthwork-bearing components. Important mound places play host to important gatherings, and gatherings are celebrated with ceremonies, ball games, and other rituals (Hayden 2001; Swanton 1911, 1931). Almost all gatherings are accompanied by feasts, and feasts require serving containers, hence warranting an easily replaceable service like pottery provides.

FIRST POTTERY AND LOCAL INTERACTION

We don't have microscopic or material details to share and, lacking them, cannot offer revelations on broad-scale ceramic diffusion or on the web of in-group and between-group social interactions responsible for it. From our armchair, it looks like pottery came into the Lower Mississippi Valley from various places in the Southeast via unfathomed means of historically slow or interrupted information transfer across the pinewood hills, along the Gulf Coast, and straight down the Tennessee-Mississippi river line. Just glancing at the sizeable number of components having fiber-tempered ware in Mississippi's Yazoo Basin compared with the mere handful on the Louisiana side of the river suggests the direction of origin (Webb 1977:table 18). First pottery's ostensibly multiple origins are connected with far-reaching events and interactions focused on Poverty Point, as Jenkins has long maintained (Jenkins et al. 1986). But precisely how information transfers are accomplished, as well as the roles of various actors and social networks involved in the transfers, has yet to be modeled explicitly (cf. Sassaman 1993a, 1995b, 2000, 2001).[9]

Function and association provide our manna, but they oblige us to focus our attention on local interaction, not on far-flung socializing and politicking. What does first pottery tell us about Poverty Point interaction, interaction between folks from the ringed inner sanctum and those from nearby neighborhoods and between greater Poverty Point in general and its surrounding hinterland (core vis-à-vis periphery, see Gibson 1998b)?

First, since we presume that all Poverty Point's neighborhoods are contemporary with its central-ring district, in whole or in part (Gibson 2000),[10] we hold pottery's confinement to the ring-enclosed center as indicating actions carried out exclusively within its inner sanctum. If pots are made and brought in by worshipers or revelers from the 'hoods, there ought to be some pottery at those residences. That there is not merely underscores the likelihood that pottery is a ritual ware or a ware used to ease the labor of mound building instead of common cookware. A similar situation exists in Poverty Point's hinterland where small amounts of pottery occur only on residential components having earthworks constructed during Poverty Point times, such as at Insley, one of the largest but most distant components in Poverty Point's hinterland (Gibson 1998b; Sassaman and Heckenberger 2004).

But what manner of interaction is suggested? As Gibson (2004) notes, raising Poverty Point's earthworks required labor far exceeding the capabilities of modern nomadic and sedentary hunter-gatherers. Estimates, based on how much work was required to build Nanih Waiya, the sacred Choctaw mound (Lincecum 1904), suggest that Poverty Point's labor force totaled between 700 and 800 dirt movers, drawn from a supporting pool of 2,000–2,500 people. Presumably, workers came not only from greater Poverty Point but from all over the homeland and possibly beyond. Poverty Point's earthworks embody standard measures and ritual counts of calendrical importance—the same set of proportions, spacing, and orientations that inheres in first monumental constructions throughout the Americas (Clark 2004; Sassaman and Heckenberger 2004). Employing that many workers and celebrating an ancient cosmic numerology point straight to sacred motives for at least some interactions, those most responsible for making Poverty Point sociality different from all preceding and contemporary formations.

We contend that feast-sponsoring ritual built Poverty Point, not directly but indirectly. How? By bringing together, physically and spiritually, family and friend, neighbor and acquaintance, ally and potential adversary, and filling them with powerful rallying casuistry, joyous friendship, and uplifting unity—the core sentiments that define a people and its allies socially and politically and that, by setting off one group, also define all others as outsiders, both real and supernatural. But ritual not only sets the stage for action and draws the lines of resistance (see Sassaman 2000, 2001), it is also the raw material of tradition itself (Pauketat 2001). There is no greater expression of a people than its rituals. And these are the contexts that give rise to first pottery. In this sense, it makes no difference whether pottery is manufactured on site or imported from afar. It makes no difference whether pottery represents a prestige or practical technology (*sensu* Hayden 1995a). The contexts that produce first pottery are the same regardless.

Scenarios that accommodate data and theory are limited only by our imagination—befeathered Poverty Point leaders toasting their counterparts from Claiborne or Jaketown with pottery mugs full of fruit wine or black drink; feast hosts serving participating family heads from clay pots; dirty, tired construction workers quenching their thirst with bayou water delivered to building sites in pottery ewers; or construction teams cooking meals in clay vessels over open fires built atop temporary surfaces on under-construction earthen rings. Trying to ascertain first pottery's origin is rendered all the more difficult because the contexts in which it occurs are not steeped with familiar signs of hereditary inequality, of prestigious exclusion (Hayden 1995b). A corporate essence permeates Poverty Point materiality to the core, or so it seems judging from the vantage of the wide-open accessibility to exotic (and local) stone that seems to be driven by function, not personage trying to outdo personage (Gibson and Griffing 1994). Yet, Poverty Point has those massive earthworks beset with cosmic design (Clark 2004; Gibson 1998a). Its exchange tentacles and enabling political diplomacy invade the far corners of the Mississippi River drainage system and produce exotic rock by the ton, not by the piece. Poverty Point sociality seems so contradictory—in terms of current archaeological rhetoric and chameleonic theory—but it's really not any more contradictory than having the magnate of the world's wealthiest company report to work carrying his lunch in a paper bag or watching the most popular American recording artist perform in a pair of worn-out blue jeans. No, the difficulty lies with us. We have not yet worked out the kinks, the seeming contradictions, in Poverty Point's social calculus.

We point out our ignorance in these matters in order to make the claim that Poverty Point sociality is inherently competitive, only not in the usual sense. Nobody loses; nobody, that is, who belongs to the local group. Everybody wins. Some just win bigger than others, but they don't flaunt the spoils or brag about their good fortunes. There are only temporary spoils anyway. Whatever largess there is quickly gets recirculated into the corporate body, keeping everyone happy and willing to lend a helping hand, working for the principles that guide the group's well being (Gibson 2004). So, it's not so much how people deal with one another that counts, it's how they handle the consequences of these negotiations. It is here amid these dealings that first pottery finds its meaning—its place in the sun.

ACKNOWLEDGMENTS

Poverty Point and Meche-Wilkes excavations were conducted between the late 1970s and the late 1990s by hundreds of university students from the University of Southwestern Louisiana (now University of Louisiana at Lafayette) and other participating universities—Northeast Louisiana University (now University of Louisiana at Monroe) and the University of Akron. Their hard work and hard play generated sufficient materials to give lifetimes of pleasure to archaeology sleuths searching for their meaning, and while we probably could have acquired the materials by our own hands, it would have taken a wee bit longer. Joe Saunders, John Clark, and Jim Stoltman provided commentary on this chapter, some helpful. So did peer reviewers Ned Jenkins and Mike O'Brien. Saunders's view of the Jaketown stratigraphy differs from ours, and we think he may be on to something. Nonetheless, we stubbornly resist changing our view. Still, Bill Haag's words ring in our ears: "We can say without equivocation that despite all our work more excavation needs to be done" (Haag 1990:31). Our friend Thurman Allen provided sediment-size data on loessial soils from Natural Resources Conservation Service analyses. Becky Saunders and Chris Hays are to be blamed for asking us to participate in the symposium that gave rise to this book and have aided and abetted our efforts since. Gibson did the pen-and-inks of the sherds from Poverty Point (Figure 8.2) and Jaketown (Figure 8.3); they were copied from pictures in Webb et al. 1970 and in Ford et al. 1955. Gibson and Mary Lee Eggart (LSU Cartographic Section) prepared Figure 8.1.

9

Petrographic Thin-Section Analysis of Poverty Point Pottery

Anthony L. Ortmann and Tristram R. Kidder

Poverty Point (16WC5), located in West Carroll Parish, Louisiana, is famous for many things, including its earthen architecture, stone artifacts, and long-distance trade. The people who built and occupied Poverty Point are not, however, renowned for their pottery vessel technology, despite being contemporary with and clearly trading with people along the Atlantic and eastern Gulf Coast regions who were producing and using pottery vessels as a regular part of their food cooking technology. Ford and Webb (1956:105–106) recognized that pottery, notably fiber-tempered ware, was an "integral" element of Poverty Point technology. Webb (1982:40–42) further noted that both fiber-tempered and temperless pottery were present at Poverty Point, Claiborne (22HA501) in southern Mississippi, and other Poverty Point sites (Bruseth 1991). These investigators, however, clearly did not feel that pottery was a significant element of Poverty Point technology, and vessel pottery was subsequently not emphasized in most discussions of the site and the culture. The pottery found at Poverty Point was typically attributed to later cultures, primarily the Early Woodland Tchefuncte culture, or to foreign imports into the Poverty Point region. Poverty Point peoples manufactured large numbers of fired-clay cooking balls and a smaller number of fired-clay figurines, indicating that the technological ability to produce fired pottery vessels was within their capacity. Over the past 25 years archaeologists have accumulated a considerable quantity of data suggesting that pottery vessel technology was a minor but important part of Poverty Point material culture (Hays and Weinstein 1999; Webb 1982).

One issue remained to be solved. What was the origin of pottery vessel technology at Poverty Point, and how was this technology maintained through time? Was it largely an indigenous process, stimulated or encouraged by nonlocal imports? Or was the pottery at Poverty Point primarily imported? Results of our thin-sectioning study tentatively suggest that Poverty Point pottery vessel technology is at least partly an indigenous development. Poverty Point people were evidently making temperless (Tchefuncte-like) pottery using local clays; sherds from these pottery vessels are present in all strata of excavated samples that we analyzed. Fiber-tempered pottery, identified as Wheeler Plain, is also present at Poverty Point. Our data suggest that some fiber-tempered vessels were also manufactured locally (see also Stoltman, this volume). In addition to the local industry, Poverty Point people appear to have been importing pottery—most notably St. Johns Plain and contemporary decorated varieties, as well as Orange series pottery, both presumably from Florida (Webb 1982:42).

METHODS

Our research represents an experimental attempt to assess whether pottery pastes can be systematically characterized in terms of their physical attributes using digital-image analysis and whether these data can then be used to assign typological classifications and determine possible origins. Our sample consisted of 19 sherds (Table 9.1). The sherds were thin-sectioned without our knowledge of provenience or typological classification. These sherds, along with seven control samples (Table 9.1), were then analyzed using a technique of computer-assisted petrographic thin-section analysis.

The sample included four wares: Tchefuncte-like, Baytown Plain, Wheeler Plain, and St. Johns Plain and Incised. In addition to the potsherds, two Poverty Point Objects were obtained from surface collections and thin-sectioned. Sediment samples were collected from two locations in Harlan Bayou on the north side of the Poverty Point site during the winter of 1999 and were fired using an electric kiln. The samples from the middle of the bank of the bayou consist of the loess soils prevalent throughout Maçon Ridge while sediments obtained from the lower portion of the Harlan Bayou bank appear macroscopically and microscopically to be much sandier than the samples taken from higher on the bank. Finally, one Weeden Island sherd from west Florida was added to the sample.

Each thin section was placed under a polarizing-light microscope at 100× magnification and sampled in five different locations using a digital camera. Each sample represents an area of approximately 2.8×2.1 mm. Micrographs of each sample area were then loaded into Image Pro-Plus, an image-analysis software application. Image Pro-Plus automatically counted all of the particles in each image and measured the average diameter and roundness/angularity of each particle. Roundness is calculated by Image Pro-Plus using the following equation: $(\text{perimeter})^2/(4 \times \pi \times \text{area})$. A value of 1.0 indicates an object is perfectly round; the greater the value, the more angular the object. The average diameter of each object was automatically classified

Table 9.1. Sample identification.

Sample Designation	Classification/ Description	Provenience	Level (depth in cm)
BP1	Baytown Plain, *var. Marksville*	N5228 E4799	1 (0–10)
TP7	Untempered (Tchefuncte Plain)	N5224 E4796	13 (120–130)
SJ1	St. Johns Incised	N5227 E4800	13 (120–130)
SJ2	St. Johns Plain	N5227 E4800	13 (120–130)
SJ3	St. Johns Plain, *var. St. Johns*	N5224 E4796	7 (60–70)
WP3	Wheeler Plain (fiber tempered)	N5638 E4999	3 (20–30)
TP1	Untempered (Tchefuncte Plain)	N5638 E4999	3 (20–30)
TP6	Untempered (Tchefuncte Plain)	N5638 E4999	1 (0–10)
TP2	Untempered (Tchefuncte Plain)	N5638 E4999	3 (20–30)
TP8	Untempered (Tchefuncte Plain)	N5227 E4800	3 (20–30)
BP2	Baytown Plain, *var. unspecified*	N5638 E4999	Root mass
WP1	Wheeler Plain (fiber tempered)	N5152 E4736	5 (40–50)
TP3	Untempered (Tchefuncte Plain)	N5638 E4999	1 (0–10)
WP2	Wheeler Plain (fiber tempered)	N5154 E4736	3 (20–30)
TP4	Untempered (Tchefuncte Plain)	N5152 E4736	4 (30–40)
TP5	Untempered (Tchefuncte Plain)	N5153 E4737	7 (60–70)
BP4	Baytown Plain	N5152 E4736	1 (0–10)
BP3	Baytown Plain	N4761 E4806	Root mass

Table 9.1. *Continued.*

Sample Designation	Classification/ Description	Provenience	Level (depth in cm)
WP4	Wheeler Plain (fiber tempered)	N5558 E4765	Root mass
SS1	Soil sample	Harlan Bayou (Poverty Point site)	Middle bank portion
SS2	Soil sample	Harlan Bayou (Poverty Point site)	Middle bank portion
SS3	Soil sample	Harlan Bayou (Poverty Point site)	Lower bank portion
SS4	Soil sample	Harlan Bayou (Poverty Point site)	Lower bank portion
TEST	Weeden Island Plain	Tampa region	Unknown
PP1	Poverty Point object	Poverty Point site	Surface collected
PP2	Poverty Point object	Poverty Point site	Surface collected

according to the Wentworth scale (Wentworth 1922). Data from the five images of each sample were then combined to produce a cumulative set of measurements.

The data obtained from this investigation were analyzed three different ways to determine whether this method of petrographic thin-section analysis could successfully discriminate between samples. First, the particles were analyzed based on the division of particle size (average diameter) into five categories: clay (0–.004 mm), silt (.004–.0625 mm), very fine sand (v.f.s.; .0625–.125 mm), fine sand (f.s.; .125–.25 mm), and medium sand (m.s.; .25–.5 mm). The data were standardized by z-scores and subjected to a linked-pair cluster analysis (Figure 9.1). Results suggest that the samples form three discrete clusters.

Principal components analysis was then conducted on the same standardized data for comparison with the linked-pair cluster analysis. The results of the principal components analysis indicate that 80 percent of the total variance in the data set can be accounted for by the first two eigenvectors (Table 9.2). Plotting these two eigenvectors against each other seems to substantiate the membership of clusters observed in the previous linked-pair cluster analysis (Figure 9.2). A few exceptions can be noted, however.

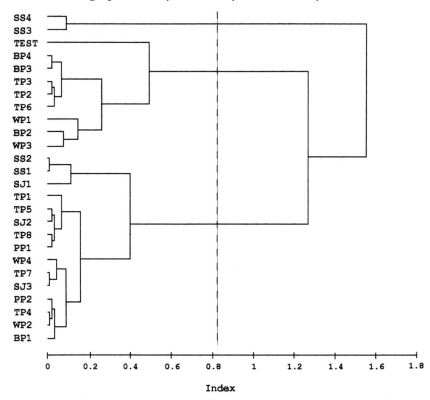

Figure 9.1. Linked-pair cluster analysis of data grouped into five particle size classes (data standardized by z-scores).

For instance, the Weeden Island sherd (TEST) appears to form its own discrete unit, whereas the disparity between other clusters appears far less substantial.

Finally, correspondence analysis was conducted on the raw counts of particles belonging to each particle size category. The results of this analysis indicate that 97 percent of the total variance in the data set can be accounted for by the first two eigenvectors (Table 9.3). A plot of these two eigenvectors (Figure 9.3) enhances the pattern observed in the principal components analysis (Figure 9.2). Three discrete clusters can be observed, with the sample TEST forming its own cluster, the samples SS3 and SS4 forming another cluster, and all other samples clustering very closely.

The particle size classification scheme was then condensed to only three categories: clay (0–.004 mm), silt (.004–.0625 mm), and sand (.0625–.5 mm). This distribution was analyzed using the same set of statistical techniques.

Table 9.2. Results of principal components analysis on data categorized in five particle size classes.

Eigenvalues[a]	1	2	3	4	5
Value	2.3360	1.6849	0.6248	0.3143	0.0400
% of variability	0.4672	0.3370	0.1250	0.0629	0.0080
Cumulative %	0.4672	0.8042	0.9291	0.9920	1.0000

Vectors[a]	1	2	3	4	5
Clay	−0.3972	0.4575	0.5130	−0.6024	0.0831
Silt	−0.4645	0.4226	0.1443	0.7608	0.0775
v.f.s.	0.3886	0.6054	−0.1336	−0.0042	−0.6816
f.s.	0.5182	0.4527	−0.1051	0.0117	0.7179
m.s.	0.4550	−0.2018	0.8289	0.2411	−0.0837

Note: Data standardized by z-scores.
[a]Eigenvalues and eigenvectors based on the correlations matrix.

First, the data were standardized by z-scores and subjected to a linked-pair cluster analysis (Figure 9.4). Results depict nearly the same situation as that observed for the five-category cluster analysis: three clusters can be observed with nearly the same membership. The major difference is samples TP4, WP2, BP1, PP2, and WP4 get placed in a different group than before.

As before, principal components analysis was then conducted on the data. The results of this analysis indicate that 89 percent of the total variance in the data set can be accounted for by the first two eigenvectors (Table 9.4). A plot of these eigenvectors reveals very little tendency for clustering (Figure 9.5). Again, however, a few outliers can be noted, particularly samples SS3, SS4, and TEST. Finally, the actual particle counts from each size category were subjected to correspondence analysis. These results indicate that 100 percent of the total variance in the data set can be accounted for by the first two eigenvectors (Table 9.5). Plotting these two eigenvectors against each other (Figure 9.6) illustrates a pattern almost identical to that obtained from correspondence analysis of the data grouped into five particle size categories (see Figure 9.3).

The final step was to evaluate the relation between the mean average diameter and mean roundness of all the particles counted in each sample. These values were standardized by z-scores before any statistical analysis was performed because of the incomparability between the units of measure. The resulting data were then analyzed using linked-pair cluster analysis

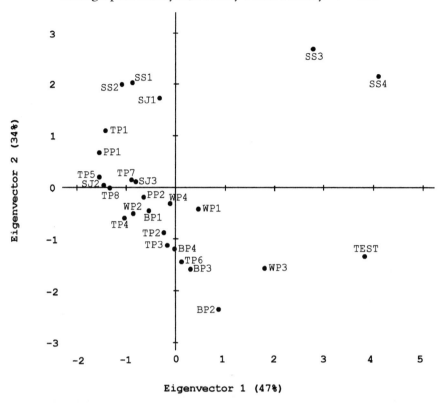

Figure 9.2. Plot of eigenvectors 1 and 2 from principal components analysis of data categorized into five particle size classes.

(Figure 9.7). As with the particle size classification analysis, results suggest that the data can best be viewed as constituting three clusters. To substantiate these results, K-means pure locational clustering analysis also was performed on the data. The greatest reduction in residual error occurred with the three-cluster solution (Table 9.6), indicating that the samples have a tendency to cluster into three discrete groups. Each case was then plotted on a two-dimensional graph to facilitate examination of the results (Figure 9.8).

RESULTS

The results of our analysis are equivocal. In each statistical analysis, the sandy sediment samples from the lower-bank portion of Harlan Bayou (SS3 and SS4) always cluster together. Our methods were able to discriminate consistently between these samples and the siltier soil samples obtained from the middle-bank portion of Harlan Bayou (SS1 and SS2). This distri-

Table 9.3. Results of correspondence analysis on data categorized into five particle size classes (raw data).

Eigenvalues and Corresponding Inertia				
Eigenvalues	1	2	3	4
Values	0.0618	0.0033	0.0014	0.0006
Inertia %	92	5	2	1
Cumulative %	92	97	99	100

Column Profiles Coordinates on Factorial Axes							
	Weight	Inertia	Normalized Inertia	1	2	3	4
Clay	0.0068	0.0015	0.0216	−0.0690	−0.1559	0.4256	−0.0495
Silt	0.9615	0.0018	0.0268	−0.0430	0.0032	−0.0030	−0.0005
v.f.s.	0.0273	0.0379	0.5654	1.1645	−0.1703	−0.0110	0.0541
f.s.	0.0040	0.0233	0.3472	2.3460	0.4672	0.0154	−0.2379
m.s.	0.0004	0.0026	0.0390	1.4660	1.9752	0.5277	0.8966

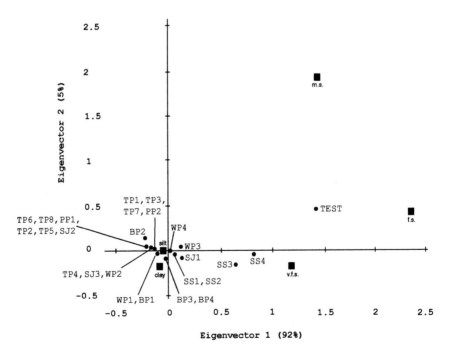

Figure 9.3. Plot of eigenvectors 1 and 2 from correspondence analysis of data categorized into five particle size classes.

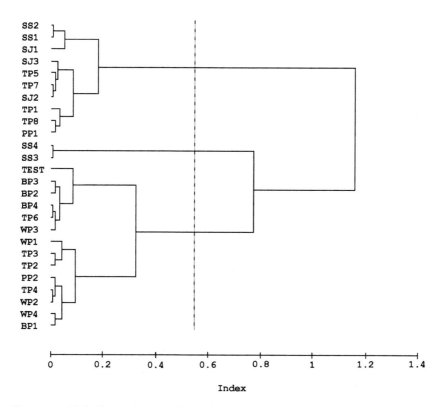

Figure 9.4. Linked-pair cluster analysis of data categorized into three particle size classes (data standardized by z-scores).

Table 9.4. Results of principal components analysis of data categorized into three particle size classes.

Eigenvalues[a]	1	2	3
Value	1.6612	1.0020	0.3368
% of variability	0.5537	0.3340	0.1123
Cumulative %	0.5537	0.8877	1.0000

Vectors[a]	1	2	3
Clay.	0.7045	0.0936	−0.7035
Silt	0.7076	−0.0159	0.7065
Sand	−0.0550	0.9955	0.0775

Note: Data standardized by z-scores.
[a]Eigenvalues and eigenvectors based on the correlations matrix.

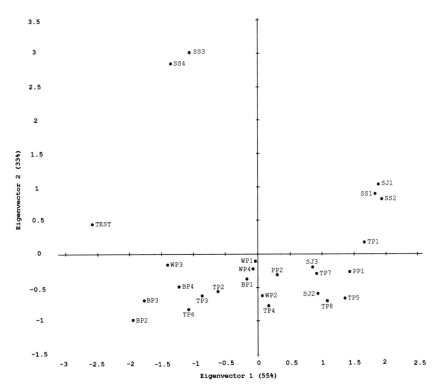

Figure 9.5. Plot of eigenvectors 1 and 2 from principal components analysis of data categorized into three particle size classes.

Table 9.5. Results of correspondence analysis of data categorized into three particle size classes (raw data).

Eigenvalues and Corresponding Inertia		
Eigenvalues	1	2
Values	0.0571	0.0014
Inertia %	98	2
Cumulative %	98	100

Column Profiles Coordinates on Factorial Axes				
	Weight	Inertia	Normalized Inertia	1	2
Clay	0.0068	0.0015	0.0248	−0.0633	0.4568
Silt	0.9615	0.0018	0.0307	−0.0431	−0.0033
Sand	0.0317	0.0553	0.9445	1.3200	0.0015

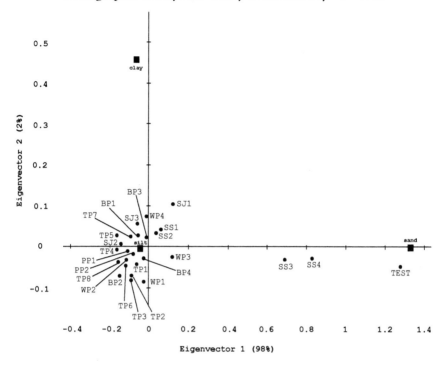

Figure 9.6. Plot of eigenvectors 1 and 2 from correspondence analysis of data categorized into three particle size classes.

bution helps substantiate the methods employed by correctly discriminating between sediments obtained from two different contexts. In addition, the one Weeden Island sherd (TEST) from Florida was consistently differentiated from the siltier sherds in the sample. This sand-tempered sherd appears very different from any other sherd in the sample both microscopically and macroscopically. In this instance, our methods were able to discriminate between sherds with different body characteristics.

The Poverty Point Objects (PP1 and PP2) display a tendency to cluster together with the sediment samples from the middle-bank portion of Harlan Bayou (SS1 and SS2) in most of the statistical analyses conducted. The similarities between Poverty Point Objects and the loess samples are important because it is reasonable to assume, given the ubiquity of Poverty Point Objects at the site and their proposed use as utilitarian cooking balls, that they represent an expedient industry manufactured on-site from locally available sediments. All of these samples (SS1, SS2, PP1, and PP2) are either known or inferred to have derived from the loess of Maçon Ridge, and most tend to cluster together. In this situation, our methods successfully grouped together samples from the same or similar contexts.

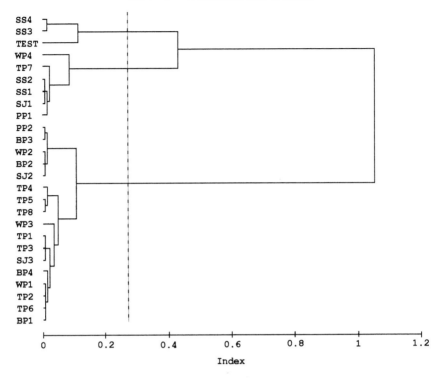

Figure 9.7. Linked-pair cluster analysis of mean average diameter vs. mean roundness (data standardized by z-scores).

The actual pottery samples, on the other hand, provide more ambiguous analytical results. In almost every statistical analysis performed on the data, all or most of the Baytown (BP1, BP2, BP3, and BP4) and St. Johns (SJ1, SJ2, and SJ3) sherds appear to cluster together. The St. Johns sherds, however, often tend to cluster with the loess soil samples (SS1 and SS2) and the Poverty Point Objects (PP1 and PP2). This distribution is somewhat confusing because St. Johns wares are thought to be imports into the Lower Mississippi Valley from Florida. In this kind of high-magnification analysis the sponge spicules visible in the St. Johns sherds appear to mimic the fine silt particles in the loess samples from Poverty Point. These sherds thus appear similar to those of the loess soil samples and the Poverty Point Objects. The Tchefuncte-like sherds (TP1, TP2, TP3, TP4, TP5, TP6, TP7, and TP8) and fiber-tempered Wheeler sherds (WP1, WP2, WP3, and WP4), however, were not discriminated into any coherent pattern by any one of the statistical analyses performed on the data.

Our method of computer-assisted petrographic thin-section analysis was

Table 9.6. K-means cluster analysis of mean average diameter vs. mean roundness/angularity.

Inertia	Values
Between group	1.4747
Within group	0.4490
Total	1.9237

Clustered Observations/Clusters Size		
Group 1	Group 2	Group 3
6	3	17
PP1	TEST	BP1
SJ1	SS3	SJ2
SS1	SS4	SJ3
SS2		WP3
WP4		TP1
TP7		TP6
		TP2
		TP8
		BP2
		WP1
		TP3
		WP2
		TP4
		TP5
		BP3
		BP4
		PP2

unable to successfully discriminate between untempered wares and between loess samples and sponge spicule–tempered wares. One reason for this may be that the image-analysis software used in our research is limited in its capacity to identify clay-sized particles (0–0.004 mm). In traditional thin-section analysis, clay particles are not individually identifiable (Stoltman 1991:110). Clay particles are therefore counted whenever the existence of a larger particle cannot be determined. As with traditional thin-section

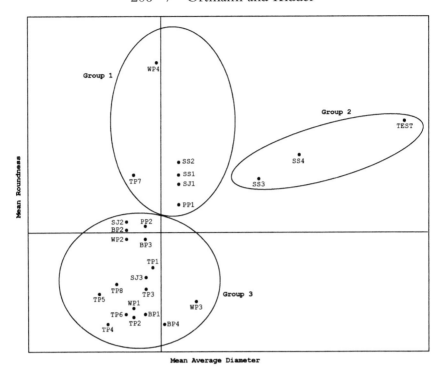

Figure 9.8. Scatterplot of mean average diameter vs. mean roundness (data standardized by z-scores).

analysis, the computer-assisted method we used was unable to identify clay particles. Our method therefore ignored these portions of each image. This resulted in inflated counts for all other particle size classes in comparison to clay. The possibility remains that if our methods could have better identified clay-sized particles the analysis might have been able to more readily discriminate samples based on their physical attributes.

DISCUSSION

Our results seem to suggest one of two situations. First, the majority of sherds in our sample were constructed of materials that are indistinguishable from the locally occurring Poverty Point soils. This possibility suggests that these samples were manufactured locally, but not necessarily at the Poverty Point site. Conversely, the people responsible for the manufacture of the sherds that we analyzed may have been selecting sediments with properties similar to those that occur locally at the Poverty Point site. Using only microscopic methods, we therefore are unable to discriminate between pottery produced locally and that which may have been imported from elsewhere. Although the microscopic method itself could not distinguish the St. Johns wares, by combining microscopic and macroscopic examination, it is possible to regularly distinguish the St. Johns wares from all others in the sample. Furthermore, macroscopic identification of all other wares did not yield any criteria that would allow us to substantiate the claim that these sherds were imported from some distant location.

More research of this sort is necessary to determine whether the methods employed in this research have any utility in the field of petrographic thin-section analysis. To further enhance our findings we would need to apply trace-element analysis or some similar discriminatory test. The available thin-section petrographic techniques are not sufficiently capable of separating sherds manufactured in different geographic locations but made from similarly textured soils.

CONCLUSION

Our data, while not conclusive, suggest that some pottery at Poverty Point was probably made locally. While questions of specific origins are interesting in and by themselves, they also bear on issues of trade patterns, the role of technology in social organization, and the organization of production at Poverty Point, as well as the emergence of later pottery-using cultures in the post–Poverty Point era. Webb and contemporary researchers at Poverty Point are largely silent on the issue of pottery origins and manufacturing, although they place a heavy emphasis on the presence of nonlocal pottery at Poverty Point and related sites (Ford and Webb 1956; Webb 1982; Webb et al. 1963). Gibson (1999, 2000), however, has recently argued that Poverty Point was an important center of terminal Archaic pottery production. He points out that pottery production was probably more important than previously thought based on the quantity of material recovered in recent excavations. Hays and Weinstein (1999) have recently demonstrated that Tchefuncte-like wares are stratigraphically earlier at Poverty Point than fiber-tempered Wheeler wares and at least as early as sponge spicule–tempered St. Johns wares.

Jenkins and his colleagues (1986) emphasize the role of the Poverty Point trade network in the movement of pottery from the Atlantic coast into the Mississippi Valley. They suggest that the development of the earliest pottery in the area (which they identified as the Wheeler series fiber-tempered wares) was "probably a byproduct of the trade created by" Poverty Point (Jenkins et al. 1986:547). Hays and Weinstein suggest that early Tchefuncte-like pottery was rare in the early levels at Poverty Point and thus may represent vessels imported into the site. These arguments imply that Poverty Point was the terminus of an east-to-west pottery trade and that the majority of pottery at the site was imported as finished vessels.

Sassaman (1993a), on the other hand, has argued that the minimal quantity of vessel pottery at Poverty Point is a result of the desire of local elites to maintain a monopoly over vessel technology, which was supposedly dominated by steatite and sandstone containers imported over long distances at considerable actual and social cost. In this model, local pottery manufacturing was "probably actively resisted by individuals who stood to lose power to appropriate social surplus" (Sassaman 1993a:225).

The models that describe the appearance of pottery at Poverty Point have emphasized its nonlocal origin. Some of the pottery is almost certainly nonlocal, most notably the Orange pottery and the distinctive St. Johns pottery with its sponge spicule paste. The presumed nonlocal origin of the majority of the pottery at Poverty Point, encompassing the Tchefuncte-like and fiber-tempered wares, is an assertion based on the assumption that it came from the east. While the initial concept is almost certainly derived from the Atlantic coastal region, the data presented here suggest that at least some of the pottery at Poverty Point was produced locally (Stoltman, this volume). Our results then challenge Sassaman's (1993a) hypothesis that Poverty Point elites may have actively resisted pottery production and/or use. Similarly, our data indicate that Poverty Point may not have been solely a terminal node for trade in finished vessels; it is possible instead to suggest that pottery vessels may have been exported from the site. Like others, we remain perplexed, however, by the low quantities of vessel pottery at Poverty Point and contemporary sites, especially given the presence of fired-clay balls in large numbers. There are no recognized taphonomic processes that can be invoked to account for the dearth of pottery vessels. Perhaps Sassaman's hypothesis can be modified to suggest that Poverty Point peoples resisted pottery vessels as a technological innovation because they had a highly developed cooking technology that was well suited to local needs. Pottery vessels may not have provided any significant adaptive advantage in this context, especially given the poor technological and thermal characteristics of much of this early pottery. In this case, innate subsistence and technological conservatism may have provided a counterweight to vessel pottery innovation, whether imported or local.

Finally, we would point out that the hypothesis that Poverty Point was a center or source of pottery production in the terminal Archaic is likely to be relevant to understanding the genesis of Early Woodland pottery manufacture and use. Gibson (1995) has argued that the presence of Tchefuncte-like pottery (what he has termed the "Old Floyd" pottery complex) in early contexts at Poverty Point is an indication that this site was the locus of later Tchefuncte pottery innovation in the Lower Mississippi Valley. Hays and Weinstein (1999) have noted that the Tchefuncte pottery assemblage at Bayou Jasmine appears to be fully developed with regard to technology, vessel shape, and decoration, even at the lowest levels of the site. Similarly, we have encountered fully developed Tchefuncte pottery at Raffman (16MA20) in contexts dated to the fifth and sixth centuries cal B.C. (Kidder 2000). Technologically and macroscopically, the untempered Tchefuncte-like pottery from Poverty Point cannot be consistently separated from later Tchefuncte pottery. We believe the development of Tchefuncte pottery in the Early Woodland reflects a local pottery industry that was mixing existing styles, such as punctation and possibly dentate stamping (presumably derived from Wheeler), with coastal design styles arriving via Bayou La Batre and farther east. We are in agreement with Gibson (1995) that the apparently rapid emergence of Tchefuncte pottery can be understood as the consequence of its having an immediate local antecedent in the Poverty Point pottery industry.

Our work on Poverty Point pottery is just beginning. This research, along with other work on early pottery, indicates that the origins and development of vessel pottery are more complex than previously acknowledged. Poverty Point was a recipient of pottery technology, but it probably should not be thought of as a passive terminal node in the movement of early pottery. It appears that craftspeople at Poverty Point adapted their existing knowledge of pottery manufacture and began to produce simple untempered and possibly fiber-tempered pottery at the site. Recognizing that Poverty Point was likely a locus of pottery vessel manufacturing requires us to rethink existing ideas about the role of pottery production in terminal Archaic societies. It does not appear that Poverty Point was simply receiving pottery made elsewhere. If this is so, then ideas about the social context and role of pottery manufacture and its relationship to steatite trade must be reevaluated. Similarly, recognizing that Poverty Point had a developed pottery industry makes it easier to understand the emergence and rapid spread of Early Woodland pottery in the Lower Mississippi Valley. These conclusions are only tentative, however, and must be further evaluated using a variety of methods and techniques.

10

Did Poverty Pointers Make Pots?

James B. Stoltman

> The principal surprise of the 1955 field season was the discovery that
> pottery is undoubtedly an element of the Poverty Point cultural complex.
>
> Ford and Webb 1956:105

Although small amounts of at least two pottery wares—clay tempered and
fiber tempered—were recovered during their excavations at Poverty Point
(16WC5), Ford and Webb (1956:105–106) made clear it was only the latter
that they felt was associated with Poverty Point culture. Subsequently, as the
radiocarbon evidence mounted documenting that fiber-tempered pottery
manufacture on the Atlantic seaboard antedated Poverty Point culture by
several hundred years (e.g., Bullen and Stoltman 1972), it became common-
place to view such pottery at Poverty Point as imported from the east rather
than as a local product (e.g., Griffin 1978:61; Jenkins et al. 1986:548; Weinstein 1995:155–158). Sassaman (1993a) not only accepted this view of the
intrusiveness of fiber-tempered pottery at Poverty Point but went further,
suggesting that Poverty Pointers actively resisted pottery container manufacture in order to preserve the social privileges that accrued to them as
controllers of the trade in soapstone vessels.

The nonfiber-tempered pottery containers recovered, albeit in small
quantities, from Poverty Point contexts are more problematic. Many writers
omit mention of them altogether, thus tacitly supporting the view that only
fiber-tempered pottery was truly associated with Poverty Point culture
(e.g., Bense 1994:100; Sassaman 1993a), while others are frankly uncertain
whether to include these sherds in Poverty Point culture or attribute them
to postdepositional mixture (e.g., Webb 1982:42).

Contrary to the trend either to ignore or deny the presence of pottery
other than fiber-tempered types in Poverty Point contexts, Jon Gibson
(1991, 1993, 2000) has long maintained that such pottery occurs in situ in
Poverty Point culture sites. To express his belief that those sherds with punctates, rocker stamping, incising, and other Tchefuncte-like design styles were
associated with Poverty Point culture, Gibson (1991:70) assigned them to
an informal category, "Old Floyd" Tchefuncte. What distinguishes the Old
Floyd series, along with its presumed early age and Tchefuncte-like decora-

tion, is its clay-grit-tempered fabric, "a catch-all grouping for early pottery that was *not* predominantly fiber-tempered, sand-tempered, or untempered" (Gibson 2000:117–118; emphasis added). Presumably "clay-grit" refers to what is conventionally termed grog or sherd temper.

The goal of this chapter is to assess the probabilities that pottery containers of any kind were manufactured at Poverty Point by employing petrography to compare the physical compositions of sherds recovered at the site with both local soils and baked-clay Poverty Point Objects (PPOs) also recovered from the site. The current study reports the findings of petrographic observations made upon 16 thin sections of soil samples and fired-clay artifacts recovered from the Poverty Point site. The three soil samples included in this study were provided by T. R. Kidder, who recovered them from beneath Mound E during the summer of 2001. Also included in this study are three PPOs housed in the collections of the Laboratory of Archaeology at the University of Wisconsin–Madison. The 10 pottery sherds analyzed in this study were selected and identified by Christopher Hays and Richard Weinstein from materials recovered in 1974 by William Haag in Excavation Unit 3 near the easternmost tip of Ridge 2 (Hays and Weinstein, this volume; Haag 1990).

The thin sections for these 16 specimens were analyzed using a basic point-counting procedure I have outlined previously (Stoltman 1989, 1991, 2001). These observations were made for the three PPOs in 1994, whereas the remaining 13 samples were studied in 2001. In this analysis, the percentages of silt-size inclusions plus the species, sizes, and percentages of mineral inclusions of sand size and larger were ascertained and used to characterize the physical composition of each thin section. Since individual clay particles are not identifiable in thin section, their presence is recorded simply as "matrix." Special precautions were taken with the 13 samples studied in 2001 (the three soil samples and the 10 potsherds) to ensure that each thin section was analyzed "blind," i.e., without knowledge of specific sample identity, and none of the quantitative data were tabulated until the analysis of all specimens had been completed.

The compositions of these 16 samples are presented in terms of a "paste" index, as previously defined (Stoltman 1991:109–110). Paste consists of only the naturally occurring minerals (i.e., exclusive of human additives) in any fired-clay product. If temper is present (fiber and sponge spicules were treated as temper in this study), it is counted separately and included as part of the body, or bulk composition, of the vessel but excluded from the paste. Paste, then, is recorded quantitatively as the percentages of the following three natural ingredients: matrix (i.e., clay); silt (i.e., all mineral inclusions that range in size between .002 mm and .0625 mm); and sand (i.e., all mineral inclusions larger in maximum diameter than .0625 mm). A sand size index is also recorded for each thin section. This particular index is presented as an ordinal scale ranging in value from 1 to 5. It is computed for each thin section by assigning a number to all sand-size grains recorded during point counting based upon maximum diameters as follows: 1 = .0625–.249 mm; 2 = .25–.499 mm; 3 = .50–.99 mm; 4 = 1.00–1.99 mm; and 5 = >2.00 mm. The index itself is a single number that is the mean of all measured grains for each thin section. These data are presented in Table 10.1 for each of the 16 samples along with mean values for four subclasses as discussed below.

The basic underlying supposition in this study is that the local manufacture of fired-clay products is the more probable alternative to importation whenever their physical properties match those of sediments from the Poverty Point site. Since the overall sample employed in this study is small, the findings are offered tentatively and in the hope that they will inspire the collection and analysis of a greater number of specimens in the future.

LOCAL POVERTY POINT SEDIMENTS

As noted above, the three samples used in this study to reflect the physical composition of sediments at the Poverty Point site were collected by Kidder from beneath Mound E, also referred to as the Ballcourt mound (Kidder 2002). Two of these samples, U.W. #16-77 and #16-78 (Table 10.1), came from depths of 287–559 cm below the surface of Mound E, within the Memphis soil that formed atop the Peoria loess that underlies the Poverty Point site (Gibson 2000:69). The third soil sample, #16-79, came from a depth of 678–712 cm below the surface of Mound E in what is referred to as "basal clay" (Figure 10.1).

As can be seen from Table 10.1, the physical compositions of these three soil samples are similar. The mean value for the three—80 percent matrix, 19 percent silt, and 1 percent sand (Table 10.1)—is here adopted as a reasonable estimate of the physical composition of the sediments that underlie the Poverty Point site. These paste values, then, will serve as the standard for comparison with paste values for the other samples in this study, all of which are humanly fired products, in order to test the hypothesis of their local manufacture.

POVERTY POINT OBJECTS

Several years ago, William Haag donated three fired-clay PPOs to the Department of Anthropology at the University of Wisconsin for inclusion in

Table 10.1. Paste values for soil samples, PPOs, and pottery vessels from the Poverty Point site.

Thin Section #	Type	Provenience	% Matrix	% Silt	% Sand	Sand Size Index
16-77	Memphis soil	Md E, 287–338 cm[a]	83	17	0	—
16-78	Memphis soil	Md E, 338–559 cm[a]	77	22	1	1.00
16-79	Basal clay	Md E, 678–712 cm[a]	80	18	2	1.00
Summary		Mean (N = 3)	80.0 ± 3.0	19.0 ± 2.6	1.0 ± 1.0	1.00 ± 0
16-1	PPO	?	77	20	3	1.00
16-2	PPO	?	75	24	1	1.50
16-3	PPO	?	76	23	1	1.50
Summary		Mean (N = 3)	76.0 ± 1.0	22.3 ± 2.1	1.7 ± 1.2	$1.33 \pm .29$
16-70	Wheeler Plain	FS 3302	84	10	6	1.25
16-71	Wheeler Punctate	FS 3190	86	10	4	1.00
16-72	Wheeler Punctate	FS 3102	78	19	3	1.00
16-73	Wheeler Punctate	FS 3306	75	23	2	1.00
Summary		Mean (N = 4)	80.8 ± 5.1	15.5 ± 6.6	3.7 ± 1.7	$1.06 \pm .12$
16-67	Tchefuncte Plain	FS 3254	82	14	4	1.00
16-68	Tammany Punctated	FS 3283	95	5	0	—
16-69	Tammany Punctated	FS 3310	97	3	0	—
Summary		Mean (N = 3)	91.3 ± 8.2	7.3 ± 5.9	1.3 ± 2.3	1.00 ± 0
16-74-1	St. Johns Plain	?	93	4	3	1.00
16-75	St. Johns Incised	FS 3053	88	8	4	1.00
16-76-1	St. Johns Incised	FS 3319	89	6	5	1.00
Summary		Mean (N = 3)	90.0 ± 2.6	6.0 ± 2.0	4.0 ± 1.0	1.00 ± 0

[a]Depth below surface.

Figure 10.1. Photomicrograph of thin section #16-78, Memphis soil beneath Mound E. Taken under crossed polars at 10× magnification. White dots are nearly all grains of quartz in the silt size range, visible against the dark clay matrix. Scale: largest quartz grain in field of view = .075 mm (i.e., very fine sand).

the teaching and reference collections of that institution. The provenience of these artifacts, other than that they were recovered at the Poverty Point site, is unknown. Thin sections were prepared from each of these artifacts (Figure 10.2), and their paste compositions are recorded in Table 10.1.

The three PPOs have closely similar compositions that, both individually and collectively, are closely similar to the paste values of the local sediments (Figure 10.3). As can be seen in Table 10.1, their mean paste value is 76 percent matrix, 22 percent silt, and 2 percent sand, leaving no reasonable doubt that they were manufactured from loessic soils, presumably those that underlie the Poverty Point site. This finding is in accord with the generally held wisdom about their manufacture (e.g., Gibson 2000:112).

FIBER-TEMPERED POTTERY

Sherds from four fiber-tempered vessels are included in this study (Table 10.1). All have been assigned to the Wheeler series on stylistic grounds by Hays and Weinstein, although this should not be taken as an expression of the belief that they are imports from the Tennessee Valley region. Indeed, it

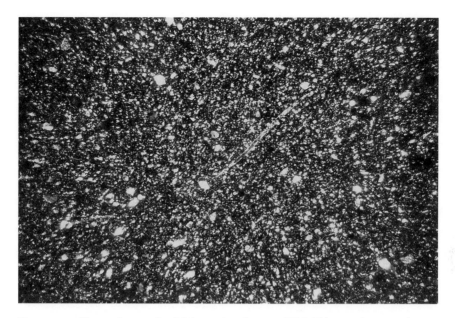

Figure 10.2. Photomicrograph of thin section #16-1, a PPO. Taken under crossed polars at 10× magnification. Scale: largest quartz grain = .10 mm (i.e., very fine sand).

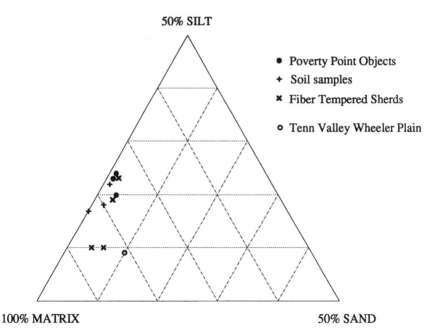

Figure 10.3. Ternary plot showing comparative paste values for three PPOs, three soil samples, and four fiber-tempered sherds from Poverty Point and one Wheeler Plain vessel from the Tennessee Valley of northern Alabama.

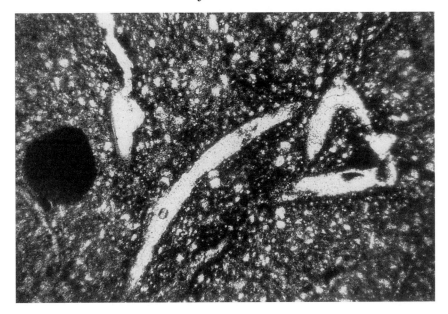

Figure 10.4. Photomicrograph of thin section #16-71, a Wheeler Punctated vessel from Poverty Point. Taken under plane-polarized light at 10× magnification. Scale: longest fiber void = 2.0 mm.

is this very question—local manufacture vs. importation—that is under investigation.

Two different pastes are represented in this sample of four vessels, suggesting the possibility of two different production sources. Two of the vessels—#16-72 and #16-73—have paste values that are completely within the range of variation of those of the local sediments and PPOs from Poverty Point (Figure 10.3). It should be noted that since the fiber (really, the distinctive voids in the paste) is presumed to have been a human additive, its presence is excluded from the paste values. When the fiber is included (as part of the body composition of the vessels), it constitutes 1–9 percent of the body volume. The most parsimonious explanation of the origins of these two vessels is that they were manufactured at Poverty Point.

By contrast, the other two fiber-tempered vessels—#16-70 and #16-71—are both sandier and much less silty than the Poverty Point sediments and PPOs (Table 10.1), indicative of production from an alluvial sediment. They most certainly were not made from the local loessic sediments (Figure 10.4). The bodies of the two vessels are composed of 5–6 percent fiber by volume. That these vessels were manufactured by Poverty Pointers who used a different material, perhaps from the floodplain to the east of the site, is, of course, a possibility. Nonetheless, at the very least, these two vessels stand out as significantly different from both the local materials and the PPOs at Poverty Point, thus rating them strong consideration as nonlocal products.

A reasonable candidate for an external source for these two fiber-tempered vessels is the Tennessee Valley. Relevant to this issue is a single thin-sectioned sherd from a Wheeler Plain vessel provided by Brian Butler from surface collections in northern Alabama. The paste composition of this vessel is 81 percent matrix, 9 percent silt, and 10 percent sand (its body has 3 percent fiber by volume). As can be seen from Figure 10.3, the pastes of the two Poverty Point fiber-tempered vessels made from alluvium are closer compositionally to this vessel than they are to the sediments and PPOs from Poverty Point. These data are insufficient to prove a Tennessee Valley derivation of the Poverty Point vessels, but they do demonstrate how an expanded study (including a compositional analysis of alluvial sediments east of Poverty Point) could provide relevant empirical evidence bearing on the origins of these vessels.

TCHEFUNCTE POTTERY

Three vessels in the current study, one plain and two punctated, were identified as Tchefuncte types by Hays and Weinstein (Hays and Weinstein, this volume, and Table 10.1). These vessels apparently conform to Gibson's informal Old Floyd Tchefuncte class (Gibson 2000:117–118), although there appears to be a difference of opinion between Hays and Weinstein and Gibson over whether these vessels have tempered bodies.

The petrographic observations of these three thin sections revealed no grog, grit, or any other kind of recognizable temper in any of them (Figure 10.5). Moreover, none of these untempered vessels was made from the local loessic soil. All three were made from what appear to be alluvial sediments, with the two Tammany Punctated vessels made from extremely fine sediments, nearly devoid of sand, that were no doubt slack-water deposits (Table 10.1 and Figure 10.6). The Tchefuncte Plain vessel (#16–67) was made from siltier and sandier clays than the other two, suggesting a different origin (Table 10.1 and Figure 10.6). None of these three vessels appears to have been locally produced at Poverty Point, although such a supposition must remain tentative in light of the absence of compositional evidence for nearby alluvial sediments.

These three vessels are technologically distinctive within the Poverty Point sample, yet at the same time have close counterparts among "real" Tchefuncte pottery from such sites as Jaketown and Norman in Mississippi (based upon observations of thin sections housed at the University of Wis-

Figure 10.5. Photomicrograph of thin section #16-69, a Tammany Punctated vessel from Poverty Point. Taken under crossed polars at 10× magnification. Scale: largest quartz grain in field of view = .075 mm (i.e., very fine sand).

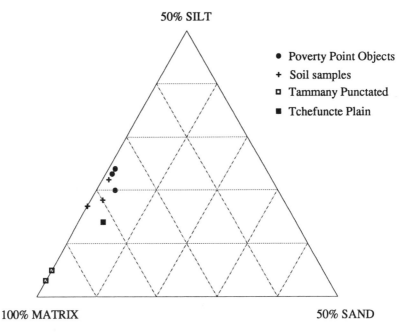

Figure 10.6. Ternary plot showing comparative paste values for the three Tchefuncte vessels vs. soil samples and PPOs from Poverty Point.

consin). That at least some Tchefuncte vessels elsewhere in the Lower Valley are known to have been manufactured from untempered alluvial clays is consistent with the hypothesis that the presence of such vessels in Poverty Point contexts is a result of postdepositional intrusion.

SPICULATE (ST. JOHNS?) POTTERY

Since its introduction by W. H. Holmes (1894), the adjective "chalky" has become virtually synonymous with the St. Johns pottery series of eastern Florida. At least by 1952, Goggin (1952:101) had noted that some of these chalky St. Johns vessels had sponge spicule inclusions, although he believed most were temperless. By 1986, Borremans and Shaak confirmed that sponge spicules were not only present but abundant inclusions in St. Johns chalky ware. Exactly when the presence of spiculate pottery was recognized at Poverty Point is uncertain. Ford and Webb (1956:106) described the texture of some of the fiber-tempered sherds in their sample as chalky, but whether they meant by this that sponge spicules were present is not known. A bit later Bullen (1971:67), in examining sherds from Poverty Point that were in the collections of the Florida State Museum, noted that "[o]ne sherd is chalky, like very early St. Johns Plain." All ambiguity over the presence of spiculate pottery at Poverty Point was ended by Haag who, in 1990, citing inspiration from Milanich and Fairbanks (1980), reported that "an electron scanning microscope examination shows the paste to contain much sponge spicule debris" (Haag 1990:23).

Three of the vessels from Poverty Point examined in this study have 26–36 percent of their body volumes composed of sponge spicules (Figure 10.7). Whether the spicules are temper or natural inclusions is an issue currently under debate in Florida (e.g., Cordell, this volume; Rolland and Bond 2003; Russo and Heide, this volume). Accepting for the sake of argument that the spicules are temper (i.e., intentional human additives), the paste compositions for these three vessels are closely similar to one another and thus can be fairly represented as a mean value: 90 percent matrix, 6 silt, and 4 percent sand (Table 10.1). Whether tempered or not, the body and paste compositions of these three vessels are so distinctive in every way that they must almost certainly be regarded as imports to the Poverty Point site.

As a suggested way to identify a presumed external source for these vessels, compositional comparisons with spiculate vessels from Florida would be helpful. I currently have access only to a single spiculate vessel thin section from Florida for use in this endeavor. It is from a St. Johns Plain vessel from the River Styx site (8AL458) in north-central Florida, where it is presumed to be from a Middle Woodland context (Milanich 1994:236–237). The River Styx vessel has 25 percent sponge spicules by volume, along with a

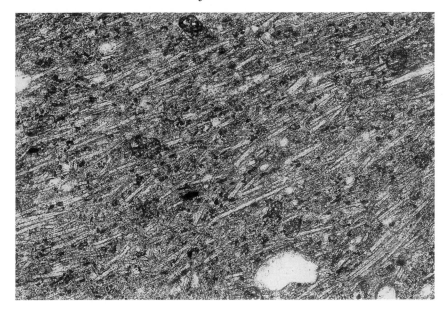

Figure 10.7. Photomicrograph of thin section #16-74-1, a St. Johns Plain vessel from Poverty Point. Taken under plane-polarized light at 25× magnification. Scale: largest quartz grain at bottom = .2 mm (i.e., very fine sand).

paste index of 87 percent matrix, 4 percent silt, and 9 percent sand (Figure 10.8). The small sample sizes involved are inadequate to sustain any strong conclusions, but these data are, at the very least, consistent with the view that spiculate vessels at Poverty Point were imported from Florida.

It is noteworthy (Hays and Weinstein, this volume) that spiculate sherds have the greatest mean depth of any of the pottery types recovered at Poverty Point and thus appear to be strong candidates for consideration as coeval with Poverty Point culture. A major problem about the contemporaneity of St. Johns pottery types with Poverty Point culture is that the St. Johns pottery series in Florida is generally regarded as postdating 2500 rcybp (e.g., Milanich 1994), that is, not appearing until after the demise of Poverty Point culture. That problem now appears to be solved with the recent discovery of spiculate pottery at the Joseph Reed Shell Ring on the Atlantic coast of Florida in contexts dating ca. 3400 B.P. (Russo and Heide, this volume).

SUMMARY AND CONCLUSIONS

In this study thin sections of 10 pottery vessels, three PPOs, and three soil samples from the Poverty Point site were analyzed to determine their physi-

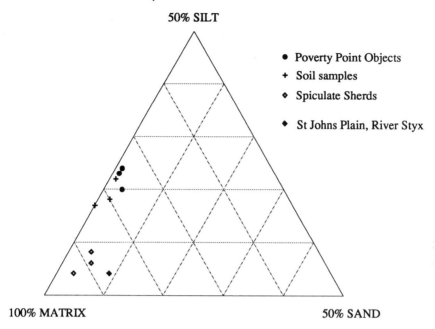

50% SILT

• Poverty Point Objects

+ Soil samples

◆ Spiculate Sherds

◆ St Johns Plain, River Styx

100% MATRIX   50% SAND

Figure 10.8. Ternary plot showing comparative paste values for the three spiculate vessels vs. soil samples and PPOs from Poverty Point. Also included is one St. Johns Plain vessel from the River Styx site, Florida.

cal compositions in order to shed light on the issue of local production vs. importation of the pottery vessels. Although sample size is lamentably small, these data, nonetheless, are valuable because they allow the empirical testing of the following proposition: if pottery containers were manufactured by Poverty Pointers (i.e., residents of the site during the time of Poverty Point culture), they can reasonably be expected to have been manufactured from the same local sediments that were used to manufacture the fired-clay balls that were so abundantly and successfully manufactured at the site.

The first step in testing this proposition was to compare the physical compositions of three PPOs, whose local manufacture is not in doubt, with those of the soil samples collected at Poverty Point. The results confirm the generally held belief that PPOs were manufactured from the loessic sediments that underlie the site.

With the physical compositions of both local sediments and local fired-clay products thus established as a baseline, the physical compositions of samples of three classes of pottery vessels previously recovered at the site by Haag—fiber-tempered (N = 4), untempered (N = 3), and spiculate (N = 3)—were compared against this local standard. Of the 10 pottery vessels involved, only two of the fiber-tempered vessels were manufactured from loessic sediments similar to those underlying the Poverty Point site. The other two fiber-tempered vessels were manufactured from a moderately silty sediment not unlike that from which a Wheeler Plain vessel from the Tennessee Valley had been made (Figure 10.3). The three spiculate vessels, whether considered tempered or not, have compositions significantly different from the local materials in every way. Their exotic origins seem highly probable, and Florida would appear to be the most likely source (Figure 10.8). As for the three Tchefuncte sherds (which are all untempered), all were made of what appear to be alluvial sediments that must have been procured beyond the limits of the Poverty Point site. That these and the other nonloessic vessels were made from alluvial sediments procured adjacent to, or at least near, the Poverty Point site remains a possibility that has yet to be disconfirmed.

This latter possibility seems improbable, however, since there is no reason to believe that the site's residents could not also have made containers of fired clay from the very same sediments that they were already employing to make fired-clay balls with considerable success. I know from personal observation of thin sections of Neolithic pottery from Belgium and Bronze Age pottery from North China that highly sophisticated pottery can be manufactured successfully from untempered loessic sediments. If the Poverty Pointers wanted to make pottery containers, they could have done so with the very same material from which they were making fired-clay balls. Thus, based upon the findings of this study, for all but some of the fiber-tempered vessels, the tentative answer to the query that titles this chapter is "no."

ACKNOWLEDGMENTS

This research could not have been done nor this chapter written without the assistance and counsel of Richard Weinstein, Christopher Hays, Rebecca Saunders, T. R. Kidder, Ann Cordell, and Jon Gibson, to each of whom I express my sincere thanks. Of course, I alone am responsible for the final written product.

Notes

CHAPTER 1

1. In this volume, *rcybp* is used for measured (uncorrected) radiocarbon dates, which are often the basis for chronologies. Corrected dates are indicated by B.P., and *cal* B.P. is used for calibrated dates. We have attempted to standardize radiocarbon discussions to a certain extent, but without imposing too much on the authors' presentations (some preferred B.C. and others B.P. dates). Wherever possible, however, a conventional date and calibrated range are offered.

2. White (2003:80) recently presented earlier radiocarbon dates and suggested a fiber-tempered presence in the lower Apalachicola River valley as early as 5000 B.P.

3. Stoltman (personal communication, 2001) confirms that the GXO dates were uncorrected. Using Calib 4.3 for correction and calibration the ages are, for GXO-343, 2cal 5569 (5045) 4654 and, for GXO-345, 2cal 5452 (5210, 5190, 5114, 5114, 5049) 4836.

4. Disregarding a date from Spanish Mount with a sigma of 350 years, the earliest conventional date on Thoms Creek pottery is 4112 ± 50, or 4290 (4151) 3960 2cal B.P. (on shell; WK-9762), from recent excavations conducted by Saunders and Russo at the Fig Island ring complex (Saunders 2000a).

5. Sutherland (who published only brief descriptions of his excavations and the materials recovered [Sutherland 1973, 1974]) found a "pure" Thoms Creek component underlying mixed Stallings and Thoms Creek ceramics at Spanish Mount (38CH62), a large, deep shell midden on Edisto Island, South Carolina. However, Cable (1993) reanalyzed the material and, on the basis of surface decoration seriation, proposed that Spanish Mount accreted laterally rather than vertically and, therefore, that the "pure" Thoms Creek component was not earlier than the mixed component. While his ceramic seriation was not based on such reasoning, Cable did "assume" that Stallings was earlier than Thoms Creek.

6. Marrinan also recovered several Tick Island Incised sherds. Tick Island motifs are extremely rare outside of the St. Johns River valley in the vicinity of the type site.

7. "St. Simons" might most appropriately be considered a phase or a series of phases with varying frequencies of Stallings, Orange, and Norwood sherds in any given component.

CHAPTER 3

1. This emphasis on northeast Florida may be more apparent than real. Taxonomic issues, such as the distinction between Orange and Norwood in the panhandle, and a hesitation to apply the Orange label to fiber-tempered wares on the central and lower Gulf coast may artificially depress the number of Orange sites in those regions.

2. These two data sets are so internally consistent that one suspects the methodologies may not be comparable. Funds are being sought to section the croaker otoliths. Russo et al. (1993) presented evidence for winter exploitation of menhaden (*Brevortia* spp.) and summer exploitation of pinfish (*Lagodon rhomboides*) in an earlier test unit at Rollins.

3. Two vessels were constructed from commercial clays, one hand modeled and one built using coils. Clay used for both vessels was tempered with dried Spanish moss. Moss was added in quantities that replicated Rollins sherd fiber abundances. Vessels were dried for two weeks (because it took that much time to schedule a firing) and then kiln fired. After firing, both vessels were broken into sherds and fiber orientation was examined on rim sherds and on vessel walls projecting up from bases (because orientation of body sherds was not preserved).

4. As for the latter, coils could not be seen in the two Coles Creek and Plaquemine (Late Woodland and Early Mississippian) sherds that were used as controls, either.

5. Trinkley (1973:154) observed that, in replicating Thoms Creek pottery, similar splits were produced when pots were insufficiently dried before firing. Our (inadvertent) prolonged drying time in the hot, dry atmosphere of the Fine Arts storage room would seem to preclude this as an explanation in our case.

6. In terms of fiber orientation, of the 12 "split" sherds, eight had predominately horizontal fibers, one had predominantly nonhorizontal fibers, and three had both.

7. Ten centimeters was chosen as the dividing point between deep and shallow vessels on the basis of Bullen's identification of Orange 3 vessels as 10 cm deep.

8. Except on miniature vessels (Bullen 1972:15).

9. The Rollins design coding system ultimately contained 93 distinct designs or design fragments. Seventeen of these were deleted as duplicates during analysis. Of the remaining 76, five were too fragmentary or too unclear to compare with Summer Haven. The large number of designs at Rollins compared to that at Summer Haven resulted from creating a new design for *all* variation, including especially the number of lines in a design (for instance, in the panels of oblique zoning). It does not appear that Bullen or Mitchell consistently created new designs for this level of variation.

10. Sixty percent of the MNV assemblage at Rollins were decorated. Bullen and Bullen (1961:5) reported 51 percent of rims were from decorated vessels, but that value does not appear to be based on MNV—in other words, the same vessel could be represented by several rims in the figure of 51 percent.

11. Rolland (Rolland and Bond 2003) looked at the pottery associated with this date and saw no evidence for spicules.

12. Dickinson and Wayne's sample from the Ribault Club site is difficult to compare because, of the 156 sherds large enough to classify, 110 were too eroded to determine surface decoration. Of the remaining 46 sherds, 11 (23.9 percent) were decorated (Dickinson and Wayne 1987; Lucy Wayne, personal communication, 2001).

13. Blitz (1993) found no significant differences in vessel decoration, ware categories, or vessel shape between mound and midden contexts at the Mississippian-period Lubbub Creek site in Alabama. However, the mound had "disproportionately" larger vessels (Blitz 1993:80).

CHAPTER 5

1. We have chosen to refer to pottery containing abundant sponge spicules as "spiculate" rather than "spicule tempered," given the fact that spicule use as temper is being debated (Cordell and Koski 2003; Rolland and Bond 2003). On the other hand, we defer to tradition and refer to pottery containing abundant sand as "sand tempered" even though the paste may in whole or part contain natural inclusions of sand.

2. Unless otherwise indicated, all radiocarbon dates from Joseph Reed Shell Ring refer to the conventional ages corrected for $^{13}C/^{12}C$ fractionation.

3. We use calibrated ages here only to show that the age, seemingly out of stratigraphic order, may appear so, in part, because of the less precise unit of conventional measure.

CHAPTER 6

1. Lazarus did identify fiber-tempered sherds at the Alligator Lake site (8WL29) as Orange series because they were so abundant and he lacked a local name. At the same time he noted that the Norwood definition was just being established, suggesting the collection might need to be reviewed at a later date.

2. The database includes all sites identified by Prentice Thomas and Associates in the study area as well as those listed on the Florida Master Site File.

CHAPTER 7

1. Gibson (e.g., 2000) defines Old Floyd Tchefuncte as a clay-grit-tempered pottery. We must note that we consider this designation to be confusing and inconsistent with findings of our research. Tchefuncte is by definition a temperless pottery (Phillips 1970), i.e., it has no intentional aplastic inclusions. Frequently one finds bits of hematite, shell, and/or bone in the matrix of some Tchefuncte sherds, but when

present these materials are few in number and a sherd may contain mixtures of several of these materials. Thus, they appear to be unintentional inclusions in the matrix of the pottery. These observations are based on many collective years of analyzing Tchefuncte pottery. Note also that Stoltman's (this volume) petrographic analysis of five of our Tchefuncte sherds from Poverty Point found no temper in the matrix. It should be noted as well that we *have* found pottery in late Tchefuncte contexts that appears to be tempered with bone, hematite, and occasionally grog. We found these sherds, mixed in with other typical Tchefuncte sherds, at the top of the Tchefuncte midden at Bayou Jasmine and in the Tchefuncte component at the Bayou Chene Blanc site (16LV43) (Hays and Weinstein 2000:66–69; Weinstein 1974). We classified this pottery as Chene Blanc Plain and consider it a transitional ware to the early Marksville period's Baytown Plain, *var. Marksville,* which has a soft laminated paste and moderate to abundant grog.

Also, as will be noted later in this chapter, there clearly are grog-tempered sherds at Poverty Point, but they can be readily sorted into standard LMV types, particularly Baytown Plain. They almost certainly represent an occupation much later than the Late/Terminal Archaic period during which most of the site was constructed. Indeed, when we plotted the vertical distribution of grog-tempered sherds in the Goad and Gibson/Connolly excavations, we found that 99 percent were present in the upper three strata of the site. Therefore, we concluded that the few grog-tempered sherds present in the lower strata (early construction zone) were the result of bioturbation while the ones in the upper strata were attributable to a later reoccupation of the site.

We suspect, moreover, that characterizing Old Floyd pottery as grit tempered is also a misnomer. Among the 641 sherds that we examined for this study we only found two sand-tempered Alexander Pinched sherds and one unclassifiable sherd containing sand/grit temper. In summary, unless the pottery sample that Gibson has examined is radically different from ours, which we believe to be highly unlikely, it seems very plausible that Gibson has conflated Tchefuncte and Baytown Plain pottery.

2. The junior author recently reviewed all of the pottery data provided in Gibson's (1984, 1987, 1989, 1990b, 1993, 1994b, 1997) seven available reports stemming from his extensive field-school research at Poverty Point. A detailed discussion of this review will be presented in a later paper to be published in a special volume of *Louisiana Archaeology* entitled *Current Research at Poverty Point.* The results of this review showed that all of Gibson's identified paste categories (Tchefuncte, Wheeler, and Baytown) were concentrated within the upper two levels (20 cm) of his excavations. Unfortunately, Gibson did not recognize a single sherd of St. Johns ware in any of his analyses, although he did have modest categories of "untempered" and "unclassified" sherds that probably included true St. Johns material. Although most of these latter items were concentrated in Level 2 (35.5 percent), an apparently significant amount was present in Levels 6 through 8 (23.9 percent), which, given the results of our study, suggests that St. Johns ware probably made up a good portion of the untempered and/or unclassified material from these lower levels. This

lends some support to the notion that St. Johns vessels were the first pottery present at Poverty Point.

3. At our request, Ann Cordell was kind enough to examine a sample of our chalky pottery with abundant sponge spicules. She concluded that in paste composition they definitely resembled typical St. Johns series sherds from northeast Florida (A. Cordell, personal communication, 2000).

4. It should be noted that freshwater sponges are present in Louisiana (Porrier 1965) and that Laura Tanley and Rebecca Saunders observed a few sponge spicules in the paste of a few Tchefuncte sherds from the Sharp site (16LV13) in southeast Louisiana (Tanley 1999). Therefore, we cannot completely dismiss the possibility that the spiculate pottery was locally made. Nonetheless, it seems highly unlikely for several reasons. First, as noted, the sherds we have classified as St. Johns contain abundant spicules like true St. Johns series sherds. Second, we found no sponge spicules at all in the pastes of any of the other pottery found at Poverty Point (e.g., Tchefuncte, Wheeler, Coles Creek Incised, and Baytown Plain). If spicules were added locally as a temper or were an unintentional inclusion because they were present in the local clays, we would expect them to show up in some of the other pottery series that certainly were local LMV products.

5. We offer one tentative hypothesis for the origin of these sherds. We suggest that they may represent a local Poverty Point attempt at making Tchefuncte pottery, and thus the chalky feel of the pottery is a result of the high silt content of the local loessial clays. This hypothesis will be tested and evaluated more rigorously in our future studies of Poverty Point–era pottery. At the Beau Mire site, Weinstein and Rivet (1978:80) classified similar sherds as a local variety of St. Johns Plain, called *var. Gonzales,* based on the soft and chalky nature of the paste. Subsequent examination of these sherds under 60× magnification showed, however, that they lack sponge spicules, thereby negating their assignment to the St. Johns series.

6. This is the exact same specimen that Gibson and Melancon (this volume) identify as an "untempered" sherd "that we suspect may be from the mother pot." If it is from the so-called mother pot, then that pot almost certainly was made somewhere in northeast Florida and not at Poverty Point.

7. It should be noted here that the junior author is somewhat skeptical of this potential early position of Tchefuncte ware at Poverty Point. The small sample size, plus the fact that most of the deep Tchefuncte sherds came from the Gibson/Connolly tree-fall excavations, gives him cause to question this possible association. Perhaps the sherds found in the tree-fall excavations had been displaced downward in the rotted-out root cavities of the trees before they fell over, or they had been dislodged in some manner during the actual fall of the tree. The relative lack of such deep sherds in Goad's non-tree-fall excavations suggests such possibilities.

8. We should note that it is possible St. Johns sherds may exist unrecognized at other Poverty Point–era sites in the region since this type is not well recognized in the LMV. However, James Matthews, of Prentice Thomas and Associates, reports that it was definitely not present in any of the small sites examined by his company along the peripheries of the Poverty Point site (James Matthews, personal commu-

nication, 2001; Thomas and Campbell 1978). We also should note that Connolly reports that the evidence for interaction of some type between Claiborne and Poverty Point is unambiguous (Robert Connolly, personal communication, 2003). He notes, for example, that at Poverty Point very sandy Poverty Point Objects of the cylindrical type with a hole perforation are occasionally found, which is a type very clearly associated with the Claiborne site.

CHAPTER 8

1. Some archaeologists adhere to the notion that Teoc Creek is older than Poverty Point. In fact, when John Connaway and associates first reported Teoc Creek's radiocarbon dates, they proved to be earlier than most of Poverty Point's (Connaway et al. 1977). Back then we regarded radiocarbon dates as fixed ages rather than as statistical probabilities, which they really are. No longer. Not only have we grown accustomed to viewing dates as statistical probabilities, but numerous, recent samples taken from Poverty Point's early construction and preconstruction phases have shown that Poverty Point is coeval with Teoc Creek (Gibson 2000). The same holds true for Cedarland, Claiborne, J. W. Copes, and other components once claimed to be older than Poverty Point. They aren't. If a site looks a lot like Poverty Point (see Webb 1968, 1977)—especially if it yields exotic materials—you might as well save your radiocarbon monies, because it is a practical certainty that it existed when Poverty Point was flourishing and was caught up in the far-reaching web of social interactions that resulted in the material cultural assemblages we identify as Poverty Point.

2. Even as we write this, we have just learned of three new radiocarbon dates from Jaketown, based on samples from the lower anthropic layers taken by Joe Saunders and Thurman Allen during their 2001 coring investigations. One date is based on organically enriched sediment and has an intercept of 2025 cal B.C. (Beta-154428), but the two charcoal dates have intercepts of 1400 cal B.C. (Beta-156646) and 1620 cal B.C. (Beta-157421) (J. Saunders 2002:76–81). These new dates show that Jaketown and Poverty Point are contemporary, as we always figured they were.

3. At Poverty Point, fiber-tempered wares, often classified as Wheeler pottery, have been shown to stratigraphically postdate other early wares in popularity (Gibson 1995, 2001). Despite conclusions to the contrary, Jaketown's ceramic stratigraphy clearly reveals that clay-tempered wares are lower than fiber-tempered materials (Phillips et al. 1951:figs. 44–45). Fiber-tempered pottery does seem to have been produced during a limited span—a horizon, if you will—only the span does not come after Poverty Point occupation but during its zenith.

4. Claims that Tchefuncte pottery lacks intentional temper abound (Phillips 1970:173; Shenkel 1980:74; Toth 1977:55; Weaver 1963:53–56; see also Hays and Weinstein, this volume). Clarence Webb refers to early Tchefuncte pottery from the Cross Bayou site near Larto Lake in central Louisiana as garbage or junk tempered because it contains iron-manganese (FeMn) masses, bone fragments, vegetal matter, and hard clay lumps. Although lacking the precision expected of today's analyses

(Stoltman 1989, 1991), Gibson's counts based on 10× magnification and point count-ing disclose that paste inclusions in Cross Bayou pottery match inclusions present in midden soil in both density and kind (Gibson 1991). Doyle Gertjejansen and asso-ciates make a strong case that Tchefuncte potters do not prepare clay before making vessels (Gertjejansen et al. 1983:46), and that includes not adding temper. Gertjejan-sen, a ceramicist, finds that he cannot make pottery as bad as Tchefuncte pottery unless he does absolutely nothing to the clay except roll the coils. If he kneads the clay or adds temper—even a little sand—laminations are eliminated, and laminated paste characterizes early clay-grit (Tchefuncte) fabrics (Ford and Quimby 1945).

Whether aplastics are deliberately added tempering or natural inclusions is an age-old question and one nearly impossible to answer without benefit of thor-ough lithological analysis of locally available soils. Loessial soils on Maçon Ridge, the landform that supports Poverty Point, as well as alluvial soils in the adjoining Tensas swamp, have natural pedogenic horizons, which contain vegetal matter, hard clay peds, grit (fine pedogenic sand and silt), hard FeMn masses and concretions, and sand (quartz) (Allen 1990), the very same inclusions identified as intentionally added tempering. Loessial topsoils are gritty (having between 2 and 6 percent very fine to very coarse sand), are covered with organic matter, and are filled with small roots (potential fiber sources); intermediate, or E, horizons are gritty too (around 2 to 4 percent sand) because clays have been stripped out (illuviated) leaving the sand and silt matrix behind (potential grit sources); and subsoils, or argillic horizons, are either concretion-filled or smooth and creamy—depending on their position on the landform—because clay and minerals illuviated from overlying horizons are rede-posited at these depths (potential source of smooth silty clay loam, silty clay, or FeMn-particle-bearing clay). Sands occur naturally in higher energy discharges in the floodplain, primarily as natural levee sediments.

By digging only a few centimeters deeper in the same hole, a potter can produce fabrics with vegetal and fiber inclusions (topsoils), sand-grit inclusions (E horizons), and FeMn inclusions or no inclusions whatever (argillic horizons). Potter's "clay" bearing heavier fractions of light to heavy sand can be secured from any natural levee in the swamp. Potters would have had to go no farther than the foot of the bluff on which Poverty Point sits to get the sandier sediment—a trip of about 30 steps. To us, telling whether aplastics are natural or intentionally added as temper involves two exercises: (a) distinguishing whether or not ceramics have ex-otic inclusions or more inclusions than are naturally present in local native soils and (b) confirming by some means that local soils are not used (also see Stoltman 1989, 1991). Even when native clays are used, analysts face the unanswerable question of whether local sources are selected because of what they naturally contain.

Nonetheless, as Ned Jenkins (personal communication, 2002) reminds us, the topper is why different Lower Mississippi fabric classes bear decorations similar to those on the same fabric classes from the Eastern Gulf region. Free punctated de-signs on fiber-tempered wares at Poverty Point and Jaketown look like free punc-tated designs on fiber-tempered wares in Alabama and Georgia (Ford and Webb 1956; Jenkins et al. 1986; Webb 1977; Webb et al. 1970). They are distinguished easily from free punctated designs on clay-grit-tempered wares, not just by dint of fabric differences alone but also because of application and pattern differences. Other decorations follow temper suit. Specific decorations go with specific fabrics, no matter whether the sherds come from the Lower Mississippi or the Tombigbee. There is minimal decoration "bleeding" across fabrics, although it does occur occasionally (Gibson 1976:fig. 4). Decorating pots the "right" way means that potters are conforming to convention and notions of properness that come from sharing or being aware of styles regardless of how many hundreds of miles intervene. Now, if we could only explain how that happened, we would instantly become front-running candidates for the Society for American Archaeology's Award for Excellence in Archaeological Research and Analysis or maybe even the Nobel Prize itself.

5. Actually, Churupa Punctated and Marksville Incised have the very lowest MVPs of all the decorated pottery at Jaketown, 9.0 and 7.0, respectively (Ford et al. 1955:table 7). But don't fret. Neither type is early; in fact, both date from Middle to Late Woodland times. So, why should later types have the largest MVPs (lowest stratigraphic positions) of all decorated types? We don't know but are acutely aware that accidents of nature and man do happen, especially to us. Phillips's explanation about sherds being dislodged by Paul Geppard's dirt-hauling bucket banging against the upper walls of the trench he was digging sounds good to us (Phillips et al. 1951:280–281). We also hold Phillips's words close to heart: "We might almost be led to think we were practicing an exast [sic] science" (Phillips et al. 1951:280). We can't blame misidentification. The guys who identified the pottery are the ones who formulated the types. But for both types, MVPs are based on only one sherd, not averages at all—lone sherds—which makes Geppard's swinging bucket very appealing.

Now, we raised hoopla earlier about the oldest (so far) piece of pottery from Poverty Point—also a single sherd (the one bracketed by radiocarbon dates on samples taken only centimeters above and below). So, we know you're thinking that if accidents can happen in one place, they can happen anywhere, right? Not to this sherd. It did not fall from above. It was found in place, lying flat, between two unbroken layers of artificial fill. No postmolds, crawfish or cicada holes, or root molds interrupted the fill layers, above or below. And when the sherd was removed, its print remained in the soil as a vivid reminder of its 3,500-year burial. Accidents happen. But the oldest sherd at Poverty Point is not one of them.

6. The classic argument against pottery "coming in" during Poverty Point times is based on the Jaketown stratigraphy. The Jaketown excavators report a wide stratigraphic separation between cooking briquette and pottery MVPs. But MVPs are averages. Pottery, albeit in small amounts, reaches bottom or near bottom in practically every excavation (Ford et al. 1955:figs. 41–45; Phillips et al. 1951:273–281), but this fact is obscured by the overwhelming quantity of cooking briquettes when percentages are converted to colored bars on graphs. Sterile bands of clay layer-cake the physical stratigraphy just where the zone of analytical separation occurs, bands that Ford and associates identify as flood deposits (Ford et al. 1955:104). Floods would indicate changing conditions—and hence passage of time—a key factor favoring the prepottery argument. But we doubt that mounds would have been

put up in regular flood zones or that people would have lived in a place that continually threatened water damage and drowning, especially when safe haven was always just around the bend or as close as the other side of the river. We suspect that both "sterile" and "midden" bands will prove to be layered mound fill. If so, whatever regional evolutionary implications they were accorded at one time will become only minor events in local history.

We would be safer deferring to Thurman Allen and Joe Saunders's opinion about Jaketown stratigraphy. In 2001, Allen and Saunders cored the area between Trenches 1 and 5 dug by Ford and associates. Allen is of the opinion that the dirt (the brown silt of Ford et al. 1955) above the lower series of buried "middens" is mound fill, but he and Saunders are not sure about the "sterile" bands separating the "midden" bands (Saunders 2002:75–82; Joe Saunders, personal communication, 2002). Anticipating an answer has never set back science, but if we play it safe and await empirical demonstration, we may be waiting a long time.

7. Orvis Scott, Coles Crossroads, Hendrix, Stockland Plantation, Alexander Point, Motley East, Steatite Field, Arledge, and Honey Hole do not have state site numbers—eds.

8. Mouth diameters are estimated from rim sherds. No whole vessels have been found.

9. Kenneth Sassaman's elegant argument stands alone in this regard (Sassaman 1993a, 1995b, 2001). He proposes that pottery jeopardizes soapstone exchange by undermining the intergroup political alliances and intragroup social obligations responsible for it. Well, it might in the Savannah River valley, home of his data. But Poverty Point presents a more complicated situation. There, pottery peaks before soapstone stratigraphically, so soapstone exchange not only manages to thrive the entire time pottery is being produced but actually increases as time goes on. From beginning to end, soapstone vessels outnumber ceramic vessels many times over. Most of Poverty Point's cooking is done in earth ovens. Pottery is so scarce that we doubt it is employed for general domestic cooking at all. If so, the isomorphism between pottery and mound building suggests that pottery's use is limited to active construction moments when needed to expedite work by providing portable, easily replaceable water buckets and open fire–proof, quick-cook utensils. Under this view, pottery and soapstone are not vying for the same practical spot around the firepit but are complementary. Similar complementarities obtain if first pottery functions as serving dishes, rather than cooking pots.

We must not forget that Poverty Point folk establish dozens of arrangements, which bring in exotic materials from near and far. Soapstone exchange is not the only activity that requires extramural alliance building and generates intramural social obligations. If we take each incoming commodity or each group of commodities that come from the same source area or that arrive along the same trade route and presume that their importation entails making arrangements and working deals similar to those consummated to procure soapstone, then the supposed "threat" homemade pottery production holds for alliance making and "controlling" the masses goes away. Any one of a number of long-distance, intergroup dealings might vie with soapstone trade, since we view it as highly unlikely that soapstone dealers also run the copper-galena trade, the Dover flint exchange, or any of the other long-distance enterprises. For one agent or family to run the whole political economy of exchange simply stretches human resources too thin. There are too many exchange vectors running in too many directions for a few people to handle all the necessary between-group diplomacy and required social conventions. Now, a single trade line or material could very well be a family business. But the point is this: pottery has negligible adverse impact on Poverty Point's intricate web of political alliances and social relations. If anything, it promotes them by serving the occasion directly (serving vessels) or indirectly (facilitating construction to celebrate the prevailing state of affairs).

    10. We are following long-standing convention by grouping early pottery into classes based on their dominant aplastic and by labeling those classes as clay-grit tempered, fiber tempered, sand tempered, and untempered (see Ford and Quimby 1945; Ford and Webb 1956; Gibson 1995; Webb 1977; Webb et al. 1970). We are not prejudging aplastics to be intentionally added. We, in fact, suspect they are natural inclusions in most cases (see our Note 4). Appeal to higher authority to bolster the case for or against intentional temper has no bearing on how we have chosen to label our classes. Besides, classes are only classes regardless of how their constituency came to exist. Gibson (1995) added the qualifier Old Floyd after discovering that pottery with Tchefuncte fabrics (clay-grit) and Tchefuncte designs reached the bottom of some of Poverty Point's rings. He opined that the Old Floyd designation would nip the impression that the rings were built or finished during a post-Poverty Point-Tchefuncte span or that building lasted for centuries and centuries—a scenario unsupported by fine-grained intrasite analyses of radiocarbon assays and relative artifact stratigraphy (see this chapter). Yet, avid typologists can resort to questioning data, observation skill, and classification rigor. Melancon and Gibson lack unswerving faith in the power of pottery typology to consistently tell who made pots by dint of fabric qualities alone. We believe native clays varied too much for potters using free-hand technology—even though tradition bound—to turn out identical fabrics over wide geographic areas. And if ever there was a centrally located, super-rich vein where all Lower Mississippi Tchefuncte potters gathered to mine their clay—thereby assuring fabric uniformity—it remains as elusive as the rainbow's gold.

    We reiterate. All four classes of early Poverty Point pottery seem to have been made from the onset of construction to the finish (Gibson 1995), and it is their relative stratigraphic position that reveals construction succession (Gibson 2001, 2002). A sample of pottery from one excavation locale does not, indeed cannot, provide *the* one and only ceramic stratigraphic succession for the colossal town. All sections of the earthworks must be taken into account, and sherd outliers, or actually underliers, cannot be waved off as accidents of sloppy excavation. Misrepresentation awaits those who would pick and choose and prejudge. Ceramic progression at Poverty Point is a matter of construction history, not evolution, and claims of being in-synch with the remainder of the Southeast is a normative moment, not lived history.

References

Aikens, C. Melvin
  1995 First in the World: The Jomon Pottery of Early Japan. In *The Emergence of Pottery: Technology and Innovation in Ancient Societies,* edited by William K. Barnett and John W. Hoopes, pp. 11–21. Smithsonian Institution Press, Washington, D.C.

Allen, E. Thurman
  1990 Soils: Poverty Point. *Louisiana Archaeology* 13:163–200.

Allen, E. Thurman, and B. Allen Touchet
  1990 Poverty Point Area: Geomorphic Evolution and Soils. In *Search for the Lost Sixth Ridge: The 1989 Excavations at Poverty Point,* by Jon L. Gibson, pp. 21–25. Report No. 9, Center for Archaeological Studies, University of Southwestern Louisiana, Lafayette.

Armit, Ian, and Bill Finlayson
  1995 Social Strategies and Economic Change: Pottery in Context. In *The Emergence of Pottery: Technology and Innovation in Ancient Societies,* edited by William K. Barnett and John W. Hoopes, pp. 267–275. Smithsonian Institution Press, Washington, D.C.

Arroyo, Barbara
  1995 Early Ceramics from El Salvador. In *The Emergence of Pottery: Technology and Innovation in Ancient Societies,* edited by William K. Barnett and John W. Hoopes, pp. 199–208. Smithsonian Institution Press, Washington, D.C.

Aten, Lawrence E.
  1999 Middle Archaic Ceremonialism at Tick Island, Florida: Ripley P. Bullen's 1961 Excavation at the Harris Creek Site. *The Florida Anthropologist* 52:131–200.

Barnett, William K.
  1995 Putting the Pot before the Horse: Earliest Ceramics and the Neolithic Transition in the Western Mediterranean. In *The Emergence of Pottery: Technology and Innovation in Ancient Societies,* edited by William K. Barnett and John W. Hoopes, pp. 79–88. Smithsonian Institution Press, Washington, D.C.

Barnett, William K., and John W. Hoopes
  1995 The Shape of Early Pottery Studies. In *The Emergence of Pottery: Technology*

and Innovation in Ancient Societies, edited by William K. Barnett and John W. Hoopes, pp. 1–7. Smithsonian Institution Press, Washington, D.C.

Bense, Judith A.

  1994   *Archaeology of the Southeastern United States.* Academic Press, New York.

Beyer, George E.

  1900   Mound Investigations at Lemar, Louisiana. *Publications of the Louisiana Historical Society* 2(3):28–33.

Binford, Lewis R.

  1962   Archaeology as Anthropology. *American Antiquity* 28(2):217–225.

Blitz, John H.

  1993   Big Pots for Big Shots: Feasting and Storage in a Mississippian Community. *American Antiquity* 58(1):80–95.

Blitz, John H., and C. Baxter Mann

  2000   *Fisherfolk, Farmers, and Frenchmen: Archaeological Explorations on the Mississippi Gulf Coast.* Archaeological Report No. 30, Mississippi Department of Archives and History, Jackson.

Borremans, Nina T., and Graig D. Shaak

  1986   Preliminary Report on Investigations of Sponge Spicules in Florida "Chalky" Paste Pottery. In *Papers in Ceramic Analysis, Ceramic Notes No. 3,* edited by Prudence M. Rice, pp. 125–132. Occasional Publications of the Ceramic Technology Laboratory, Florida State Museum, Gainesville.

Bradley, Richard B.

  1984   *The Social Foundations of British Prehistory.* Longman, London.

Brain, Jeffrey P., and Drexel A. Peterson

  1971   Palmetto Tempered Pottery. *Southeastern Archaeological Conference Bulletin* 13:70–76.

Brose, David S.

  1985   "Willey-Nilly" or the Archaeology of Northwest Florida and Adjacent Borderlands Revisited. *The Florida Anthropologist* 38(1–2, pt. 2):156–162.

Brown, James A.

  1989   The Beginnings of Pottery as an Economic Process. In *What's New? A Closer Look at the Process of Innovation,* edited by S. E. van der Leeuw and Robin Torrence, pp. 203–224. Unwin Hyman, London.

Bruseth, James E.

  1991   Poverty Point Development as Seen at the Cedarland and Claiborne Sites, Southern Mississippi. In *The Poverty Point Culture: Local Manifestations, Subsistence Practices, and Trade Networks,* edited by Kathleen M. Byrd, pp. 7–25. Geoscience and Man 29. Louisiana State University, Baton Rouge.

Buckley, James, and Eric H. Willis

  1972   Isotopes' Radiocarbon Measurements IX. *Radiocarbon* 14(1):114–139.

Bullen, Adelaide K., and Ripley P. Bullen

  1953   The Battery Point Site, Bayport, Hernando County, Florida. *The Florida Anthropologist* 6(3):85–92.

Bullen, Ripley P.

1954 Culture Changes during the Fiber-Tempered Period of Florida. *Southern Indian Studies* 6:45–48.

1955 Stratigraphic Tests at Bluffton, Volusia County. *The Florida Anthropologist* 8(1):1–16.

1958a More Florida Radiocarbon Dates and Their Significance. *The Florida Anthropologist* 11(4):97–110.

1958b *Six Sites near the Chattahoochee River in the Jim Woodruff Reservoir Area, Florida.* River Basin Surveys Papers No. 14, pp. 315–358. Bulletin 169, Bureau of American Ethnology, Washington, D.C.

1959 The Transitional Period of Florida. *Southeastern Archaeological Conference Newsletter* 6:43–53.

1961 Radiocarbon Dates for Southeastern Fiber-Tempered Pottery. *American Antiquity* 27:104–106.

1968 Report of the Florida–South Georgia Group. *Southeastern Archaeological Conference Bulletin* 8:7–10.

1969 *Excavations at Sunday Bluff, Florida.* Contributions of the Florida State Museum, No. 15, Gainesville.

1971 The Transitional Period of Southern Southeastern United States as Viewed from Florida, or the Roots of the Gulf Tradition. *Southeastern Archaeological Conference Bulletin* 13:63–70.

1972 The Orange Period of Peninsular Florida. In *Fiber-Tempered Pottery in Southeastern United States and Northern Colombia: Its Origins, Context, and Significance,* edited by Ripley P. Bullen and James B. Stoltman, pp. 9–33. Florida Anthropological Society Publications, No. 6, Gainesville.

Bullen, Ripley P., and Walter Askew

1965 Tests at the Askew Site, Citrus County, Florida. *The Florida Anthropologist* 18(4):201–217.

Bullen, Ripley P., Walter Askew, Lee Feder, and Richard L. McDonnell

1978 *The Canton Street Site, St. Petersburg, Florida.* Florida Anthropological Society Publications, No. 9, Gainesville.

Bullen, Ripley P., and Adelaide K. Bullen

1956 *Excavations on Cape Haze Peninsula, Florida.* Contributions of the Florida State Museum, No. 1, Gainesville.

1961 The Summer Haven Site, St. Johns County, Florida. *The Florida Anthropologist* 14:1–15.

1976 *The Palmer Site.* Florida Anthropological Society Publications, No. 8, Gainesville.

Bullen, Ripley P., and James B. Stoltman, eds.

1972 *Fiber-Tempered Pottery in Southeastern United States and Northern Colombia: Its Origins, Context, and Significance.* Florida Anthropological Society Publications, No. 6, Gainesville.

Cable, John S.

1993 Prehistoric Chronology and Settlement Patterns of Edisto Beach State

Park. In *Cultural Resources Survey and Archaeological Site Evaluation of the Edisto Beach State Park, Colleton County, South Carolina,* pp. 158–205. Report prepared by New South Associates, Stone Mountain, Georgia; on file with South Carolina Department of Parks, Recreation, and Tourism, Columbia.

1997 The Ceremonial Mound Theory: New Evidence for the Possible Ceremonial Function of Shell Rings. From South Carolina Archaeology Week poster, *Shell Rings of the Late Archaic.* South Carolina Institute of Archaeology and Anthropology, University of South Carolina, Columbia.

Cable, John S., and G. Ishmael Williams

1993 Prehistoric Background. In *Cultural Resources Survey and Archaeological Site Evaluation of the Edisto Beach State Park, Colleton County, South Carolina,* pp. 9–51. Report prepared by New South Associates, Stone Mountain, Georgia; on file with South Carolina Department of Parks, Recreation, and Tourism, Columbia.

Caldwell, Joseph R.

1958 *Trend and Tradition in the Prehistory of the Eastern United States.* American Anthropological Association, Memoir No. 88, Menasha, Wisconsin.

Caldwell, Joseph R., and Antonio J. Waring, Jr.

1939 Some Chatham County Pottery Types and Their Sequence. *Southeastern Archaeological Conference Newsletter* 1:5–6.

Calvert, P. M., D. S. Introne, and J. J. Stipp

1979 University of Miami Radiocarbon Dates XIV. *Radiocarbon* 21:107–112.

Carr, Christopher

1995 A Unified Middle-Range Theory of Artifact Design. In *Style, Society, and Person: Archaeological and Ethnological Perspectives,* edited by Christopher Carr and Jill E. Neitzel, pp. 171–258. Plenum Press, New York.

Carr, Robert S., and John G. Beriault

1984 Prehistoric Man in South Florida. In *Environments of South Florida: Present and Past II,* edited by Patrick J. Gleason, pp. 1–14. Memoir 2, Miami Geological Society, Coral Gables.

Chagnon, Napolean A.

1968 *Yanomamö: The Fierce People.* Holt, Rinehart and Winston, New York.

Chase, David

1972 Evidence of Bayou La Batre–Archaic Contact. *Journal of Alabama Archaeology* 18(2):151–161.

Claassen, Cheryl

1996 A Consideration of the Social Organization of the Shell Mound Archaic. In *Archaeology of the Mid-Holocene Southeast,* edited by Kenneth E. Sassaman and David G. Anderson, pp. 235–258. University Press of Florida, Gainesville.

Claflin, William H., Jr.

1931 *The Stallings Island Mound, Columbia County, Georgia.* Papers of the Peabody Museum of American Archaeology and Ethnology, Vol. 14, No. 1, Harvard University, Cambridge, Massachusetts.

Clark, John E.

2004 Surrounding the Sacred: Geometry and Design of Early Mound Groups as Meaning and Function. In *Signs of Power: The Rise of Cultural Complexity in the Southeast,* edited by Jon L. Gibson and Phillip J. Carr, pp. 162–213. University of Alabama Press, Tuscaloosa.

Clark, John E., and Michael Blake

1994 The Power of Prestige: Competitive Generosity and the Emergence of Rank Societies in Lowland Mexico. In *Factional Competition and Political Development in the New World,* edited by Elizabeth M. Brumfiel and John W. Fox, pp. 17–30. Cambridge University Press, Cambridge, United Kingdom.

Clark, John E., and Dennis Gosser

1995 Reinventing Mesoamerica's First Pottery. In *The Emergence of Pottery: Technology and Innovation in Ancient Societies,* edited by William K. Barnett and John W. Hoopes, pp. 209–221. Smithsonian Institution Press, Washington, D.C.

Cockrell, Wilburn A.

1970a Glades I and Pre-Glades Settlement and Subsistence Patterns on Marco Island (Collier County, Florida). Unpublished Master's thesis, Department of Anthropology, Florida State University, Tallahassee.

1970b *Interim Report on Archaeological Salvage Excavations, Marco Island, Florida, 1967–1970.* Division of Archives, History, and Records Management, Bureau of Historic Sites and Properties, Tallahassee, Florida.

Connaway, John M., Samuel O. McGahey, and Clarence H. Webb

1977 *Teoc Creek, A Poverty Point Site in Carroll County, Mississippi.* Archaeological Report No. 3, Mississippi Department of Archives and History, Jackson.

Connolly, Robert P.

1999 *1999 Annual Report: Station Archaeology Program at the Poverty Point State Commemorative Area.* Poverty Point State Commemorative Area. Submitted to Division of Archaeology, Louisiana Department of Culture, Recreation and Tourism, Baton Rouge.

2001 *2001 Annual Report: Station Archaeology Program at the Poverty Point State Historic Site.* Poverty Point State Commemorative Area. Submitted to Division of Archaeology, Louisiana Department of Culture, Recreation and Tourism, Baton Rouge.

2002 *2002 Annual Report: Station Archaeology Program at the Poverty Point State Historic Site.* Poverty Point State Commemorative Area. Submitted to Division of Archaeology, Louisiana Department of Culture, Recreation and Tourism, Baton Rouge.

Cooke, Richard

1995 Monagrillo, Panama's First Pottery: Summary of Research, with New Interpretations. In *The Emergence of Pottery: Technology and Innovation in Ancient Societies,* edited by William K. Barnett and John W. Hoopes, pp. 169–184. Smithsonian Institution Press, Washington, D.C.

Cordell, Ann S.

1984 *Ceramic Notes No. 2: Ceramic Technology at a Weeden Island Period Archaeological Site in North Florida.* Occasional Publications of the Ceramic Technology Laboratory, Museum of Natural History, University of Florida, Gainesville.

1985 Pottery Variability and Site Chronology in the Upper St. Johns River Basin. In *Archaeological Site Types, Distribution, and Preservation within the Upper St. Johns River Basin, Florida,* edited by Brenda Sigler-Eisenberg, pp. 114–134. Miscellaneous Project and Report Series, No. 27, Florida State Museum, Gainesville.

1992 Technological Investigation of Pottery Variability in Southwest Florida. In *Culture and Environment in the Domain of the Calusa,* edited by William H. Marquart, pp. 105–189. Monograph No. 1, Institute of Archaeology and Paleoenvironmental Studies, University of Florida, Gainesville.

2000 Appendix 7: Analysis of Pottery from the Joseph Reed Shell Ring. In *The Joseph Reed Shell Ring,* by Michael Russo and Gregory Heide, pp. 83–84. Submitted to Hobe Sound National Wildlife Refuge by the Southeast Archeological Center, National Park Service, Tallahassee, Florida.

2001 *Report on the Investigation of Daub Construction Materials from San Luis de Talimali.* Prepared for Dr. Bonnie McEwan, Mission San Luis de Talimali.

2002 *Paste Variability and Clay Resource Utilization in Pottery from the Gulfstream Project: 8PO6486 and 8PO6111.* Prepared for Janus Research, St. Petersburg, Florida.

2003 *Paste Variability and Clay Resource Utilization in Pottery from the Ten Mile Creek Project, St. Lucie County, Florida.* Prepared for New South Associates, Stone Mountain, Georgia.

2005 Technological Investigation of Pottery Variability at the Pineland Site Complex. In *The Archaeology of Pineland: A Coastal Southwest Florida Village Complex,* edited by Karen J. Walker and William H. Marquardt. Monograph No. 4, Institute of Archaeology and Paleoenvironmental Studies, University of Florida, Gainesville.

Cordell, Ann S., and Steven H. Koski

2003 Analysis of a Spiculate Clay from Lake Monroe, Volusia County, Florida. *The Florida Anthropologist* 56(2):113–124.

Crown, Patricia L., and W. H. Wills

1995 Economic Intensification and the Origins of Ceramic Containers in the American Southwest. In *The Emergence of Pottery: Technology and Innovation in Ancient Societies,* edited by William K. Barnett and John W. Hoopes, pp. 241–254. Smithsonian Institution Press, Washington, D.C.

Crusoe, Donald L.

1971a Fiber-Tempered Ceramic Fabrics and Late Archaic Culture Historical Problems. Paper presented at the Southeastern Archaeological Conference, Macon, Georgia. Copy on file at the Southeastern Archaeological Center, National Park Service, Tallahassee, Florida.

1971b A Study of Aboriginal Trade: A Petrographic Analysis of Certain Types from Florida and Georgia. *The Florida Anthropologist* 24(1):31–43.

Cumbaa, Stephen L.
1976 A Reconsideration of Freshwater Shellfish Exploitation in the Florida Archaic. *The Florida Anthropologist* 29:49–59.

Davis, Thomas W., Jeffrey H. Maymon, Michael P. Hornum, Lance B. Trask, John Calabrese, Thomas F. Majarov, Timothy A. Silva, Amy K. Fanz, Conne Capozo-zola, John G. Clarke, Clifford A. Brown, Donald J. Maher, Meril Dunn, Ellen S. Onge, J. Hampton Tucker, and S. Justine Woodard
1994 *Phase II Archaeological Survey Evaluation of Thirteen Sites for the Proposed Florida Gas Transmission Phase III Expansion Project, Jefferson and Madison Counties, Florida.* Report prepared by R. Christopher Goodwin & Associates, Inc.

DeBoer, Warren R., and James A. Moore
1982 The Measurement and Meaning of Stylistic Diversity. *Nawpa Pacha* 20: 147–162.

DePratter, Chester B.
1979 Ceramics. In *The Anthropology of St. Catherines Island 2: The Refuge-Deptford Mortuary Complex,* edited by David H. Thomas and Clark S. Larson, pp. 109–132. Anthropological Papers Vol. 56, Pt. 1, American Museum of Natural History, New York.

1991 *W.P.A. Archaeological Excavations in Chatham County, Georgia: 1937–1942.* Laboratory of Archaeology Series, Report No. 29, University of Georgia, Athens.

DePratter, Chester B., Richard W. Jeffries, and Charles Pearson
1973 A Review of Early Pottery from the South Carolina Coast. *The Notebook* 5(2):45–53. Institute of Archaeology and Anthropology, University of South Carolina, Columbia.

DesJean, Thomas
1985 The Archaic Stage Occupation at Kings Bay: An Overview. In *Aboriginal Subsistence and Settlement Archaeology of the Kings Bay Locality,* vol. 1, *The Kings Bay and Devils Walkingstick Sites,* edited by William Hampton Adams, pp. 17–34. Reports of Investigations 1, Department of Anthropology, University of Florida, Gainesville.

Dickel, David
1992 *An Archaeological and Historical Survey of Bonita Springs, Parcel Three, Lee County, Florida.* AHC Technical Report 43, The Archaeological and Historical Conservancy, Inc., Davie, Florida.

Dickinson, Martin F., and Lucy B. Wayne
1987 *Archaeological Survey and Testing Phase I Development Areas Fairfield Fort George, Fort George Island, Duval County, Jacksonville, Florida.* Water and Air Research, Inc., Gainesville, Florida.

Douglass, Andrew E.
1882 A Find of Ceremonial Axes in a Florida Mound. *American Antiquarian and Oriental Journal* 4:100–109.

Dye, David H., and Jerry R. Galm

1986 Alexander, Tchefuncte, and Black Sand: An Early Gulf Tradition in the Mississippi Valley. In *The Tchula Period in the Mid-South and Lower Mississippi Valley,* edited by David H. Dye and Ronald C. Brister, pp. 28–39. Archaeological Report No. 17, Mississippi Department of Archives and History, Jackson.

Elliott, Daniel T., R. Jerald Ledbetter, and Elizabeth A. Gordon

1994 *Data Recovery at Lovers Lane, Phinizy Swamp and the Old Dike Sites, Bobby Jones Expressway Extension Corridor, Augusta, Georgia.* Occasional Papers in Cultural Resource Management 7, Georgia Department of Transportation, Atlanta.

Elliott, Daniel T., and Kenneth E. Sassaman

1995 *Archaic Period Archaeology of the Georgia Coastal Plain and Coastal Zone.* University of Georgia Laboratory of Archaeology Series Report No. 35, Georgia Archaeological Research Design Paper No. 11, Athens.

Endonino, Jon C.

2000 *The Determination of Orange Period Pottery Manufacturing Techniques Using Experimental and Radiographic Approaches.* On file, Florida Museum of Natural History, Gainesville.

Feathers, James P.

2000 *Luminescence Dating of Pottery from Poverty Point.* Report on file, Regional Archaeology Program, Museum of Natural Science, Louisiana State University, Baton Rouge.

Ferguson, Vera Masius

1951 *Chronology at South Indian Fields, Florida.* Yale University Publications in Anthropology, No. 45, New Haven, Connecticut.

Ford, James A.

1952 *Measurements of Some Prehistoric Design Developments in the Southeastern States.* Anthropological Papers Vol. 44, Pt. 3, American Museum of Natural History, New York.

1954 The Type Concept Revisited. *American Anthropologist* 56:42–54.

1966 Early Formative Cultures in Georgia and Florida. *American Antiquity* 31: 781–799.

1969 *A Comparison of Formative Cultures in the Americas: Diffusion or the Psychic Unity of Man.* Smithsonian Contributions to Anthropology Vol. 2. Smithsonian Institution Press, Washington, D.C.

Ford, James A., Philip Phillips, and William G. Haag

1955 *The Jaketown Site in West-Central Mississippi.* Anthropological Papers Vol. 45, Pt. 1, American Museum of Natural History, New York.

Ford, James A., and George I. Quimby, Jr.

1945 *The Tchefuncte Culture, an Early Occupation of the Lower Mississippi Valley.* Memoir No. 2, Society of American Archaeology, Menasha, Wisconsin.

Ford, James A., and Clarence H. Webb

1956 *Poverty Point, A Late Archaic Site in Louisiana.* Anthropological Papers Vol. 46, Pt. 1, American Museum of Natural History, New York.

Fradkin, Arlene
  1976 The Wightman Site: A Study of Prehistoric Culture and Environment on
        Sanibel Island, Lee County, Florida. Unpublished Master's thesis, Depart-
        ment of Anthropology, University of Florida, Gainesville.
Fryman, Mildred L., David Swindell, and James J. Miller
  1980 *Cultural Resource Reconnaissance of Hobe Sound National Wildlife Refuge, Mar-
        tin County, Florida.* Submitted to Interagency Archeological Services–Atlanta
        and U.S. Fish and Wildlife Service, Contract A-55034(79). On file at the
        Office of the State Historic Preservation Officer, Tallahassee, Florida.
Fullen, Steven
  2001 *Manufacture of Fiber Tempered Slab Molded Pot.* Report on file, Anthropology
        Division, Museum of Natural Science, Louisiana State University, Baton
        Rouge.
Fuller, Richard S., and Diane Silvia Fuller
  1987 *Excavations at Morgan: A Coles Creek Mound Complex in Coastal Louisiana.*
        Lower Mississippi Survey Bulletin No. 11, Peabody Museum, Harvard
        University, Cambridge, Massachusetts.
Gagliano, Sherwood M., and Clarence H. Webb
  1970 Archaic and Poverty Point Transition at the Pearl River Mouth. In *The
        Poverty Point Culture,* edited by Betty J. Broyles and Clarence H. Webb, pp.
        42–72. Bulletin No. 12, Southeastern Archaeological Conference, Morgan-
        town, West Virginia.
Gebauer, Anne Birgitte
  1995 Pottery Production and the Introduction of Agriculture in Southern Scan-
        dinavia. In *The Emergence of Pottery: Technology and Innovation in Ancient So-
        cieties,* edited by William K. Barnett and John W. Hoopes, pp. 99–112. Smith-
        sonian Institution Press, Washington, D.C.
Gertjejansen, Doyle J., J. Richard Shenkel, and Jesse O. Snowden
  1983 Laboratory Simulation of Tchefuncte Period Ceramic Vessels from the Pont-
        chartrain Basin. *Southeastern Archaeology* 2(1):37–63.
Gibson, Jon L.
  1973 Social Systems at Poverty Point, an Analysis of Intersite and Intrasite Varia-
        bility. Ph.D. dissertation, Southern Methodist University, Dallas.
  1976 *Archaeological Survey of Bayou Teche, Vermilion River, and Freshwater Bayou,
        South Central Louisiana.* Report No. 2, Center for Archaeological Studies,
        University of Southwestern Louisiana, Lafayette.
  1984 *The Earthen Face of Civilization: Mapping and Testing at Poverty Point, 1983.*
        Center for Archaeological Studies, University of Southwestern Louisiana,
        Lafayette.
  1987 *The Ground Truth about Poverty Point: The Second Season, 1985.* Report No.
        7, Center for Archaeological Studies, University of Southwestern Louisiana,
        Lafayette.
  1989 *Digging on the Dock of the Bay(ou): The 1988 Excavations at Poverty Point,
        Louisiana.* Report No. 8, Center for Archaeological Studies, University of
        Southwestern Louisiana, Lafayette.

1990a *Archaeological Survey of the Mid-Teche Ridge, South Louisiana: From Bayou Gerimond to Bayou Portage Guidry.* Center for Archaeological Studies, University of Southwestern Louisiana, Lafayette.

1990b *Search for the Lost Sixth Ridge: The 1989 Excavations at Poverty Point.* Report No. 9, Center for Archaeological Studies, University of Southwestern Louisiana, Lafayette.

1991 Catahoula—An Amphibious Poverty Point Period Manifestation in Eastern Louisiana. In *The Poverty Point Culture: Local Manifestations, Subsistence Practices, and Trade Networks,* edited by Kathleen M. Byrd, pp. 61–87. Geoscience and Man Vol. 29. Louisiana State University, Baton Rouge.

1993 *In Helona's Shadow: Excavations in the Western Rings at Poverty Point, 1991.* Report No. 11, Center for Archaeological Studies, University of Southwestern Louisiana, Lafayette.

1994a Ceramics. In *The Development of Southeastern Archaeology,* edited by Jay K. Johnson, pp. 18–35. University of Alabama Press, Tuscaloosa.

1994b *Cool Dark Woods, Poison Ivy, and Maringoins: The 1993 Excavations at Poverty Point, Louisiana.* Report No. 12, Center for Archaeological Studies, University of Southwestern Louisiana, Lafayette.

1995 Things That Count: Mean Vertical Position and Poverty Point Archaeology. In *"An' Stuff Like That There": In Appreciation of William G. Haag,* edited by Jon L. Gibson, Robert W. Neuman, and Richard A. Weinstein, pp. 61–83. Louisiana Archaeology No. 18. Louisiana Archaeological Society, Lafayette.

1996a The Orvis Scott Site: A Poverty Point Component on Joes Bayou, East Carroll Parish, Louisiana. *Midcontinental Journal of Archaeology* 21:1–48.

1996b Poverty Point Archaeology and Greater Southeastern Prehistory: The Culture That Did Not Fit. In *Archaeology of the Mid-Holocene Southeast,* edited by Kenneth E. Sassaman and David G. Anderson, pp. 288–305. University Press of Florida, Gainesville.

1997 *By the Shining Bayou Waters: The 1995 Excavations at Poverty Point, Louisiana.* Report No. 13, Center for Archaeological Studies, University of Southwestern Louisiana, Lafayette.

1998a Broken Circles, Owl Monsters, and Black Earth Midden: Separating Sacred and Secular at Poverty Point. In *Ancient Earthen Enclosures of the Eastern Woodlands,* edited by Robert C. Mainfort, Jr., and Lynne P. Sullivan, pp. 17–30. University Press of Florida, Gainesville.

1998b Elements and Organization of Poverty Point Political Economy: High-Water Fish, Exotic Rocks, and Sacred Earth. In *Research in Economic Anthropology,* edited by Barry L. Issac, pp. 291–340. JAI Press, Stamford, Connecticut.

1999 *Poverty Point: A Terminal Archaic Culture in the Lower Mississippi Valley.* 2nd ed. Anthropological Study 7. Department of Culture, Recreation and Tourism, Louisiana Archaeological Survey and Antiquities Commission, Baton Rouge.

2000 *Ancient Mounds of Poverty Point: Place of Rings.* University Press of Florida, Gainesville.

2001   The Chicken or the Egg B.C. (Before Chickens): Building Progression at Poverty Point, Louisiana. Paper presented to the 27th Annual Meeting of the Louisiana Archaeological Society, Natchitoches.

2002   Behold the Wonderful Work of Their Hands: Poverty Point History and Sociality. Paper presented to the 58th Southeastern Archaeological Conference, Biloxi, Mississippi.

2004   The Power of Beneficent Obligation in First Mound-Building Societies. In *Signs of Power: The Rise of Cultural Complexity in the Southeast,* edited by Jon L. Gibson and Phillip J. Carr, pp. 254–269. University of Alabama Press, Tuscaloosa.

Gibson, Jon L., and David L. Griffing

1994   Only a Stone's Throw Away: Exchange in the Poverty Point Hinterland. In *Exchange in the Lower Mississippi Valley and Contiguous Areas in 1100 B.C.,* edited by Jon L. Gibson, pp. 207–250. Louisiana Archaeology No. 17. Louisiana Archaeological Society, Lafayette.

Goggin, John M.

1939   A Ceramic Sequence in South Florida. *New Mexico Anthropologist* 3:35–40.

1940   The Distribution of Pottery Wares in the Glades Archaeological Area of South Florida. *New Mexico Anthropologist* 4:22–23.

1947   A Preliminary Definition of Archaeological Areas and Periods in Florida. *American Antiquity* 13:114–127.

1949   Cultural Traditions in Florida Prehistory. In *The Florida Indian and His Neighbors,* edited by John W. Griffin, pp. 13–44. Rollins College, Winter Park, Florida.

1952   *Space and Time Perspective in Northern St. Johns Archeology, Florida.* Publications in Anthropology, No. 47, Yale University Press, New Haven, Connecticut.

Goldsmith, Victor

1966   The Recent Sedimentary Environment of Choctawhatchee Bay, Florida. Master's thesis, Florida State University, Tallahassee.

Goodyear, Albert C.

1988   On the Study of Technological Change. *Current Anthropology* 29:320–323.

Greene, Glen S.

1990   *The Deep Six Paleosol: The Incipient Poverty Point Occupation, 1983 Excavations.* Northeast Louisiana State University, Monroe. Submitted to the Louisiana Division of Archaeology, Baton Rouge.

Gregory, Hiram F., Jr.

1991   Terral Lewis: Recapitulation. In *The Poverty Point Culture: Local Manifestations, Subsistence Practices, and Trade Networks,* edited by Kathleen M. Byrd, pp. 121–127. Geoscience and Man Vol. 29. Louisiana State University, Baton Rouge.

Gregory, Hiram F., Jr., and Clarence H. Webb

1971   European Trade Beads from Six Sites in Natchitoches Parish, Louisiana. *The Florida Anthropologist* 18(3):15–44.

Griffin, James B.

1939   Report on the Ceramics of the Wheeler Basin. In *An Archaeological Survey of Wheeler Basin on the Tennessee River in Northern Alabama,* by William S. Webb. Bulletin 122, Bureau of American Ethnology, Washington, D.C.

1943   *An Analysis and Interpretation of the Ceramic Remains from Two Sites near Beaufort, South Carolina.* Anthropological Papers No. 22, pp. 155–168. Bulletin 133, Bureau of American Ethnology, Smithsonian Institution, Washington, D.C.

1945a Ceramic Collections from Two South Carolina Sites. *Papers of the Michigan Academy of Science, Arts and Letters* 30:465–476.

1945b The Significance of Fiber-Tempered Pottery of the St. Johns Area in Florida. *Journal of the Washington Academy of Sciences* 35(7):218–223.

1978   Eastern United States. In *Chronologies in New World Archaeology,* edited by R. E. Taylor and Clement W. Meighan, pp. 51–70. Academic Press, New York.

Griffin, John W.

1974   Archeology and Environment in South Florida. In *Environments of South Florida: Present and Past,* edited by Patrick J. Gleason, pp. 342–346. Memoir 2, Miami Geological Society, Miami.

1988   *The Archeology of the Everglades National Park: A Synthesis.* Contract CX5000-5-0049, National Park Service, Southeast Archeological Center, Tallahassee, Florida.

Griffin, John W., and Hale G. Smith

1949   Nocoroco, a Timucuan Village of 1605 Now in Tomoka State Park. *Florida Historical Quarterly* 27:340–361.

1954   The Cotten Site: An Archaeological Site of Early Ceramic Times in Volusia County, Florida. *Florida State University Studies* 16:27–60.

Griffing, David L.

1990   Surface Surveys of the Insley Site in Franklin Parish. *Louisiana Archaeology* 12:219–240.

Haag, William G.

1939   Pickwick Basin Pottery Type Descriptions. *Southeastern Archaeological Conference Newsletter* 1(1):1–17.

1978   A Prehistory of the Lower Mississippi Valley. In *Man and Environment in the Lower Mississippi Valley,* edited by Sam B. Hilliard, pp. 1–8. Geoscience and Man Vol. 19. Louisiana State University, Baton Rouge.

1990   Excavations at the Poverty Point Site: 1972–1975. In *Recent Research at the Poverty Point Site,* edited by Kathleen M. Byrd, pp. 1–36. Louisiana Archaeology No. 13. Louisiana Archaeological Society, Lafayette.

Hally, David J.

1983   Use Alterations of Pottery Vessel Surfaces: An Important Source of Evidence for the Identification of Vessel Function. *North American Archaeologist* 4:3–26.

1986   The Identification of Vessel Function: A Case Study from Northwest Georgia. *American Antiquity* 51:267–295.

Hayden, Brian

1990 Nimrods, Piscators, Pluckers and Planters: The Emergence of Food Production. *Journal of Anthropological Archaeology* 9:31–69.

1995a The Emergence of Prestige Technologies and Pottery. In *The Emergence of Pottery: Technology and Innovation in Ancient Societies,* edited by William K. Barnett and John W. Hoopes, pp. 257–265. Smithsonian Institution Press, Washington, D.C.

1995b Pathways to Power: Principles for Creating Socioeconomic Inequalities. In *Foundations of Social Inequality,* edited by T. Douglas Price and Gary M. Feinman, pp. 15–86. Plenum Press, New York.

1996a Feasting in Prehistoric and Traditional Societies. In *Food and the Status Quest: An Interdisciplinary Perspective,* edited by Polly Wiessner and Wulf Schiefenhövel, pp. 127–148. Berghahn Books, New York.

1996b Thresholds of Power in Emergent Complex Societies. In *Emergent Complexity: The Evolution of Intermediate Societies,* edited by Jeanne E. Arnold, pp. 50–58. Archaeological Series 9. International Monographs in Prehistory, Ann Arbor, Michigan.

1998 Practical and Prestige Technologies: The Evolution of Material Systems. *Journal of Archaeological Method and Theory* 5(1):1–55.

2001 Fabulous Feasts: A Prolegomenon to the Importance of Feasting. In *Feasts: Archaeological and Ethnographic Perspectives on Food, Politics, and Power,* edited by Michael Dietler and Brian Hayden, pp. 23–64. Smithsonian Institution Press, Washington, D.C.

Hays, Christopher T.

1995 *1995 Annual Report for Management Units IV and V.* Regional Archaeology Program, Museum of Natural Science, Louisiana State University. Submitted to Division of Archaeology, Louisiana Department of Culture, Recreation and Tourism, Baton Rouge.

1997 Fort Butler and Other Projects: Regional Archaeology in Southeast Louisiana. In *1997 Annual Report for Management Units IV and V.* Regional Archaeology Program, Museum of Natural Science, Louisiana State University. Submitted to Division of Archaeology, Louisiana Department of Culture, Recreation and Tourism, Baton Rouge.

Hays, Christopher T., and Richard A. Weinstein

1999 Ceramics at the Poverty Point Site: Contexts and Origins. Paper presented at the 56th Annual Meeting of the Southeastern Archaeological Conference, Pensacola, Florida.

2000 Perspectives on Tchefuncte Cultural Chronology: A View from the Bayou Jasmine Site, St. John the Baptist Parish, Louisiana. *Louisiana Archaeology* 23:49–89.

Heckenberger, Michael J.

1998 Manioc Agriculture and Sedentism in Amazonia: The Upper Xingu Example. *Antiquity* 72:633–648.

Heckenberger, Michael J., James B. Peterson, and Eduardo Goes Neves
   1999   Village Size and Permanence in Amazonia: Two Archaeological Examples from Brazil. *Latin American Antiquity* 10(4):353–376.

Heide, Gregory
   2000   The Transitional Period in Florida: An Overview. In *The Joseph Reed Shell Ring,* by Michael Russo and Gregory Heide, pp. 93–108. Submitted to Hobe Sound National Wildlife Refuge by the Southeast Archeological Center, National Park Service, Tallahassee, Florida.

Helms, Mary W.
   1988   *Ulysses' Sail: An Ethnographic Odyssey of Power, Knowledge and Geographical Distance.* Princeton University Press, Princeton, New Jersey.

Hemphill, Keith, L. Janice Campbell, and James R. Morehead
   1995   *Completing the Evaluation Process at Eglin Air Force Base, Okaloosa, Santa Rosa and Walton Counties; Volume XXII: Testing and Evaluation of the Stone Vessel Site—8WL1005.* Report of Investigations No. 290, Prentice Thomas and Associates, Inc., Fort Walton Beach, Florida.

Hillman, Mitchell M.
   1987   *The 1985 Test Excavations of the "Dock" Area of Poverty Point.* Poverty Point State Commemorative Area, Epps, Louisiana.

Holder, Preston
   1938   Excavations on Saint Simons Island and Vicinity (Winter 1936–37). *Proceedings of the Society for Georgia Archaeology* 1:8–9.

Holmes, William H.
   1894   Earthenware of Florida. *Journal of the Academy of Natural Sciences of Philadelphia* 10(1):106–128.

Hoopes, John W.
   1995   Interaction in Hunting and Gathering Societies as a Context for the Emergence of Pottery in the Central American Isthmus. In *The Emergence of Pottery: Technology and Innovation in Ancient Societies,* edited by William K. Barnett and John W. Hoopes, pp. 185–198. Smithsonian Institution Press, Washington, D.C.

Hoopes, John W., and William K. Barnett
   1995   The Shape of Early Pottery Studies. In *The Emergence of Pottery: Technology and Innovation in Ancient Societies,* edited by William K. Barnett and John W. Hoopes, pp. 1–7. Smithsonian Institution Press, Washington, D.C.

Houck, Brett A.
   1996   *Archaeological Excavations at 8LL717, Bonita Springs, Lee County, Florida.* Archaeological Historical Conservancy Technical Report 78, 1993 report revised in 1996. Submitted to Bonita Bay Properties. Copy on file, Bureau of Archaeological Research, Tallahassee, Florida.

Hunter, Donald G.
   1975   Functional Analysis of Poverty Point Objects. *The Florida Anthropologist* 28:57–71.

Iceland, Harry
   2000   Appendix 4: Joseph Reed Shell Ring Lithics Report. In *The Joseph Reed Shell Ring,* by Michael Russo and Gregory Heide, pp. 67–68. Submitted to Hobe Sound National Wildlife Refuge by the Southeast Archeological Center, National Park Service, Tallahassee, Florida.

Jahn, Otto L., and Ripley P. Bullen
   1978   *The Tick Island Site, St. Johns River, Florida.* Florida Anthropological Society Publications, No. 10, Gainesville.

Janus Research
   1998   *Cultural Resource Assessment Survey of the Indian River Park in Martin County, Florida.* Janus Research, St. Petersburg, Florida.

Jenkins, Ned J.
   1982   Archaeology of the Gainesville Lake Area: Synthesis. In *Archaeological Investigations in the Gainesville Lake Area of the Tennessee-Tombigbee Waterway,* Vol. 5. Report of Investigations 23, Office of Archaeological Research, University of Alabama, University.

Jenkins, Ned J., David H. Dye, and John A. Walthall
   1986   Early Ceramic Development in the Coastal Plain. In *Early Woodland Archaeology,* edited by Kenneth B. Farnsworth and Thomas E. Emerson, pp. 546–563. Center for American Archaeology Press, Kampsville, Illinois.

Jenkins, Ned J., and Richard A. Krause
   1986   *The Tombigbee Watershed in Southeastern Prehistory.* University of Alabama Press, Tuscaloosa.

Jeter, Marvin D., Jerome C. Rose, G. Ishmael Williams, Jr., and Anna M. Harmon
   1989   *Archaeology and Bioarchaeology of the Lower Mississippi Valley and Trans-Mississippi South in Arkansas and Louisiana.* Arkansas Archeological Survey Research Series No. 37, Fayetteville.

Johnson, Jay K.
   1993   Poverty Point Period Quartz Crystal Drill Bits, Microliths, and Social Organization in the Yazoo Basin. *Southeastern Archaeology* 12:59–64.

Johnson, Robert E.
   2000   *Archaeological Testing and Monitoring of Site 8DU76 for the Ribault Clubhouse Foundation Repairs Project, Duval County, Florida.* Florida Archaeological Services, Inc., Jacksonville.

Johnson, William, Prentice M. Thomas, Jr., and Glen Fredlund
   1986   The Impact of Sea-Level Changes on the Cultural Prehistory of the Choctawhatchee Bay Area, Florida. Paper presented at the 51st Annual Meeting of the Society for American Archaeology, New Orleans.

Jones, Reca
   1997   Replicating Fire-Cracked Rock. Paper presented to the 23th Annual Meeting of the Louisiana Archaeological Society, Alexandria.

Kelly, A. R.
   1938   *A Preliminary Report on Archaeological Excavation at Macon, Georgia.* Anthro-

pological Papers No. 1. Bulletin 119, Bureau of American Ethnology, Smithsonian Institution, Washington, D.C.

Kelly, Robert L.

1991   Sedentism, Sociopolitical Inequality, and Resource Fluctuations. In *Between Bands and States,* edited by Susan A. Gregg, pp. 135–158. Occasional Paper No. 9, Center for Archaeological Investigations, Southern Illinois University, Carbondale.

Kennedy, Jerald, and Skye Wheeler

1998   *Hobe Sound National Wildlife Refuge: Narrative Description and Literature Citations.* Prepared for the U.S. Fish and Wildlife Service Comprehensive Conservation Plan. Copy on file, Hobe Sound National Wildlife Refuge, Stuart, Florida.

Kennedy, William Jerald

1980   Map of Joseph Reed Site. In *Cultural Resource Reconnaissance of Hobe Sound National Wildlife Refuge, Martin County, Florida,* by Mildred L. Fryman, David Swindell, and James J. Miller. Cultural Resource Management, Inc. Submitted to Interagency Archeological Services, National Park Service, Atlanta, Contract A-55034(79). On file, Division of Archives, History, and Records Management, Tallahassee, Florida.

Kidder, Tristram R.

2000   *A Brief Summary of the Archaeology of the Raffman Locality, Madison Parish, Louisiana.* Report submitted to Anderson-Tully Co., Vicksburg, Mississippi.

2002   Mapping Poverty Point. *American Antiquity* 67:89–101.

Kimbrough, Rhonda L.

1990   Norwood Period Sites in the Apalachicola National Forest, Florida. Paper presented at the 47th Southeastern Archaeological Conference, Mobile.

1999   A Norwood Simple Stamped Vessel from the Apalachicola National Forest, Florida. Paper presented at the Annual Meeting of the Florida Anthropological Society, Fort Walton Beach.

Knoblock, Byron

1939   *Banner-Stones of the North American Indian.* Published by the author, LaGrange, Illinois.

Krieger, Alex D.

1944   The Typological Concept. *American Antiquity* 9:271–288.

Kuttruff, Carl

1975   The Poverty Point Culture: North Sector Test Excavations. *Louisiana Archaeology* 2:129–152.

Kuttruff, Jenna, Marie Standifer, and Carl Kuttruff

1993   *Radiocarbon Dating of Cordage from Bayou Jasmine.* Report on file, Louisiana Archaeological Conservancy, Baton Rouge.

Lazarus, William C.

1958   A Poverty Point Complex in Florida. *The Florida Anthropologist* 11:23–32.

1965   Alligator Lake, a Ceramic Horizon Site on the Northwest Florida Coast. *The Florida Anthropologist* 23(2):83–124.

Lear, Phyllis M.

1998 A Stylistic Analysis of Poverty Point Objects. Unpublished Master's thesis, Department of Fine Arts, Louisiana State University, Baton Rouge.

Ledbetter, R. Jerald

1995 *Archaeological Investigations at Mill Branch Sites 9WR4 and 9WR11, Warren County, Georgia.* Technical Report No. 3, Interagency Archeological Services Division, National Park Service, Atlanta.

Lee, Arthur R., John G. Beriault, Walter Buschelman, and Jean Belknap

1993 A Small Site—Mulberry Midden, 8CR697—Contributes to Knowledge of Transitional Period. *The Florida Anthropologist* 46:43–52.

Lehmann, Geoffrey R.

1982 *The Jaketown Site, Surface Collections from a Poverty Point Regional Center in the Yazoo Basin, Mississippi.* Archaeological Report No. 9, Mississippi Department of Archives and History, Jackson.

Lincecum, Gideon

1904 Choctaw Traditions about Their Settlement in Mississippi and the Origin of Their Mounds. *Publications of the Mississippi Historical Society* 8:521–542.

Linton, Ralph

1944 North American Cooking Pots. *American Antiquity* 9:369–380.

Lockett, Samuel H.

1873 Mounds in Louisiana. In *Annual Report of the Board of Regents for 1872,* Smithsonian Institution, pp. 429–430. U.S. Government Printing Office, Washington, D.C.

Lowe, Gareth W.

1971 The Civilizational Consequences of Varying Degrees of Agricultural and Ceramic Dependency within the Basic Ecosystems of Mesoamerica. In *Observations on the Emergence of Civilization in Mesoamerica,* edited by Robert F. Heizer and John A. Graham, pp. 212–248. Contributions of the University of California Archaeological Research Facility 11. University of California, Department of Anthropology, Berkeley.

Luer, George M.

1989 Notes on the Howard Shell Mound and Calusa Island, Lee County, Florida. *The Florida Anthropologist* 42(3):249–254.

1999 *Cedar Point: A Late Archaic through Safety Harbor Occupation on Lemon Bay, Charlotte County, Florida.* Florida Anthropological Society Publication, No. 14, pp. 43–56, Gainesville.

McGimsey, Charles R., and Josette van der Koogh

2001 *Louisiana's Archaeological Radiometric Database.* Special Publication No. 3, Louisiana Archaeological Society, Lafayette.

McMichael, Alan

1982 *A Cultural Resource Assessment of Horrs Island, Collier County, Florida.* Miscellaneous Project Report Series, No. 15, Florida State Museum, Gainesville.

Manson, Joni L.
  1995 Starčevo Pottery and Neolithic Development in the Central Balkans. In *The Emergence of Pottery: Technology and Innovation in Ancient Societies,* edited by William K. Barnett and John W. Hoopes, pp. 65–77. Smithsonian Institution Press, Washington, D.C.

Marquardt, William H. (editor)
  1992 *Culture and Environment in the Domain of the Calusa.* Monograph 1 of the Institute of Archaeology and Paleoenvironmental Studies, University of Florida, Gainesville.
  1999 *The Archaeology of Useppa Island.* Monograph 3 of the Institute of Archaeology and Paleoenvironmental Studies, University of Florida, Gainesville.

Marrinan, Rochelle A.
  1975 *Ceramics, Molluscs, and Sedentism: The Late Archaic Period on the Georgia Coast.* Unpublished Ph.D. dissertation, Department of Anthropology, University of Florida, Gainesville.

Meggers, Betty, Clifford Evans, and E. Estrada
  1965 *The Early Formative Period of Coastal Ecuador.* Smithsonian Contributions in Anthropology 1, Washington, D.C.

Melancon, Mark A.
  1999 Seriation of Certain Tchefuncte Ceramic Decoration Styles in Avoyelles, Lafayette, St. Landry, and St. Martin Parishes, Louisiana. *Louisiana Archaeology* 22:37–47.

Michie, James L.
  1979 *The Bass Pond Site: Intensive Archaeological Testing at a Formative Period Base Camp on Kiawah Island, South Carolina.* Research Manuscript Series 154, South Carolina Institute of Archaeology and Anthropology, University of South Carolina, Columbia.

Milanich, Jerald T.
  1994 *Archaeology of Precolumbian Florida.* University Press of Florida, Gainesville.

Milanich, Jerald T., and Charles H. Fairbanks
  1980 *Florida Archaeology.* Academic Press, New York.

Mills, Barbara
  1989 Integrating Functional Analysis of Vessels and Sherds through Models of Ceramic Assemblage Formation. *World Archaeology* 21(1):133–147.

Milner, George R., and Richard W. Jefferies
  1998 The Read Archaic Shell Midden in Kentucky. *Southeastern Archaeology* 17(2): 119–132.

Mitchell, Scott
  1993 *An Analysis of the Ceramics from the Summer Haven Site.* Report on file, Janus Research, St. Petersburg, Florida.

Moore, A. M. T.
  1995 The Inception of Potting in Western Asia and Its Impact on Economy and Society. In *The Emergence of Pottery: Technology and Innovation in Ancient So-*

cieties, edited by William K. Barnett and John W. Hoopes, pp. 39–53. Smithsonian Institution Press, Washington, D.C.

Moore, Clarence B.

1894   Certain Sand Mounds of the St. John's River, Florida. Part II. *Journal of the Academy of Natural Sciences of Philadelphia* 10:129–246.

1913   Some Aboriginal Sites in Louisiana and Arkansas: Atchafalaya River, Lake Larto, Tensas River, Bayou Maçon, Bayou D'Arbonne, in Louisiana; Saline River, in Arkansas. *Journal of the Academy of Natural Sciences of Philadelphia* 16:5–93.

Morgan, Lewis H.

1878   *Ancient Society.* World, New York.

Morrell, L. Ross

1969   Fiber-Tempered Pottery from Southwestern Florida. Paper presented at the 68th Annual Meeting of the American Anthropological Association, New Orleans.

O'Hear, John W.

2001   Early Pottery in the Tombigbee and Tennessee Valleys. Paper presented in the symposium "Early Pottery in the Lower Southeast: Stylistic and Technological Approaches to Function and Interaction." Society for American Archaeology 66th Annual Meeting, New Orleans.

O'Shea, John

1981   Coping with Scarcity: Exchange and Social Storage. In *Economic Archaeology: Towards an Integrated Approach,* edited by Alison Sheriden and Geoff Bailey, pp. 167–183. British Archaeological Reports 96, Oxford.

Oyuela-Caycedo, Augusto

1995   Rock versus Clay: The Evolution of Pottery Technology in the Case of San Jacinto 1, Colombia. In *The Emergence of Pottery: Technology and Innovation in Ancient Societies,* edited by William K. Barnett and John W. Hoopes, pp. 133–144. Smithsonian Institution Press, Washington, D.C.

Pauketat, Timothy P.

2001   A New Tradition in Archaeology. In *The Archaeology of Traditions,* edited by Timothy P. Pauketat, pp. 1–16. University Press of Florida, Gainesville.

Pepe, James P.

1999   Jupiter Inlet (8PB34): A Test Case in the Use of Ceramic Frequencies and Discriminant Analysis in Determining Cultural Affinity. Unpublished Master's thesis, Department of Anthropology, Florida Atlantic University, Boca Raton.

Pepe, James, and Linda Jester

1995   *An Archaeological Survey and Assessment of the Mt. Elizabeth Site, 8MT30, Martin County, Florida.* AHC Technical Report 126, The Archaeological and Historical Conservancy, Inc., Davie, Florida.

Phelps, David S.

1965   The Norwood Series of Fiber-Tempered Ceramics. *Southeastern Archaeological Conference Bulletin* 2:65–69.

1966   Early and Late Components of the Tucker Site. *The Florida Anthropologist* 19(1):11–38.

1968   Thom's Creek Ceramics in the Central Savannah River Locality. *The Florida Anthropologist* 21(1):17–30.

1969   The Norwood Phase of North Florida and Its Extra-Regional Relationships. Paper presented at the 68th Annual Meeting of the American Anthropological Association, New Orleans.

Phillips, Philip

1970   *Archaeological Survey in the Lower Yazoo Basin, Mississippi, 1949–1955.* Papers of the Peabody Museum of Archaeology and Ethnology, Vol. 60, Harvard University, Cambridge, Massachusetts.

Phillips, Philip, James A. Ford, and James B. Griffin

1951   *Archaeological Survey in the Lower Mississippi Alluvial Valley, 1940–1947.* Papers of the Peabody Museum of Archaeology and Ethnology, Vol. 25, Harvard University, Cambridge, Massachusetts.

Piatak, Bruce J.

1994   The Tomoko Mound Complex in Northeast Florida. *Southeastern Archaeology* 12:109–118.

Porrier, Michael A.

1965   Ecological Variation in *Spongilla lacustris.* Unpublished Master's thesis, Department of Zoology, Louisiana State University, Baton Rouge.

Purdy, Barbara A.

1996   *Indian Art of Ancient Florida.* University Press of Florida, Gainesville.

Quitmyer, Irvy R.

2000   *Size vs. Season of Modern and Zooarchaeological Menhaden (*Brevoortia *spp.), Atlantic Croaker (*Micropogonias undulates*), and Coquina (*Donax variabilis*): Technical Data Used to Determine Season of Resource Exploitation during the Archaic Period at Jacksonville, Florida, Duval County.* Report on file, Louisiana State University Museum of Natural Science, Baton Rouge, Louisiana.

Reichel-Dolmatoff, Geraldo

1972   The Cultural Context of Early Fiber-Tempered Pottery in Northern Columbia. In *Fiber-Tempered Pottery in Southeastern United States and Northern Colombia: Its Origins, Context, and Significance,* edited by Ripley P. Bullen and James B. Stoltman, pp. 1–8. Florida Anthropological Society Publication, No. 6, Gainesville.

Rice, Prudence M.

1987   *Pottery Analysis: A Sourcebook.* University of Chicago Press, Chicago.

1999   On the Origins of Pottery. *Journal of Archaeological Method and Theory* 6:1–54.

Rodríguez, Camilo

1995   Sites with Early Ceramics in the Caribbean Littoral of Colombia: A Discussion of Periodization and Typologies. In *The Emergence of Pottery: Technology and Innovation in Ancient Societies,* edited by William K. Barnett and John W. Hoopes, pp. 145–156. Smithsonian Institution Press, Washington, D.C.

Rolland, Vickie L., and Paulette Bond
  2003 The Search for Spiculate Clays near Aboriginal Village Sites in the Lower St. Johns River. *The Florida Anthropologist* 56(2):91–111.

Roosevelt, Anna C.
  1995 Early Pottery in the Amazon. In *The Emergence of Pottery: Technology and Innovation in Ancient Societies,* edited by William K. Barnett and John W. Hoopes, pp. 115–131. Smithsonian Institution Press, Washington, D.C.

Rouse, Irving
  1939 *Prehistory in Haiti: A Study in Method.* Publications in Anthropology, No. 1, Yale University, New Haven, Connecticut.
  1951 *A Survey of Indian River Archeology, Florida.* Yale University Publications in Anthropology, No. 44, Yale University Press, New Haven, Connecticut.

Russo, Michael
  1991 Archaic Sedentism on the Florida Coast: A Case Study from Horr's Island. Unpublished Ph.D. dissertation, Department of Anthropology, University of Florida, Gainesville.
  1992 Chronologies and Cultures of the St. Marys Region of Northeast Florida and Southern Georgia. *The Florida Anthropologist* 45:107–126.
  1996a Southeastern Archaic Mounds. In *Archaeology of the Mid-Holocene Southeast,* edited by Kenneth E. Sassaman and David G. Anderson, pp. 259–287. University Press of Florida, Gainesville.
  1996b Southeastern Mid-Holocene Coastal Settlements. In *Archaeology of the Mid-Holocene Southeast,* edited by Kenneth E. Sassaman and David G. Anderson, pp. 177–199. University Press of Florida, Gainesville.
  2004 Measuring Shell Rings for Social Inequality. In *Signs of Power: The Rise of Cultural Complexity in the Southeast,* edited by Jon L. Gibson and Phillip J. Carr, 26–70. University of Alabama Press, Tuscaloosa.

Russo, Michael, Ann S. Cordell, and Donna L. Ruhl
  1993 *The Timucuan Ecological and Historic Preserve: Phase III Final Report.* SEAC Accession No. 899, Florida Museum of Natural History. Submitted to the Southeast Archeological Center, National Park Service, Tallahassee, Florida, Contract CA-5000-9-8011. Copies available from the Southeast Archeological Center, Tallahassee.

Russo, Michael, and Gregory Heide
  2000 *Draft: The Joseph Reed Shell Ring.* Submitted to Hobe Sound National Wildlife Refuge, Stuart, Florida. Copy on file, Southeast Archeological Center, National Park Service, Tallahassee, Florida.
  2001 Shell Rings of the Southeast US. *Antiquity* 75(289):491–492.
  2002 The Joseph Reed Shell Ring. *The Florida Anthropologist* 55(2):67–88.

Russo, Michael, Barbara A. Purdy, Lee A. Newsome, and Ray M. McGee
  1992 A Reinterpretation of Late Archaic Adaptations in Central-East Florida: Grove's Orange Midden (8Vo2601). *Southeastern Archaeology* 11:95–108.

Russo, Michael, and Rebecca Saunders
  1999 *Identifying the Early Use of Coastal Fisheries and the Rise of Social Complexity*

in Shell Rings and Arcuate Middens on Florida's Northeast Coast. Report submitted to the National Geographic Society, Washington, D.C. Copies available from Michael Russo, Southeast Archeological Center, Tallahassee, Florida.

Sassaman, Kenneth E.

1993a *Early Pottery in the Southeast: Tradition and Innovation in Cooking Technology.* University of Alabama Press, Tuscaloosa.

1993b *Early Woodland Settlement in the Aiken Plateau: Archaeological Investigations at 38AK157, Savannah River Site, Aiken County, South Carolina.* Savannah River Archaeological Research Papers 3, South Carolina Institute of Archaeology and Anthropology, University of South Carolina, Columbia.

1994 Production for Exchange in the Mid-Holocene Southeast: A Savannah River Valley Example. *Lithic Technology* 19:42–51.

1995a The Cultural Diversity of Interactions among Mid-Holocene Societies of the American Southeast. In *Native American Interactions: Multiscalar Analyses and Interpretations in the Eastern Woodlands,* edited by Michael S. Nassaney and Kenneth E. Sassaman, pp. 174–204. University of Tennessee Press, Chattanooga.

1995b The Social Contradictions of Traditional and Innovative Cooking Technologies in the Prehistoric American Southeast. In *The Emergence of Pottery: Technology and Innovation in Ancient Societies,* edited by William K. Barnett and John W. Hoopes, pp. 223–240. Smithsonian Institution Press, Washington, D.C.

1998 Crafting Cultural Identity in Hunter-Gatherer Economies. In *Craft and Social Identity,* edited by Cathy L. Costin and Rita P. Wright, pp. 93–107. Archeological Papers of the American Anthropological Association, No. 8, American Anthropological Association, Arlington, Virginia.

1999a A Southeastern Perspective on Soapstone Vessel Technology in the Northeast. In *The Archaeological Northeast,* edited by Mary A. Levine, Kenneth E. Sassaman, and Michael S. Nassaney, pp. 75–95. Bergin and Garvey, Westport, Connecticut.

1999b *Stallings Island Revisited: Modern Investigation of Stratigraphy and Chronology.* Report submitted to the National Geographic Society, Washington, D.C., in partial fulfillment of Grant #6411-99.

2000 Agents of Change in Hunter-Gatherer Technology. In *Agency in Archaeology,* edited by Marcia-Anne Dobres and John E. Robb, pp. 148–168. Routledge, London.

2001 Hunter-Gatherers and Traditions of Resistance. In *The Archaeology of Traditions,* edited by Timothy Pauketat, pp. 218–236. University Press of Florida, Gainesville.

2002 Woodland Ceramic Beginnings. In *The Woodland Southeast,* edited by David G. Anderson and Robert C. Mainfort, Jr., pp. 398–420. University of Alabama Press, Tuscaloosa.

2003a New AMS Dates on Orange Fiber-Tempered Pottery from the Middle St. Johns Valley and Their Implications for Culture History in Northeast Florida. *The Florida Anthropologist* 56(1):5–13.

2003b *St. Johns Archaeological Field School 2000–2001: Blue Spring and Hontoon Island State Parks.* Technical Report Series, No. 4, Laboratory of Southeastern Archaeology, Department of Anthropology, University of Florida, Gainesville.

Sassaman, Kenneth E., I. Randolph Daniel, Jr., and Christopher R. Moore

2002 *G. S. Lewis-East: Early and Late Archaic Occupations along the Savannah River, Aiken County, South Carolina.* Savannah River Archaeological Research Papers 12, South Carolina Institute of Archaeology and Anthropology, University of South Carolina, Columbia.

Sassaman, Kenneth E., and Michael J. Heckenberger

2004 Crossing the Symbolic Rubicon in the Southeast. In *Signs of Power: The Rise of Cultural Complexity in the Southeast,* edited by Jon L. Gibson and Phillip J. Carr, pp. 214–233. University of Alabama Press, Tuscaloosa.

Sassaman, Kenneth E., and Wictoria Rudolphi

2001 Communities of Practice in the Early Pottery Traditions of the American Southeast. *Journal of Anthropological Research* 57(4):407–425.

Saunders, Joe W.

2002 *2001 Annual Report for Management Unit 2.* Regional Archaeology Program, Department of Geosciences, University of Louisiana at Monroe.

Saunders, Joe W., Thurman Allen, and Roger T. Saucier

1994 Four Archaic? Mound Complexes in Northeast Louisiana. *Southeastern Archaeology* 13(2):134–152.

Saunders, Rebecca

1985 The Fiber Tempered Area. In *Aboriginal Subsistence and Settlement Archaeology of the Kings Bay Locality,* vol. 1, *The Kings Bay and Devils Walkingstick Sites,* edited by William Hampton Adams, pp. 152–168. Reports of Investigations 1, Department of Anthropology, University of Florida, Gainesville.

1994 The Case for Archaic Period Mounds in Southeastern Louisiana. *Southeastern Archaeology* 13(2):118–133.

1999 Feast or Quotidian Fare?: Rollins Shell Ring and the Question of Site Function. Paper presented at the 56th Annual Meeting of the Southeastern Archaeological Conference, Pensacola, Florida.

2002a Field Excavation: Methods and Results. In *The Fig Island Ring Complex (38CH42): Coastal Adaptation and the Question of Ring Function in the Late Archaic,* edited by Rebecca Saunders, pp. 98–140. Report prepared for the South Carolina Department of Archives and History under Grant #45-01-16441. On file, South Carolina Department of Archives and History, Columbia.

2002b Previous Archaeological Research. In *The Fig Island Ring Complex (38CH42): Coastal Adaptation and the Question of Ring Function in the Late Archaic,* edited by Rebecca Saunders, pp. 43–63. Report prepared for the South Carolina

Department of Archives and History, Grant #45-01-16441. On file, South Carolina Department of Archives and History, Columbia.

2003 *Feast or Quotidian Fare?: Rollins Shell Ring and the Question of Ring Function.* Report submitted to the Florida Department of Archives and History, permit #1A-32 9697.04.

Saunders, Rebecca, and Michael Russo

2000 Late Archaic Monumental Architecture on the Lower Atlantic Coast. Paper presented in the symposium "Monuments in Intermediate-Scale Societies: New World and Old World Perspectives" at the 65th Annual Meeting of the Society for American Archaeology, Philadelphia.

Sears, William H.

1973 The Sacred and the Secular in Prehistoric Ceramics. In *Variation in Anthropology,* edited by Donald Lathrop and John Douglass, pp. 31–42. Illinois Archaeological Survey, Urbana.

1982 *Fort Center: An Archaeological Site in the Lake Okeechobee Basin.* Ripley P. Bullen Monographs in Anthropology and History, No. 4, Florida State Museum, Gainesville.

Sears, William H., and James B. Griffin

1950 Fiber-Tempered Pottery of the Southeast. In *Prehistoric Pottery of the Eastern United States,* edited by James B. Griffin, unpaginated. Museum of Anthropology, University of Michigan, Ann Arbor.

Shannon, George W.

1986 The Southeastern Fiber-Tempered Ceramic Tradition Reconsidered. In *Papers in Ceramic Analysis, Ceramic Notes No. 3,* edited by Prudence M. Rice, pp. 47–80. Occasional Publications of the Ceramic Technology Laboratory, Florida State Museum, Gainesville.

1987 A Reconsideration of Formative Cultural Development in the Southeastern United States. Ph.D. dissertation, Department of Anthropology, Michigan State University, East Lansing.

Shenkel, J. Richard

1980 *Oak Island Archaeology: Prehistoric Estuarine Adaptation in the Mississippi River Delta.* Archaeological and Cultural Research Program, University of New Orleans. Submitted to Jean Lafitte National Historic Park, National Park Service, U.S. Department of the Interior, New Orleans.

Shepard, Anna O.

1980 *Ceramics for the Archaeologist.* Publication 609, Carnegie Institution of Washington, Washington, D.C.

Simpkins, Daniel L.

1975 A Preliminary Report on Test Excavations at the Sapelo Island Shell Ring, 1975. *Early Georgia* 3(2):15–37.

Simpkins, Daniel L., and Dorothy J. Allard

1986 Isolation and Identification of Spanish Moss Fiber from a Sample of Stallings and Orange Series Ceramics. *American Antiquity* 51:102–117.

Simpkins, Daniel L., and D. A. Scoville

1981 Isolation and Identification of Fiber Inclusions from a Sample of Stallings and Orange Series Ceramics. Paper presented at the 38th Annual Meeting of the Southeastern Archaeological Conference, Asheville.

Skibo, James M.

1992 *Pottery Function: A Use-Alteration Perspective.* Plenum Press, New York.

Smith, Bruce D.

1986 The Archaeology of the Southeastern United States: From Dalton to de Soto, 10,500–500 B.P. In *Advances in World Archaeology,* Vol. 5, edited by Fred Wendorf and Angela Close, pp. 1–92. Academic Press, New York.

Smith, Marvin T., and Mark Williams

1994 Mississippian Mound Refuse Disposal Patterns and Implications for Archaeological Research. *Southeastern Archaeology* 13(1):27–35.

Snow, Frankie

1977 *An Archaeological Survey of the Ocmulgee Big Bend Region.* Occasional Papers from South Georgia, No. 3, South Georgia College, Douglas.

Spinden, Herbert J.

1917 The Origin and Distribution of Agriculture in America. *Proceedings of the International Congress of Americanists* 19:269–276.

State of Florida, Department of Transportation

1995 *Archaeological Investigations at the Summer Haven Site (8SJ46), an Orange Period and St. Johns Period Midden Site in Southeastern St. Johns County, Florida.* Environmental Management Office, Tallahassee, Florida.

Stoltman, James B.

1966 New Radiocarbon Dates for Southeastern Fiber-Tempered Pottery. *American Antiquity* 31:872–874.

1972a The Late Archaic in the Savannah River Region. In *Fiber-Tempered Pottery in Southeastern United States and Northern Colombia: Its Origins, Context, and Significances,* edited by Ripley P. Bullen and James B. Stoltman, pp. 37–62. Florida Anthropological Society Publications, No. 6, Gainesville.

1972b Preface. In *Fiber-Tempered Pottery in Southeastern United States and Northern Colombia: Its Origins, Context, and Significance,* edited by Ripley P. Bullen and James B. Stoltman, pp. i–iv. Florida Anthropological Society Publications, No. 6, Gainesville.

1974 *Groton Plantation: An Archaeological Study of a South Carolina Locality.* Monographs of the Peabody Museum, No. 1. Harvard University, Cambridge, Massachusetts.

1989 A Quantitative Approach to the Petrographic Analysis of Ceramic Thin Sections. *American Antiquity* 54(1):147–160.

1991 Ceramic Petrography as a Technique for Documenting Cultural Interaction: An Example from the Upper Mississippi Valley. *American Antiquity* 56(1):103–120.

2001 The Role of Petrography in the Study of Archaeological Ceramics. In *Earth Sciences and Archaeology,* edited by Paul Goldberg, Vance T. Holliday, and C. Reid Ferring, pp. 297–326. Kluwer Academic/Plenum Publishers, New York.

Stuiver, Minze, and Henry A. Polach
  1977 Discussion Reporting of ^{14}C Data. *Radiocarbon* 19(3):355–363.

Stuiver, Minze, and Paula J. Reimer
  1993 Extended ^{14}C Database and Revised CALIB Radiocarbon Calibration Program. *Radiocarbon* 35:215–230.

Stuiver, Minze, Paula J. Reimer, Edouard Bard, J. Warren Beck, G. S. Burr, Konrad A. Hughen, Bernd Kromer, Gerry McCormac, Johannes van der Plicht, and Marco Spurk
  1998 INTCAL98 Radiocarbon Age Calibrations 24,000–0 cal BP. *Radiocarbon* 40:1041–1083.

Stuiver, Minze, Paula J. Reimer, and Thomas F. Braziunas
  1998 High-Precision Radiocarbon Age Calibration for Terrestrial and Marine Samples. *Radiocarbon* 40:1127–1151.

Sutherland, Donald R.
  1973 A Preliminary Analysis of Ceramic Materials Recovered from the Spanish Mount Site, Edisto Island, S.C. *South Carolina Antiquities* 5:46–50.
  1974 Excavations at the Spanish Mount Shell Midden, Edisto Island, S.C. *South Carolina Antiquities* 6:25–36.

Swanton, John R.
  1911 *Indian Tribes of the Lower Mississippi Valley and Adjacent Coast of the Gulf of Mexico.* Bulletin 43, Bureau of American Ethnology, Smithsonian Institution, Washington, D.C.
  1931 *Source Material for the Social and Ceremonial Life of the Choctaw Indians.* Bulletin 103, Bureau of American Ethnology, Smithsonian Institution, Washington, D.C.

Tanley, Laura C.
  1999 Archaeological Investigation of Unit Two at the Sharp Site (16LV13), Livingston Parish, Louisiana. Unpublished Master's thesis, Department of Geography and Anthropology, Louisiana State University, Baton Rouge.

Tesar, Louis
  1980 *The Leon County Bicentennial Survey Report: An Archaeological Survey of Selected Portions of Leon County, Florida.* Miscellaneous Project Report Series 49. Performed for the Florida Bicentennial Commission, City of Tallahassee, and National Park Service by the Bureau of Historic Sites and Properties, Division of Archives, History and Records Management, Tallahassee.

Thomas, Prentice M., Jr., and L. Janice Campbell
  1978 *The Peripheries of Poverty Point.* New World Research, Inc., Report of Investigations No. 12. Submitted to EMANCO, Inc., Houston.
  1985 *The Deptford to Santa Rosa/Swift Creek Transition in the Florida Panhandle.* Paper presented at the 42nd Southeastern Archaeological Conference, Pensacola.
  1993 *Eglin Air Force Base Historic Preservation Plan, Technical Synthesis of Cultural Resources Investigations at Eglin, Santa Rosa, Okaloosa and Walton Counties,*

Florida. New World Research, Inc., Report of Investigations No. 192, Fort Walton Beach, Florida.

Toth, Edwin A.

1977 Early Marksville Phases in the Lower Mississippi Valley: A Study of Culture Contact Dynamics. Ph.D. dissertation, Harvard University, Cambridge, Massachusetts.

Trickey, E. Bruce, and Nicholas Holmes, Jr.

1971 A Chronological Framework for the Mobile Bay Region: Revised, 1970. *Journal of Alabama Archaeology* 17:116–128.

Trinkley, Michael B.

1973 A Study in the Manufacture of Early Aboriginal Pottery in the Edisto Region of South Carolina. *South Carolina Antiquities* 2:149–155.

1976 A Typology of Thom's Creek Pottery for the South Carolina Coast. Unpublished Master's thesis, Department of Anthropology, University of North Carolina, Chapel Hill.

1980 A Typology of Thom's Creek Pottery for the South Carolina Coast. *South Carolina Antiquities* 12(1):1–31.

1983 Ceramics of the Central South Carolina Coast. *South Carolina Antiquities* 15:43–54.

1985 The Form and Function of South Carolina's Early Woodland Shell Rings. In *Structure and Process in Southeastern Archaeology,* edited by Roy S. Dickens and H. Trawick Ward, pp. 102–118. University of Alabama Press, Tuscaloosa.

1986 *Indian and Freeman Occupation at the Fish Haul Site (38BU805), Beaufort County, South Carolina.* Research Series 7, Chicora Foundation, Columbia, South Carolina.

Tylor, Edward B.

1871 *Primitive Culture: Researches into the Development of Mythology, Philosophy, Religion, Language, Art and Custom.* J. Murray, London.

Vitelli, Karen D.

1989 Were Pots First Made for Foods? Doubts from Franchthi. *World Archaeology* 21:17–29.

1995 Pots, Potters, and the Shaping of Greek Neolithic Society. In *The Emergence of Pottery: Technology and Innovation in Ancient Societies,* edited by William K. Barnett and John W. Hoopes, pp. 55–64. Smithsonian Institution Press, Washington, D.C.

Walthall, John, and Ned J. Jenkins

1976 The Gulf Formational Stage in Southeastern Prehistory. *Southeastern Archaeological Conference Bulletin* 19:43–49.

Waring, Antonio J., Jr.

1968a The Archaic and Some Shell Rings. In *The Waring Papers: The Collected Works of Antonio J. Waring, Jr.,* edited by Stephen Williams, pp. 253–255. Papers of the Peabody Museum of Archaeology and Ethnology, No. 58, Harvard University, Cambridge, Massachusetts.

1968b The Bilbo Site, Chatham County, Georgia. In *The Waring Papers: The Col-*

lected Works of Antonio J. Waring, Jr., edited by Stephen Williams, pp. 152–197. Papers of the Peabody Museum of Archaeology and Ethnology, No. 58, Harvard University, Cambridge, Massachusetts.

Waring, Antonio J., Jr., and Lewis Larson

1968 The Shell Ring on Sapelo Island. In *The Waring Papers: The Collected Works of Antonio J. Waring, Jr.,* edited by Stephan Williams, pp. 263–278. Papers of the Peabody Museum of Archaeology and Ethnology, No. 58, Harvard University, Cambridge, Massachusetts.

Weaver, Elizabeth C.

1963 Technological Analysis of Prehistoric Lower Mississippi Ceramic Materials: A Preliminary Report. *American Antiquity* 29:49–56.

Webb, Clarence H.

1968 The Extent and Content of Poverty Point Culture. *American Antiquity* 33:297–321.

1977 *The Poverty Point Culture.* Geoscience and Man Vol. 17. Louisiana State University, Baton Rouge.

1982 *The Poverty Point Culture.* Geoscience and Man Vol. 17, 2nd ed. (rev.). Louisiana State University, Baton Rouge.

Webb, Clarence H., James A. Ford, and Sherwood M. Gagliano

1963 *Poverty Point and the American Formative.* On file, Center for Archaeology, Tulane University, New Orleans.

1970 *Poverty Point Culture and the American Formative,* pt. 1. On file, Poverty Point State Historic Site, Epps, Louisiana.

Webb, Malcolm C.

1989 Functional and Historical Parallelisms between Mesoamerica and Mississippian Cultures. In *The Southeastern Ceremonial Complex: Artifacts and Analysis,* edited by Patricia Galloway, pp. 279–293. University of Nebraska Press, Lincoln.

Webb, William S., and David L. DeJarnette

1942 *An Archaeological Survey of Pickwick Basin in the Adjacent Portions of the States of Alabama, Mississippi, and Tennessee.* Bulletin 129, Bureau of American Ethnology, Smithsonian Institution, Washington, D.C.

Weinstein, Richard A.

1974 An Archaeological Survey of the Lower Amite River, Louisiana. Unpublished Master's thesis, Department of Geography and Anthropology, Louisiana State University, Baton Rouge.

1986 Tchefuncte Occupation in the Lower Mississippi Delta and Adjacent Coastal Zone. In *The Tchula Period in the Mid-South and Lower Mississippi Valley: Proceedings of the 1982 Mid-South Archaeological Conference,* edited by David H. Dye and Ronald C. Brister, pp. 102–127. Archaeological Report 17, Mississippi Department of Archives and History, Jackson.

1995 The Tchula Period in the Lower Mississippi Valley and Adjacent Coastal Zone: A Brief Summary. In *"An' Stuff Like That There": In Appreciation of William G. Haag,* edited by Jon L. Gibson, Robert W. Neuman, and Richard

A. Weinstein, pp. 153–187. Louisiana Archaeology No. 18. Louisiana Archaeological Society, Lafayette.

Weinstein, Richard A., and Philip G. Rivet

1978 *Beau Mire: A Late Tchula Period Site of the Tchefuncte Culture, Ascension Parish, Louisiana.* Anthropological Report No. 1, Department of Culture, Recreation and Tourism, Louisiana Archaeological Survey and Antiquities Commission, Baton Rouge.

Wentworth, Chester K.

1922 A Scale of Grade and Class Terms for Clastic Sediments. *Journal of Geology* 30(5):377–392.

Whatley, John S.

2002 An Overview of Georgia Projectile Points and Selected Cutting Tools. *Early Georgia* 30:7–133.

Wheeler, Skye, Annette Snapp, and Scott Lewis

1997 *Phase II Report: Archaeological Investigations of the Scheurich Midden Site (8PB9261), Jupiter, Palm Beach County, Florida.* On file with SPLHPS Inc., Ft. Lauderdale, Florida.

White, Nancy M.

1981 *Archaeological Survey at Lake Seminole, Jackson and Gadsden Counties, Florida, Seminole and Decatur Counties, Georgia.* Archaeological Research Report 29, Cleveland Museum of Natural History, Cleveland.

1999 Late Archaic Adaptation in the Apalachicola–Lower Chattahoochee Valley, Northwest Florida–South Georgia/Alabama. Paper presented at the 56th Annual Meeting of the Southeastern Archaeological Conference, Pensacola.

2003 Late Archaic in the Apalachicola/Lower Chattahoochee Valley, Northwest Florida, Southwest Georgia, and Southeast Alabama. *The Florida Anthropologist* 56(2):69–90.

Widmer, Randolph J.

1974 *A Survey and Assessment of Archaeological Resources on Marco Island, Collier County, Florida.* Miscellaneous Projects Report Series, No. 19, Florida Division of Archives, History, and Records Management, Tallahassee.

1988 *The Evolution of the Calusa: A Nonagricultural Chiefdom on the Southwest Florida Coast.* University of Alabama Press, Tuscaloosa.

Willey, Gordon R.

1949a *Archeology of the Florida Gulf Coast.* Smithsonian Miscellaneous Collections 113, Washington, D.C.

1949b *Excavations in Southeast Florida.* Yale University Publications in Anthropology, No. 42, New Haven, Connecticut.

Williams, Stephen

1968 Appendix: Radiocarbon Dates from the Georgia Coast. In *The Waring Papers: The Collected Works of Antonio J. Waring, Jr.,* edited by Stephen Williams, pp. 329–332. Papers of the Peabody Museum of Archaeology and Ethnology, No. 58, Harvard University, Cambridge, Massachusetts.

Williams, Stephen, and Jeffery P. Brain

1983   *Excavations at the Lake George Site, Yazoo County, Mississippi, 1958–1966.* Papers of the Peabody Museum of Archaeology and Ethnology, Vol. 74, Harvard University, Cambridge, Massachusetts.

Wimberly, Steve B.

1950   Bayou La Batre Tchefuncte Pottery Series. In *Prehistoric Pottery of the Eastern United States,* edited by James B. Griffin, unpaginated. Museum of Anthropology, University of Michigan, Ann Arbor.

1960   *Indian Pottery from Clarke County and Mobile County, Southern Alabama.* Museum Paper No. 36, Alabama Museum of Natural History, Tuscaloosa.

Wobst, H. Martin

1977   Stylistic Behavior and Information Exchange. In *Papers for the Director: Research Essays in Honor of James B. Griffin,* edited by Charles E. Cleland, pp. 317–342. Anthropological Papers 61, University of Michigan, Museum of Anthropology, Ann Arbor.

Wood, W. Dean, Dan T. Elliott, Teresa P. Rudolph, and Dennis B. Blanton

1986   *Prehistory in the Richard B. Russell Reservoir: The Archaic and Woodland Periods of the Upper Savannah River.* Russell Papers. Archaeological Services Branch, National Park Service, Atlanta.

Woodburn, James

1981   Egalitarian Societies. *Man* 17(3):431–451.

Wunderlin, Richard P.

1998   *Guide to the Vascular Plants of Florida.* University of Florida Press, Gainesville.

Wyman, Jeffries

1875   *Fresh-water Shell Mounds of the St. Johns River, Florida.* Peabody Academy of Science Memoir 4, pp. 3–94. Salem, Massachusetts.

Contributors

L. Janice Campbell is vice president of Prentice Thomas & Associates, Inc. She is actively engaged in research related to Gulf Formational developments, interregional relations, and the influence of Poverty Point contact on Florida's Gulf Coast.

Ann S. Cordell is a staff archaeologist at the University of Florida's Florida Museum of Natural History in Gainesville. She manages the FLMNH's Ceramic Technology Laboratory and conducts pottery analyses for FLMNH curators. She has studied prehistoric and historic aboriginal pottery from Florida, the southeastern United States, and the Caribbean.

Jon L. Gibson has retired from teaching at the University of Louisiana at Lafayette and spends his time wondering what people used to do with their time a long time ago.

Christopher T. Hays is an assistant professor of anthropology at the University of Wisconsin–Washington County. He has published articles on the Adena and Tchefuncte cultures.

Gregory Heide is an archaeologist for the National Park Service, Southeast Archeological Center, Tallahassee, Florida. He has worked on a number of Late Archaic shell rings in Florida and South Carolina.

Tristram R. Kidder is a professor of anthropology at Washington University. He is director of the Raffman Project, which has among its goals analysis of the effects of climate change on Poverty Point and later cultures in the Mississippi Valley.

James H. Mathews is a senior archaeologist with Prentice Thomas & Associates, Inc. He is a specialist in prehistoric ceramic traditions, with continued interest in the development and spread of ceramic traits.

Mark A. Melancon is a graduate student in the Department of Geography and Anthropology at Louisiana State University. He has been extensively involved in Late Archaic research at the Poverty Point and Meche-Wilkes sites and is using information from the latter in his M.A. thesis.

Anthony L. Ortmann is a graduate student in the Department of Anthropology at Tulane University. His graduate research focuses on the construction and use of earth architecture at the Poverty Point site.

Michael Russo is an archaeologist for the National Park Service, Southeast Archeological Center, Tallahassee, Florida. He has reported extensively on shell rings and mounds of the Middle and Late Archaic periods in the southeastern United States.

Kenneth E. Sassaman is an associate professor with the Department of Anthropology at the University of Florida. His research into social theory is often directed at Middle and Late Archaic cultures in the Savannah and St. Johns River valleys.

Rebecca Saunders is curator of anthropology at the Louisiana State University Museum of Natural Science. She has been studying cultural interaction vis-à-vis pottery traditions for over 15 years.

James B. Stoltman is Professor Emeritus at the Department of Anthropology, University of Wisconsin–Madison.

Prentice M. Thomas, Jr., is president of Prentice Thomas & Associates, Inc. He has spent the past 30 years directing cultural resources investigations in the Southeast, with a specialization in the dynamics of prehistoric settlement and exchange mechanisms.

Richard A. Weinstein is a principal investigator with Coastal Environments, Inc., in Baton Rouge, Louisiana. He has investigated sites of all descriptions in the Lower Mississippi River Valley and coastal Texas.

Index